The Structure of
Spherical Buildings

The Structure of
Spherical Buildings

Richard M. Weiss

PRINCETON UNIVERSITY PRESS

PRINCETON AND OXFORD

Library of Congress Cataloguing-in-Publication Data

Weiss, Richard M. (Richard Mark), 1946–
    The structure of spherical buildings / by Richard M. Weiss.
        p. cm.
    Includes bibliographical references and index.
    ISBN 0-691-11733-0 (acid-free paper)
        1. Buildings (Group theory). I. Title.

    QA179 .W45 2004
    512'.2—dc21   2003050674

British Library Cataloguing-in-Publication Data is available

This book has been composed in Times and LucidaSans
Typeset by T&T Productions Ltd, London
Printed on acid-free paper ⊗
www.pupress.princeton.edu

Printed in the United States of America

10   9   8   7   6   5   4   3   2   1

I am not interested in constructing a building, so much as in having a perspicuous view of the foundations of possible buildings.

Ludwig Wittgenstein, *Culture and Value*

Contents

Preface

Jacques Tits's classification of thick irreducible spherical buildings of rank at least three (published in 1974 as Volume 386 of the Springer Lecture Notes [14]) is no doubt one of the great accomplishments of 20th century mathematics. At the heart of Tits's classification is the famous Theorem 4.1.2 of [14], which states that every 'local isomorphism' (in a suitable sense) from one thick irreducible spherical building to another extends to an isomorphism. Only with this result in hand does Tits invoke Coxeter's classification of finite reflection groups and begin a case-by-case analysis of buildings having a given irreducible spherical diagram.

Our main goal in this monograph is to give a detailed introduction to the theory of buildings culminating (in Chapter 10) in a proof of Theorem 4.1.2. Since the first four chapters of Tits's Lecture Notes accomplish this same goal quite beautifully, it behooves us to explain our purpose more carefully.

In 1981 Tits introduced his 'local approach' to buildings [16], central to which was the idea of viewing buildings as chamber systems. In the introduction to this paper, Tits wrote:

> So far, buildings have always been described as incidence geome-
> tries or simplicial complexes. The results of the present paper find
> their simplest expression in a somewhat more abstract framework,
> that of *chamber systems*.

In fact, a chamber system can be viewed as nothing more abstract than a certain class of edge-colored graphs, and the 'local approach' offers an indisputably more elementary way to learn about buildings than the 'complex' point of view taken in the Lecture Notes (but at a price: the important connection to the classical geometries is more difficult to describe in terms of chamber systems).

A basic aspect of the chamber system point of view is the notion of an isom-etry which can be found only implicitly in the Lecture Notes. The apartments of a building are the thin subbuildings having the same type as the building itself. In [16] Tits looked at an apartment as the image of an isometry from the corresponding Coxeter chamber system to the building. This suggested results about extensions of isometries which turned out to be crucial. In [6] and [8], Bernhard Mühlherr and Mark Ronan developed these ideas in order to extend Theorem 4.1.2 to a large class of twin buildings. In particular, Ronan proved results in [8] which yielded an elegant simplified proof of Theorem 4.1.2 as a special case. (A spherical building can always be twinned with itself.) Ronan's proof follows the same basic lines as Tits's original proof, but his focus on extensions of isometries allowed him to circumvent a large portion of the technical difficulties encountered by Tits. Ronan's proof (with some minor simplifications of our own) forms the centerpiece of this book.

Another, more recent, development in the theory of buildings is the classification of Moufang polygons by Tits and the author [20]. In the addenda to his Lecture Notes, Tits introduced the Moufang property for spherical buildings, a certain symmetry property expressed in terms of apartments and roots. He also observed that, as a consequence of Theorem 4.1.2, all thick irreducible spherical buildings of rank at least three, as well as all the irreducible residues *of rank at least two* of such a building, have the Moufang property. This means, in particular, that the irreducible residues of rank two of such a building are Moufang polygons. Theorem 4.1.2 itself says that a thick irreducible spherical building of rank at least three is uniquely determined by the union (in an appropriate sense) of the residues of rank two containing a given chamber. These observations led Tits to suggest that a classification of Moufang polygons should make it possible to prove the classification of thick irreducible spherical buildings of higher rank in a simpler and more uniform fashion. This goal is also realized in [20].

In Chapter 11 of these notes, we introduce the Moufang property and show how it can be used to examine the structure of a spherical building and its automorphism group. In Chapter 12, we give an overview of the classification of thick irreducible spherical buildings as it is carried out in [20].

In [9] Ronan and Tits gave an existence criterion for buildings which applied, in particular, to all spherical buildings (thick, irreducible and of rank at least three). In the Lecture Notes, Tits proved existence by referring either to classical geometries (involving vector spaces, pseudo-quadratic forms, etc.) or to the theory of algebraic groups (with some additional effort for the buildings 'of mixed type'). The results of [9] allowed, by contrast, a completely elementary and uniform solution to the problem of existence. The way of looking at spherical buildings which we adopt in Chapters 11 and 12 reflects these ideas.

The first nine chapters of this book are heavily influenced by Ronan's beautiful monograph [7]. In Chapter 1 we introduce the language of chamber systems. In Chapters 2–6 we examine the structure of Coxeter chamber systems (whose role in the theory of buildings is, in some geometrical sense, analogous to the role played by bases in the theory of vector spaces). Chapter 6 is devoted to a result of Mühlherr, which we use in Chapter 11 to link Theorem 4.1.2 to the Moufang property. Buildings and apartments are introduced in Chapters 7–8 and in Chapter 9 we specialize to spherical buildings.

We have tried to make this monograph accessible to as wide an audience as possible. In the theory of buildings there are often alternative definitions and different ways of reaching the same goal. This reflects the richness of the subject but is also a source of difficulty for the beginner. For the sake of simplicity we have, for the most part, refrained from giving alternatives. The only prerequisite for the first eleven chapters is a slight familiarity with the notion of a group defined by generators and relations; in fact, even this familiarity is needed only in the proof of two preliminary lemmas which the beginning reader would do just as well to accept as axioms. In the last chapter, we refer to results from [20], but it is of course hoped that the reader is keen to start looking at other sources by this point.

Virtually all the results in this book can be found in their original form in one of the sources in the bibliography. To be sure not to have overlooked anything, we have included [19], which contains a complete list of Tits's books and articles.

It is a pleasure to thank Pierre-Emmanuel Caprace, Jon Hall, George Leger, Tom De Medts, Bernhard Mühlherr and Katrin Tent for their comments, assistance and encouragement.

The Structure of
Spherical Buildings

Chapter One

Chamber Systems

In the first six chapters of this book we introduce Coxeter groups and study them via properties of their Cayley graphs. These Cayley graphs, it will turn out, are a special (but very important!) class of buildings. Arbitrary buildings will be described in terms of certain edge-colored graphs called chamber systems. (The edges of the Cayley graph of a Coxeter group are canonically 'colored' by the generators.) We could postpone introducing chamber systems until Chapter 7 when we really need them, but there is some idiosyncratic usage which comes along with chamber systems ('chambers' instead of 'vertices,' 'galleries' instead of 'paths,' etc.), and it makes sense to introduce this vocabulary right away.

Let $\Delta = (V, E)$ be a graph. By this we mean simply that V is a set and E is a subset of the set of two-element subsets of V. The elements of V are called *vertices* and the elements of E are called *edges*. (If E is the set of *all* two-element subsets of V, then Δ is called a *complete graph*.) A *subgraph* of Δ is a graph (V', E') such that $V' \subset V$ and $E' \subset E$. The subgraph *spanned* by a subset X of V is the subgraph (X, E_X), where E_X consists of *all* the two-element subsets of X which lie in E.

An *edge coloring* of a graph $\Delta = (V, E)$ is a map from the edge set E to a set I whose elements we think of as colors. We will always assume that this map is surjective, so that the set I is unambiguous. An *edge-colored graph* is a graph Δ endowed with an edge coloring. The image I of the edge coloring will be called the *index set* of the edge-colored graph Δ.

Suppose that $\Delta = (V, E)$ is an edge-colored graph with index set I. Rather than give a name to the edge coloring, we will write

$$x \sim_i y$$

(for $x, y \in V$ and $i \in I$) as abbreviation for the statement

'$\{x, y\}$ is an edge of Δ whose color is i.'

Two vertices x and y will be called *i-adjacent* (for some $i \in I$) if $x \sim_i y$, and two vertices will be called *adjacent* if they are i-adjacent for some $i \in I$. (Since E consists of two-element subsets of V, a vertex is never adjacent to itself.)

If a graph $\Delta = (V, E)$ has an edge coloring, we will refer to the elements of V as *chambers* rather than vertices and we will write Δ in place of V, so Δ will refer both to the set of chambers and to the edge-colored graph itself. A subgraph (V', E') of an edge-colored graph Δ will always be assumed to have the edge coloring obtained by restricting the edge coloring of Δ to E'; its index set is a subset of the index set of Δ.

For each set I, we will denote by M_I the *free monoid* on I, i.e. the set of all finite sequences of elements of I including the empty sequence, or equivalently, the set of all words in the alphabet I including the empty word, with multiplication given by concatenation.

Definition 1.1. Let Δ be an edge-colored graph with index set I, let $x, y \in \Delta$ and let $J \subset I$. A *gallery* of length k (for some $k \geqslant 0$) from x to y is a sequence $\gamma = (u_0, u_1, \ldots, u_k)$ of $k + 1$ chambers $u_0, u_1, \ldots, u_k$ such that $u_0 = x$, $u_k = y$ and

$$u_{j-1} \sim_{i_j} u_j$$

for some $i_j \in I$ for all $j \in [1, k]$, and the *type* of the gallery γ is the word $i_1 \cdots i_k$ (an element of the free monoid M_I). A *J-gallery* is a gallery whose type is in M_J. The *distance* from x to y is the length of a shortest gallery from x to y if there are galleries from x to y, and ∞ otherwise. We will denote the distance from x to y by $\mathrm{dist}(x, y)$. A gallery from x to y is called *minimal* if its length is $\mathrm{dist}(x, y)$. The *diameter* of Δ is the supremum of the set

$$\{\mathrm{dist}(u, v) \mid u, v \in \Delta\};$$

it will be denoted by $\mathrm{diam}\,\Delta$. Two chambers x and y of Δ are said to be *opposite* if $\mathrm{dist}(x, y) = \mathrm{diam}\,\Delta < \infty$ (so if $\mathrm{diam}\,\Delta = \infty$, there are no opposite chambers in Δ).

Definition 1.2. Let Δ be an edge-colored graph with index set I and let $J \subset I$. Then Δ is *connected* (respectively, *J-connected*) if for any two chambers x and y there exists a gallery (respectively, a J-gallery) from x to y. A *connected component* of Δ is the subgraph spanned by an equivalence class with respect to the equivalence relation 'there exists a gallery from x to y' on Δ. A *J-residue* of Δ is a connected component of the subgraph of Δ obtained from Δ by discarding all the edges whose color is *not* in J. (Thus, in particular, for each chamber u of Δ there is a unique J-residue R such that u is a chamber of R.) A *residue* of Δ is a J-residue for some $J \subset I$.

1.3. Note that the notions 'distance,' 'diameter,' 'connected' and 'gallery' (but not the type of a gallery) as defined in 1.1 and 1.2 are (for a given graph Δ)

independent of the edge coloring and are really aspects of the graph Δ itself (i.e. without an edge coloring).

We come now to the main definition of this chapter.

Definition 1.4. A *chamber system* is an edge-colored graph Δ with index set I such that for each $i \in I$, all $\{i\}$-residues of Δ are complete graphs with at least two chambers.

An edge of a chamber system is usually permitted to have more than one color and $\{i\}$-residues of a chamber system are usually permitted to consist of a single chamber. Since neither of these possibilities occur in any of the examples which interest us, we have modified the usual definition of a chamber system to rule them out.

Definition 1.5. A *sub-chamber system* of a chamber system Δ is a subgraph (V', E') of Δ (with the edge coloring obtained by restricting the edge coloring of Δ to E'), which is also a chamber system. It would be more accurate to write 'sub-(chamber system)' rather than 'sub-chamber system,' but we will not, of course, do this.

Note that residues of a chamber system are sub-chamber systems.

Definition 1.6. Let Δ be a chamber system with index set I as defined in 1.4. The cardinality of I is called the *rank* of Δ. If R is a J-residue of Δ, then each chamber of R is contained in at least one edge of every color in J and hence J is the index set of R and the rank of R is $|J|$. We call the set J the *type* of R. A *panel* is a residue of rank one. More precisely, an *i-panel* or *panel of type i* (for some $i \in I$) is a residue of type $\{i\}$. We say that two chambers are *i-equivalent* for some $i \in I$ if they lie on the same i-panel. Thus two chambers are i-equivalent for some $i \in I$ if and only if they are either i-adjacent or equal.

By 1.4 and 1.6, the panels of a chamber system Δ are maximal complete monochromatic subgraphs, panels contain at least two chambers and i-equivalence is, in fact, an equivalence relation for each $i \in I$.

Definition 1.7. A chamber system is *thin* if every panel contains exactly two chambers, *thick* if every panel contains at least three chambers.

Note that a thin chamber system is just an edge-colored graph with the property that each chamber is contained in exactly one edge of each color.

A chamber system of rank zero is just a collection of chambers with no edges (and no colors).

A chamber system of rank one is a graph with edges all of the same color, each of whose connected components is a complete graph with at least two chambers.

A chamber system of rank two can be viewed as a bipartite graph. In fact, chamber systems of rank two and bipartite graphs are essentially the same thing, as we explain in the next two paragraphs.

1.8. Let $\Gamma = (V, E)$ be a bipartite graph (with no edge coloring). This means that there exists a partition of V into subsets V_1 and V_2 such that each edge contains one vertex of V_1 and one of V_2 (equivalently, such that each edge 'joins' a vertex of V_1 to a vertex of V_2). (If Γ is connected, then two vertices are in the same subset if and only if the distance between them is even. It follows that the partition of V is unique in this case.) Suppose, too, that every vertex of Γ has at least two neighbors. Let $\Delta_\Gamma = E$ and let $I = \{1, 2\}$. We set $x \sim_i y$ for $x, y \in \Delta_\Gamma$ and $i \in I$ whenever the edges x and y are distinct but have a vertex in V_i in common. This makes Δ_Γ into a chamber system with index set I which is connected if and only if Γ is connected—thin if and only if every vertex of Γ has exactly two neighbors and thick if and only if every vertex of Γ has at least three neighbors. The chamber system Δ_Γ depends on the choice of V_1 and V_2, but if Γ is connected, it is unique up to a relabeling of the index set.

1.9. Let Δ be a chamber system of rank two and let Γ_Δ denote the graph whose vertices are the panels of Δ, where two panels are joined by an edge if and only if they have a non-empty intersection. Then Γ_Δ is a bipartite graph (since two panels can have a non-empty intersection only if they have different types) all of whose vertices have at least two neighbors. If we restrict our attention to connected bipartite graphs and connected chamber systems of rank two, this construction is the inverse of the construction described in 1.8.

We will need the following definition in 7.32 and 7.33.

Definition 1.10. Let $\Delta_1, \ldots, \Delta_k$ be (a finite number of) edge-colored graphs with pairwise disjoint index sets $I_1, \ldots, I_k$. The *direct product* $\Delta_1 \times \cdots \times \Delta_k$ is the edge-colored graph with index set $I_1 \cup \cdots \cup I_k$ whose chambers are all k-tuples $(x_1, \ldots, x_k) \in \Delta_1 \times \cdots \times \Delta_k$ such that for each $t \in [1, k]$ and each $i \in I_t$,

$$(x_1, \ldots, x_k) \sim_i (y_1, \ldots, y_k)$$

whenever $x_t \sim_i y_t$ in Δ_t and $x_s = y_s$ for all $s \in [1, k]$ distinct from t. If $\Delta_1, \ldots, \Delta_k$ are chamber systems, then so is their direct product.

We now give a number of additional definitions. We have formulated them all for chamber systems rather than for arbitrary edge-colored graphs only because we will have no need for the more general case.

Definition 1.11. Let Δ be a chamber system and let

$$\gamma = (x_0, x_1, \ldots, x_k)$$

be a gallery in Δ. Then $[\gamma]$ denotes the (edge-colored) subgraph of Δ whose vertex set is

$$\{u \mid u = x_i \text{ for some } i \in [0, k]\}$$

and whose edge set is

$$\big\{\{u, v\} \mid \{u, v\} = \{x_{i-1}, x_i\} \text{ for some } i \in [1, k]\big\}.$$

Definition 1.12. Let Δ be a chamber system and let $\Delta' = (V', E')$ be a subgraph of Δ. Then Δ' will be called *convex* if for every two chambers u and v of Δ' and every minimal gallery $(x_0, x_1, \ldots, x_k)$ in Δ from u to v,

$$[\gamma] \subset \Delta',$$

where $[\gamma]$ is as defined in 1.11 (equivalently, $x_i \in V'$ for all $i \in [0, k]$ and $\{x_{i-1}, x_i\} \in E'$ for all $i \in [1, k]$).

Definition 1.13. Let

$$\gamma = (x_0, \ldots, x_{k-1}, x_k) \quad \text{and} \quad \gamma' = (x_0', x_1', \ldots, x_m')$$

be galleries of a chamber system such that either $x_k = x_0'$ or x_k is adjacent to x_0'. The *concatenation* of γ and γ' is the gallery

$$(x_0, \ldots, x_{k-1}, x_k, x_1', \ldots, x_m')$$

in the first case and

$$(x_0, \ldots, x_{k-1}, x_k, x_0', x_1', \ldots, x_m')$$

in the second; in both cases, it will be denoted by (γ, γ'). If u is a chamber adjacent to x_0 and v a chamber adjacent to x_k, then we will write simply (u, γ) and (γ, v) to denote the concatenations $((u), \gamma)$ and $(\gamma, (v))$.

Definition 1.14. Two chamber systems Δ and Δ' with index sets I and I' will be called *isomorphic* if there exist bijections σ from I to I' and ϕ from Δ to Δ' (i.e. from chambers to chambers) such that

$$x \sim_i y \text{ if and only if } \phi(x) \sim_{\sigma(i)} \phi(y)$$

for all $x, y \in \Delta$ and all $i \in I$. If (ϕ, σ) is such a pair of bijections, we will say that ϕ is a σ-*isomorphism* from Δ to Δ'. By *isomorphism* we mean a σ-isomorphism for some σ. An isomorphism is *special* (or *type preserving*) if $I = I'$ and the corresponding map σ from I to I is the identity map.

Since isomorphisms map galleries to galleries of the same length, they preserve the distance between chambers (i.e. they are *isometries* with respect to the distance defined in 1.1).

Notation 1.15. Let Δ be a chamber system with index set I. A σ-*automorphism* is a σ-isomorphism from Δ to itself for some permutation σ of I. An *automorphism* of Δ is a σ-automorphism for some σ. The set of all automorphisms of Δ forms a group (under composition of functions) which we denote by $\text{Aut}(\Delta)$. We denote by $\text{Aut}^\circ(\Delta)$ the subgroup of $\text{Aut}(\Delta)$ consisting of just the special automorphisms, i.e. the σ-automorphisms such that $\sigma = 1$. The group $\text{Aut}^\circ(\Delta)$ is a normal subgroup of $\text{Aut}(\Delta)$.

Isomorphisms are a special case of homomorphisms.

Definition 1.16. Let Δ and Δ' be chamber systems with index sets I and I' and let σ be a map from I to I'. A σ-*homomorphism* from Δ to Δ' is a map ρ from chambers to chambers which sends each i-panel of Δ into some $\sigma(i)$-panel of Δ' for all $i \in I$, i.e. such that $\rho(x)$ and $\rho(y)$ are $\sigma(i)$-equivalent chambers of Δ' whenever x and y are i-adjacent chambers of Δ. A σ-*endomorphism* of Δ is a σ-homomorphism from Δ to itself. A *homomorphism* (or *endomorphism*) is a σ-homomorphism (or σ-endomorphism) for some σ. A homomorphism (or endomorphism) is *special* if $I = I'$ and the corresponding map σ from I to I is the identity map.

Definition 1.17. Let Δ be a chamber system. A *pre-gallery* in Δ is a sequence $(u_0, u_1, \ldots, u_k)$ of chambers $u_0, u_1, \ldots, u_k$ such that for each $i \in [1, k]$, the chamber u_i is either adjacent or equal to the chamber u_{i-1}. The *gallery underlying* the pre-gallery γ is the gallery obtained from γ by deleting every chamber which is equal to its successor.

Before going on to the next chapter, we make a few elementary observations about homomorphisms of chamber systems to which we will later refer a number of times, specifically, in the proofs of 3.18, 3.22, 8.5, 8.21 and 9.4.

1.18. Let Δ and Δ' be chamber systems with index sets I and I' and let ρ be a σ-homomorphism from Δ to Δ' for some map σ from I to I'. If γ is a gallery of type $i_1 \cdots i_k$ in Δ, then $\rho(\gamma)$ is a pre-gallery in Δ' and the type of its underlying gallery can be obtained from the word $\sigma(i_1) \cdots \sigma(i_k)$ by deleting letters. In particular,

$$\text{dist}(\rho(x), \rho(y)) \leqslant \text{dist}(x, y)$$

for all $x, y \in \Delta$ (where 'dist' on the left refers to distance in Δ' and 'dist' on the right refers to distance in Δ), and if x, y are two chambers both in the same J-residue of Δ for some $J \subset I$, then $\rho(x)$ and $\rho(y)$ lie in the same $\sigma(J)$-residue of Δ'.

Proposition 1.19. *Let ρ be a special endomorphism of a chamber system Δ and let R be a residue of Δ such that $R \cap \rho(R) \neq \emptyset$. Then $\rho(R) \subset R$.*

Proof. Let J denote the type of R, choose a chamber $x \in R$ such that $\rho(x) \in R$ and let $y \in R$ be arbitrary. Since $x, y \in R$, there is a J-gallery from x to y. By 1.18, therefore, there is a J-gallery from $\rho(x)$ to $\rho(y)$. Since $\rho(x) \in R$, also $\rho(y) \in R$. $\qquad\square$

Chapter Two

Coxeter Groups

In this chapter we introduce Coxeter chamber systems. As we will see, a Coxeter chamber system is just the Cayley graph of a Coxeter group constructed with respect to (and with edges colored by) the given generators.

Definition 2.1. A *Coxeter matrix* is a symmetric array $[m_{ij}]$ with i, j in some index set I (of arbitrary cardinality) such that for all i, $j \in I$, m_{ij} is either a positive integer or the symbol ∞, and $m_{ij} = 1$ if and only if $i = j$. The *Coxeter diagram* of a Coxeter matrix $[m_{ij}]$ is the graph with vertex set I and edge set consisting of all unordered pairs $\{i, j\}$ such that $m_{ij} \geqslant 3$ (including $m_{ij} = \infty$) together with the labeling which assigns the label m_{ij} to each edge $\{i, j\}$. A Coxeter diagram is called *irreducible* if its underlying graph is connected. The *rank* of a Coxeter diagram is the cardinality of its vertex set.

We will always use the standard conventions of omitting each label equal to three in a Coxeter diagram and replacing each label equal to four by a second edge, i.e. we draw $\bullet\!\!-\!\!\!-\!\!\!-\!\!\bullet$ in place of $\bullet\!\!\overset{3}{-\!\!\!-\!\!\!-}\!\!\bullet$ and $\bullet\!\!=\!\!=\!\!\bullet$ in place of $\bullet\!\!\overset{4}{-\!\!\!-\!\!\!-}\!\!\bullet$.

Definition 2.2. Let $[m_{ij}]$ be a Coxeter matrix with index set I and let Π denote the corresponding Coxeter diagram. The *Coxeter group of type Π* is the group W having a set of generators $\{r_i \mid i \in I\}$ indexed by I such that W is defined by the relations

$$\{(r_i r_j)^{m_{ij}} = 1 \mid i, j \in I, \ m_{ij} \neq \infty\}.$$

(In particular, $r_i^2 = 1$ for all $i \in I$.) Let $f \mapsto r_f$ denote the unique extension of the map $i \mapsto r_i$ to a homomorphism r from the free monoid M_I to W. (Thus $r_\emptyset = 1$.) The pair (W, r) is called the *Coxeter system of type Π*. A Coxeter diagram is called *spherical* if the corresponding Coxeter group W is finite.

The order of an element g in a group will be denoted by $|g|$ and the set of non-trivial elements of a group G will be denoted by G^*.

The proof of the next result is unlike anything else we do in this book.

Theorem 2.3. *Let* $[m_{ij}]$ *be a Coxeter matrix with index set* I *and let* (W, r) *denote the corresponding Coxeter system. Then the following hold.*

(i) $|r_i| = 2$ *for all* $i \in I$ *and* $|r_i r_j| = m_{ij}$ *for all* $i, j \in I$.

(ii) *If* $r_i \in \langle r_j \mid j \in J \rangle$ *for some* $i \in I$ *and some* $J \subset I$, *then* $i \in J$.

Proof. Let V be a real vector space having a basis $\{e_i \mid i \in I\}$ in one-to-one correspondence with the set I. We define a bilinear form $(\cdot, \cdot)$ on V by setting

$$(e_i, e_j) = -\cos(\pi/m_{ij})$$

for all i, j. Thus, in particular, $(e_i, e_j) = -1$ if and only if $m_{ij} = \infty$ and $(e_i, e_j) = 1$ if and only if $i = j$. Let

$$U^\perp = \{v \in V \mid (u, v) = 0 \text{ for all } u \in U\}$$

for all $U \subset V$. For each $i \in I$ let S_i denote the automorphism of V given by

$$S_i(v) = v - 2(v, e_i)e_i$$

for all $v \in V$. Then $S_i^2 = 1$ and $S_i(e_i) = -e_i$ (so $|S_i| = 2$) for all $i \in I$.

Choose $i, j \in I$ distinct. We claim that $|S_i S_j| = m_{ij}$. Let V_{ij} denote the subspace spanned by e_i and e_j. Then S_i and S_j both map V_{ij} to itself. Suppose that $m_{ij} = \infty$. In this case, the matrices representing S_i and S_j in their action on V_{ij} with respect to the ordered basis e_i, e_j are

$$\begin{pmatrix} -1 & 2 \\ 0 & 1 \end{pmatrix} \quad \text{and} \quad \begin{pmatrix} 1 & 0 \\ 2 & -1 \end{pmatrix}.$$

The Jordan normal form of the product of these two matrices is

$$\begin{pmatrix} 1 & 1 \\ 0 & 1 \end{pmatrix}.$$

Since this matrix has infinite order, so does $S_i S_j$.

Now suppose that m_{ij} is finite. Let

$$f = -(e_i, e_j)e_i + e_j.$$

Thus $(f, f) = 1 - (e_i, e_j)^2 > 0$ and hence

$$e_i, \frac{f}{\sqrt{(f, f)}}$$

is an orthonormal basis of V_{ij} with respect to $(\cdot, \cdot)$. From the existence of an orthonormal basis of V_{ij}, it follows that $V = V_{ij} \oplus V_{ij}^\perp$. (It is not true that

$V = V_{ij} \oplus V_{ij}^{\perp}$ if $m_{ij} = \infty$; in fact, $f = e_i + e_j \in V_{ij} \cap V_{ij}^{\perp}$ in this case.)
Let $\langle \cdot, \cdot \rangle$ denote the standard inner product on $\mathbb{R}^2$, let E_i and E_j denote the
elements $(1, 0)$ and $(-\cos(\pi/m_{ij}), \sin(\pi/m_{ij}))$ of $\mathbb{R}^2$ and let ϕ denote the
unique linear transformation from V_{ij} to $\mathbb{R}^2$ which sends e_i to E_i and e_j to E_j.
Since $\sin(\pi/m_{ij}) \neq 0$, the map ϕ is an isomorphism. Let $T_k = \phi \cdot S_k \cdot \phi^{-1}$
for $k = i$ and j. (The composition of functions, which will be denoted by
either $\cdot$ or juxtaposition, is to be read from right to left; thus, for example,
$T_k(x) = \phi(S_k(\phi^{-1}(x)))$ for all $x \in \mathbb{R}^2$. See, however, 11.9.) Then

$$T_k(x) = x - 2\langle x, E_k \rangle E_k$$

for $k = i$ and j and for all $x \in \mathbb{R}^2$, i.e. T_i and T_j are two reflections of the
Euclidean plane $\mathbb{R}^2$ whose axes make an angle of π/m_{ij}. Their product is thus
a rotation by $2\pi/m_{ij}$ radians. In particular, $|T_i T_j| = m_{ij}$. Thus $S_i S_j$ induces
an element of order m_{ij} on V_{ij}. Since both S_i and S_j act trivially on $V_{ij}^{\perp}$ and
$V = V_{ij} \oplus V_{ij}^{\perp}$, it follows that $|S_i S_j| = m_{ij}$.

Hence $|S_i| = 2$ for all $i \in I$ and $|S_i S_j| = m_{ij}$ for all $i, j \in I$. In particular,
$(S_i S_j)^{m_{ij}} = 1$ for all $i, j \in I$, so by 2.2, there exists a surjective homomorphism
ψ from W to

$$\langle S_i \mid i \in I \rangle$$

mapping r_i to S_i for all $i \in I$. Thus (i) holds.

Choose $J \subset I$, let G_J denote the group $\langle S_j \mid j \in J \rangle$ and let V_J denote the
subspace of V spanned by $\{e_j \mid j \in J\}$ (so $e_i \notin V_J$ for all $i \in I \backslash J$). Then
$T(v) \in v + V_J$ for all $T \in G_J$ and all $v \in V$. Now suppose that $r_i \in \langle r_j \mid j \in J \rangle$
for some $i \in I$. Applying the homomorphism ψ from the previous paragraph,
we obtain $S_i \in G_J$. Since $S_i(e_i) = -e_i$, it follows that $-e_i \in e_i + V_J$, hence
$e_i \in V_J$ and therefore $i \in J$. Thus (ii) holds. $\square$

We will apply 2.3 (i) only twice, once in 2.4 and a second time in the proof
of 2.6. We will need 2.3 (ii) in the proof of 2.7.

Our real interest is not so much in Coxeter groups as in certain chamber
systems on which they act. Here is the main definition of this chapter.

Definition 2.4. Let Π be a Coxeter diagram with vertex set I and let (W, r) be
the Coxeter system of type Π. By 2.3 (i), the map $f \mapsto r_f$ restricted to words
of length at most one is injective. We can thus define a thin chamber system
(i.e. an edge-colored graph such that each vertex is contained in exactly one
edge of each color) with index set I whose chambers are the elements of W by
setting

$$x \sim_i y \text{ for } i \in I \text{ if and only if } x^{-1}y = r_i.$$

(Since $r_i \neq 1$, $x \sim_i y$ implies that $x \neq y$, since $r_i^2 = 1$, the relation $\sim_i$ is symmetric and since $r_i \neq r_j$ whenever $i \neq j$, the color of an edge is well defined.) We denote this chamber system by Σ_Π. Thus I is both the vertex set of Π and the set of colors of Σ_Π. A *Coxeter chamber system* of type Π is a chamber system Σ with index set I such that there exists a special isomorphism from Σ to Σ_Π. (Thus Σ_Π is the unique Coxeter chamber system of type Π up to a special isomorphism.)

The Coxeter chamber system Σ_Π defined in 2.4 is just the Cayley graph of the group W with respect to the generating set

$$\{r_i \mid i \in I\}$$

with each edge labeled by the corresponding generator. (We will not, however, mention Cayley graphs again.) We emphasize that Σ_Π is a *thin* chamber system, i.e. each chamber is i-adjacent to exactly one chamber for each $i \in I$.

Proposition 2.5. *Let Π be a Coxeter diagram with vertex set I, let (W, r) be the corresponding Coxeter system and let $\Sigma = \Sigma_\Pi$ be the corresponding Coxeter chamber system. Then for all $x \in \Sigma$ and all $f \in M_I$, there is a unique gallery of type f in Σ beginning at x; its last chamber is xr_f. (Thus for all $x, y \in \Sigma$, there is a gallery of type f from x to y in Σ if and only if $x^{-1}y = r_f$, and this gallery, if it exists, is unique. In particular, Σ is connected.)*

Proof. Let $x \in \Sigma$ and let $f = ijk \cdots \in M_I$. By 2.4,

$$(x, xr_i, xr_{ij}, xr_{ijk}, \ldots)$$

is the unique gallery of type f which begins at x. $\square$

It is in the following form that we will apply 2.3 (i). This basic result will be needed in the proofs of 4.2 and 6.13; see also 4.6.

Proposition 2.6. *Let $[m_{ij}]$, I, (W, r) and Σ_Π be as above and let $i, j \in I$ be distinct. Then every $\{i, j\}$-residue of Σ_Π contains exactly $2m_{ij}$ chambers.*

Proof. Let W_{ij} denote the subgroup of W generated by r_i and r_j and let w denote the product $r_i r_j$. By 2.3 (i), $|w| = m_{ij}$, so $r_i \neq r_j$, and $|r_i| = 2$. We have $W_{ij} = \langle r_i, w \rangle$ and $r_i^{-1} w r_i = r_j r_i = w^{-1}$, so $\langle w \rangle$ is a normal subgroup of W_{ij}. Since $\langle w \rangle$ is cyclic, it cannot contain two subgroups of the same order and hence it cannot contain both r_i and r_j. Therefore $r_i \notin \langle w \rangle$. It follows that $|W_{ij}| = 2m_{ij}$. (In fact, W_{ij} is a dihedral group; see Section 1.2 of Chapter 4 of [1].) By 2.5, the chambers of the $\{i, j\}$-residue containing a given chamber x are precisely the elements of the left coset xW_{ij}. $\square$

Chapter Three

Roots

Roots, which we introduce in 3.10, and the projection map, which we introduce in 3.22 and 3.23, play a fundamental role in Tits's approach to Coxeter groups.

To begin our study of these things, we first have to take a careful look at the defining relations of a Coxeter group. Let $[m_{ij}]$ be a Coxeter matrix with index set I, let Π denote the corresponding Coxeter diagram, let (W, r) denote the corresponding Coxeter system, and let $\Sigma = \Sigma_\Pi$ denote the corresponding Coxeter chamber system.

Definition 3.1. Let

$$p(i, j) = \begin{cases} (ij)^{m_{ij}/2} & \text{if } m_{ij} \text{ is even,} \\ j(ij)^{(m_{ij}-1)/2} & \text{if } m_{ij} \text{ is odd} \end{cases}$$

(a word in the free monoid M_I of length m_{ij} ending in j) for all ordered pairs of distinct $i, j \in I$ such that $m_{ij} < \infty$. (If $m_{ij} = \infty$, the word $p(i, j)$ is undefined.) An *elementary homotopy* is a transformation of a word of the form $f_1 p(i, j) f_2$ into the word $f_1 p(j, i) f_2$. (Here f_1 and f_2 are arbitrary elements of M_I.) A *contraction* is a transformation of a word of the form $f_1 i i f_2$ into the word $f_1 f_2$. The inverse of a contraction is called an *expansion*. Two words are called *equivalent* if one can be transformed into the other by a sequence of elementary homotopies, expansions and contractions. We emphasize that all of these notions depend on the given Coxeter matrix $[m_{ij}]$, or equivalently, on the given Coxeter diagram Π.

Our first goal in this chapter is to prove 3.4. This is not a deep result, but its proof requires a bit of reflection on the notion of a group defined by generators and relations. We start by introducing two different notions of conjugation in a free monoid in 3.2 and 3.3.

Notation 3.2. Let f be an arbitrary word in M_I. We denote by $|f|$ the length of a word f and by $\bar{f}$ the word f written in reverse. *Conjugation by f* (for $f \in M_I$) is the map $x \mapsto f x \bar{f}$ from M_I to itself.

By 2.5, a gallery of type f in Σ is minimal if and only if $|f| = \|r_f\|$, where $|f|$ is as defined in 3.2 and $\|r_f\|$ is as defined in 2.9.

In 2.2 we have already assumed that the reader is familiar with the notion of defining relations and, in particular, with the notion of a free group. For the proof of 3.4, however, it will be helpful to have a precise definition of a free group at hand.

Definition 3.3. Let I be a set and let $I^{-1} = \{i^{-1} \mid i \in I\}$ be a disjoint set in one-to-one correspondence with I. Two words of the free monoid $M_{I \cup I^{-1}}$ are *free equivalent* if one can be transformed into the other by a finite sequence of deletions and insertions. A *deletion* is a transformation of a word of the form $f_1 i i^{-1} f_2$ or $f_1 i^{-1} i f_2$ into the word $f_1 f_2$. An *insertion* is the inverse of a deletion. Let F_I denote the set of free-equivalence classes. Then F_I has a unique multiplication $\cdot$ which makes the natural map from $M_{I \cup I^{-1}}$ onto F_I into a homomorphism from a monoid into a group. The pair $(F_I, \cdot)$ is (up to isomorphism) the *free group on the set I*. For each word f in the free monoid $M_{I \cup I^{-1}}$, we denote by f^{-1} the word f written in reverse with every letter i (for $i \in I$) replaced by i^{-1} and every letter i^{-1} (for $i^{-1} \in I^{-1}$) replaced by i. *Conjugation by f* (for $f \in M_{I \cup I^{-1}}$) is the map $x \mapsto f x f^{-1}$.

Proposition 3.4. *Two words f and g in M_I are equivalent (with respect to Π) as defined in 3.1 if and only if $r_f = r_g$.*

Proof. Let f and g be words in M_I. If f and g are equivalent, then $r_f = r_g$ since $r_{ii} = r_i^2 = 1$ and $r_{p(i,j)} = r_{p(j,i)}$ for all i, j. Now suppose, conversely, that $r_f = r_g$ and let $h = f\bar{g}$ (in M_I), where $\bar{g}$ is as in 3.2. Since $r_{\bar{g}} = r_g^{-1}$, we have $r_h = 1$. By 2.2, this means that the image of h (via the canonical embedding of M_I in $M_{I \cup I^{-1}}$) in the free group F_I on I lies in the normal subgroup of F_I generated by X, where X denotes the set of words of the form $(ij)^{m_{ij}}$ for all i, $j \in I$ (possibly equal) such that $m_{ij} < \infty$. We can thus choose an element h_1 in $M_{I \cup I^{-1}}$ which is built up out of words in X, multiplication and conjugation (by arbitrary words) as defined in 3.3 such that h and h_1 have the same image in F_I. This means that h_1 can be obtained from h by a finite sequence of insertions and deletions:

$$h \to g_1 \to g_2 \to \cdots \to g_k \to h_1.$$

Let h_1^+ (respectively, $g_1^+, g_2^+, \ldots, g_k^+$) denote the word in M_I obtained from h_1 (respectively, $g_1, g_2, \ldots, g_k$) by replacing every letter of I^{-1} which appears in it by the corresponding letter in I. Then

$$h \to g_1^+ \to g_2^+ \to \cdots \to g_k^+ \to h_1^+$$

is a sequence of expansions and contractions from h to h_1^+. Moreover, h_1^+ is built up out of words in X, multiplication and conjugation (by arbitrary words) as defined in 3.2. If $1 < m_{ij} < \infty$ for some $i, j \in I$, then

$$(ij)^{m_{ij}} = p(i, j)^2 \qquad \text{and} \qquad p(j, i) = \overline{p(i, j)}$$

if m_{ij} is even and

$$(ij)^{m_{ij}} = p(j, i)p(i, j) \quad \text{and} \quad p(i, j) = \overline{p(i, j)}$$

if m_{ij} is odd, and thus in both cases, the word $(ij)^{m_{ij}}$ can be transformed into the empty word by an elementary homotopy followed by several contractions. It follows that h_1^+ is equivalent to the empty word. Thus h is also equivalent to the empty word and hence hg is equivalent to g. Since f is equivalent to hg (via a sequence of expansions), it follows that f is equivalent to g. $\qquad\square$

Corollary 3.5. *If $r_f = r_g$ for two words f and g in M_I, then $|f|$ and $|g|$ have the same parity.*

Proof. This holds by 3.4 since the lengths of two equivalent words differ by an even number. $\qquad\square$

Proposition 3.6. *Let x, y, z be chambers of Σ. If y and z are adjacent, then $\mathrm{dist}(x, y) = \mathrm{dist}(x, z) \pm 1$.*

Proof. Since y and z are adjacent, we have

$$\mathrm{dist}(x, z) - 1 \leqslant \mathrm{dist}(x, y) \leqslant \mathrm{dist}(x, z) + 1.$$

It is thus necessary to show only that $\mathrm{dist}(x, y) \neq \mathrm{dist}(x, z)$. Let γ be a gallery from x to y, let f denote the type of γ and let i be the type of the panel containing y and z. Then (γ, z) is a gallery of type fi from x to z. Hence, by 2.5, $r_f = x^{-1}y = r_g$ for all $g \in M_I$ such that there is a gallery of type g from x to y. Similarly, $r_{fi} = x^{-1}z = r_h$ for all $h \in M_I$ such that there is a gallery of type h from x to z. By 3.5, therefore, $\mathrm{dist}(x, y)$ has the same parity as $|f|$ and $\mathrm{dist}(x, z)$ has the same parity as $|fi|$. $\qquad\square$

Next we introduce reflections.

Definition 3.7. We identify W with its image under the isomorphism from W to $\mathrm{Aut}^\circ(\Sigma)$ described in 2.8. A *reflection* is a non-trivial element of W which fixes edges (i.e. panels) of Σ. By 2.8, only the trivial element fixes a chamber of Σ. It follows that if s is a reflection and $\{x, y\}$ is an edge of Σ fixed by s, then s interchanges x and y, $|s| = 2$ and s is uniquely determined by $\{x, y\}$. In fact, for each edge $\{x, y\}$, there exists an $i \in I$ such that $y = xr_i$ and hence there exists a reflection which fixes $\{x, y\}$, namely, the product $x r_i x^{-1}$. The set of edges fixed by a reflection s will be called the *wall* of s and will be denoted by M_s.

Let s be a reflection. We will say that a gallery $\gamma = (c_0, c_1, \ldots, c_k)$ *crosses the wall* M_s at the panel $\{c_{i-1}, c_i\}$ for some $i \in [1, k]$ if the panel $\{c_{i-1}, c_i\}$ is contained in M_s. We will say that γ *crosses* M_s m *times* if m is the number of indices $i \in [1, k]$ such that γ crosses M_s at $\{c_{i-1}, c_i\}$.

Lemma 3.8. *A minimal gallery cannot cross a wall more than once.*

Proof. Let s be a reflection and let $\gamma = (c_0, c_1, \ldots, c_k)$ be a gallery which crosses the wall M_s at the panels $\{c_{i-1}, c_i\}$ and $\{c_{j-1}, c_j\}$ for $i, j \in [1, k]$ such that $i < j$. Then s interchanges c_{m-1} and c_m for $m = i$ and j. Since s is an automorphism of Σ, it preserves distances. Thus $\text{dist}(c_i, c_{j-1}) = \text{dist}(c_{i-1}, c_j)$. Since the subgallery of γ from c_i to c_{j-1} is of length $j - i - 1$ and the length of the subgallery of γ from c_{i-1} to c_j is $j - i + 1$, the gallery γ cannot be minimal. $\square$

Lemma 3.9. *Let* $x, y \in \Sigma$ *and let* s *be a reflection of* Σ. *For each gallery* γ *from* x *to* y *let* $n(\gamma)$ *denote the number of times* γ *crosses* M_s. *Then the parity of* $n(\gamma)$ *depends only on* x, y *and* s *and not on* γ.

Proof. Let γ and γ' be two galleries from x to y; we denote their types by f and g. By 2.5, $r_f = x^{-1} y = r_g$. By 3.4, therefore, f and g are equivalent. If f and g differ by a contraction or an expansion, then either $n(\gamma) = n(\gamma')$ or $n(\gamma) = n(\gamma') \pm 2$. It suffices to assume, therefore, that f and g differ by an elementary homotopy. By 2.5 again, there are galleries $\gamma_1, \gamma_2, \gamma_2', \gamma_3$ and distinct $i, j \in I$ such that γ_2 and γ_2' both start at the last chamber of γ_1 and both end at the first chamber of γ_3, γ_2 is of type $p(i, j)$, γ_2' is of type $p(j, i)$, $\gamma = (\gamma_1, \gamma_2, \gamma_3)$ and $\gamma' = (\gamma_1, \gamma_2', \gamma_3)$. Let X denote the union of the chamber sets of $[\gamma_2]$ and $[\gamma_2']$. Then X is the chamber set of an $\{i, j\}$-residue and, by 2.6, $|X| = 2m_{ij}$. Let R denote this $\{i, j\}$-residue and suppose that some edge of R lies in M_s and is thus mapped to itself by s. Since s is a special automorphism, it must map the residue R to itself. It follows that s fixes a unique edge of the subgraph $[\gamma_2]$ and a unique edge of the subgraph $[\gamma_2']$. In other words, $n(\gamma_2) = n(\gamma_2') = 1$. We conclude that $n(\gamma) = n(\gamma')$. $\square$

We come now to the definition of a root.

Definition 3.10. Let s be a reflection of Σ. We define a relation $\equiv_s$ on Σ by setting $x \equiv_s y$ for $x, y \in \Sigma$ if and only if there is a gallery in Σ from x to y which crosses the wall M_s an even number of times. By 3.9, $x \equiv_s y$ for

$x, y \in \Sigma$ if and only if *every* gallery in Σ from x to y crosses the wall M_s an even number of times. The relation $\equiv_s$ is an equivalence relation. A *root* of Σ is an equivalence class with respect to $\equiv_s$ for some reflection s.

Proposition 3.11. *There are exactly two roots associated with a reflection s of Σ. For each panel $\{x, y\} \in M_s$, the two roots are*

$$\{u \mid \mathrm{dist}(u, x) < \mathrm{dist}(u, y)\}$$

and its complement. They are interchanged by s.

Proof. Let s be a reflection and let $\{x, y\}$ be a panel in M_s. The gallery (x, y) crosses M_s once. By 3.9, therefore, x and y are inequivalent with respect to $\equiv_s$. Let $u \in \Sigma$. Suppose that $\mathrm{dist}(u, x) < \mathrm{dist}(u, y)$. Let γ be a minimal gallery from u to x. Then (γ, y) is also a minimal gallery. Hence, by 3.8, γ does not cross M_s (since the last edge of the minimal gallery (γ, y) crosses M_s at $\{x, y\}$). Thus $u \equiv_s x$. By symmetry, $u \equiv_s y$ if $\mathrm{dist}(u, y) < \mathrm{dist}(u, x)$. By 3.6, every chamber is either nearer to x than to y or nearer to y than to x. Since s preserves distances and interchanges x and y, it also interchanges the set of chambers nearer to x than to y with its complement. $\qquad\square$

By 3.11, the complement of a root is also a root. If α is an arbitrary root, we will denote its complement by $-\alpha$ and we will say that $-\alpha$ is the root *opposite* α (or that α and $-\alpha$ are opposite roots).

Proposition 3.12. *Let s be a reflection of Σ. Then a panel is contained in the wall M_s if and only if it contains one chamber from each of the two roots associated with s.*

Proof. Let P be a panel and let x and y be the two chambers in P. By 3.10, the panel P contains one chamber from each of the two roots associated with s if and only if the gallery (x, y) crosses M_s an odd number of times, i.e. if and only if $P \in M_s$. $\qquad\square$

Notation 3.13. Let α be one of the two roots associated with a reflection s of Σ. By 3.7 and 3.12, s is the unique non-trivial element of $\mathrm{Aut}^\circ(\Sigma)$ which fixes any given panel having exactly one chamber in α, and the wall M_s is precisely the set of all such panels. Thus s and M_s are uniquely determined by α. We denote by $\mathrm{refl}_\Sigma(\alpha)$ the reflection s and by M_α the wall M_s. Thus $\mathrm{refl}_\Sigma(-\alpha) = \mathrm{refl}_\Sigma(\alpha)$ and $M_{-\alpha} = M_\alpha$. We denote by $\partial\alpha$ the set of chambers of α contained in a panel which is contained in the wall M_α. (In [7], $\partial\alpha$ is used to denote the wall M_α itself.)

Corollary 3.14. *Let α be a root of Σ and let $\mathrm{refl}_\Sigma(\alpha)$ and $\partial\alpha$ be as in 3.13. Let $s = \mathrm{refl}_\Sigma(\alpha)$. For each $x \in \partial\alpha$, the product sx (i.e. the image of x under s) is the only chamber adjacent to x which lies in $-\alpha$.*

Proof. This holds by 3.12. $\square$

We will often use these basic results about roots in the following form.

Corollary 3.15. *For all ordered pairs (x, y) of adjacent chambers, let*

$$\Sigma_{(x\backslash y)} = \{u \mid \mathrm{dist}(u, x) < \mathrm{dist}(u, y)\}.$$

Then for all ordered pairs (x, y) of adjacent chambers, $\Sigma_{(x\backslash y)}$ is the unique root of Σ containing x but not y and $\mathrm{refl}_\Sigma(\Sigma_{(x\backslash y)})$ is the unique reflection of Σ interchanging x and y.

Proof. By 3.7, there is a unique reflection s interchanging x and y. By 3.11, there is a unique root α such that $\mathrm{refl}_\Sigma(\alpha) = s$ and $x \in \alpha$, and the root α contains precisely those chambers of Σ which are nearer to x than to y. In particular, $y \notin \alpha$. If β is an arbitrary root containing x but not y, then $\{x, y\} \in M_\beta$ by 3.12, thus $\mathrm{refl}_\Sigma(\beta) = s$ by 3.7 and hence $\beta = \alpha$. $\square$

At this point, it might be instructive to consider the reflections and roots of the Coxeter chamber systems of type A_3 and C_3 using the models described in 2.10. In both cases, a reflection in the Coxeter group act on Ξ_Π as the restriction to Ξ_Π of a reflection of the ambient Euclidean space, and a root corresponding to a reflection consists of all the chambers of Ξ_Π on one side of the corresponding plane of reflection. In the first case, there are six reflections (and thus 12 roots) and the intersection of each plane of reflection with Ω is made up of lines (i.e. boundaries of chambers) having all three colors. The group $G = \langle S_i \mid i \in I \rangle$ acts transitively on the set of these intersections, hence W acts transitively on the set of roots in Ξ_Π and thus the set of reflections forms a single conjugacy class in W. In the second case, there are six planes of reflection intersecting Ω in lines colored black and gray and three planes of reflection intersecting Ω only in lines colored red, and the group G acts transitively on the set of black–gray intersections and on the set of red intersections. There are thus nine reflections altogether (and hence 18 roots) forming two conjugacy classes in W, one of size six and the other of size three. There are two kinds of roots: 12 have walls containing only black and gray panels and the remaining 6 have walls made up entirely of red panels.

We now turn to foldings.

Definition 3.16. For each root α of Σ, let $\rho_{\Sigma,\alpha}$ denote the map from Σ to Σ given by

$$\rho_{\Sigma,\alpha}(u) = \begin{cases} u & \text{if } u \in \alpha, \\ su & \text{if } u \notin \alpha, \end{cases}$$

where $s = \text{refl}_\Sigma(\alpha)$. The map $\rho_{\Sigma,\alpha}$ will be called the *folding* corresponding to α. By 3.11, the image of $\rho_{\Sigma,\alpha}$ is α.

Proposition 3.17. *Let α be a root of Σ. The folding $\rho_{\Sigma,\alpha}$ is a special endomorphism of Σ as defined in 1.16 and adjacent chambers have the same image under $\rho_{\Sigma,\alpha}$ if and only if the panel which contains them lies in M_α.*

Proof. Let $\rho = \rho_{\Sigma,\alpha}$ and let x and y be i-adjacent chambers for some $i \in I$. If x and y are contained both in α or both in $-\alpha$, then $\rho(x)$ and $\rho(y)$ are i-adjacent since $\text{refl}_\Sigma(\alpha)$ is a special automorphism. By 3.12, $\text{refl}_\Sigma(\alpha)$ interchanges x and y (i.e. $\{x, y\} \in M_\alpha$) if and only if x and y are contained neither both in α nor both in $-\alpha$. It follows that $\rho(x) = \rho(y)$ if and only if $\{x, y\} \in M_\alpha$. $\square$

Proposition 3.18. *Let α be a root of Σ and let $x \in \alpha$. Then*

$$\text{dist}(x, \rho_{\Sigma,\alpha}(y)) < \text{dist}(x, y)$$

for all $y \in -\alpha$.

Proof. Let $y \in -\alpha$ and let $\gamma = (x, \ldots, y)$ be a minimal gallery from x to y. By 3.10, γ must cross M_α. By 1.18 and 3.17, $\rho_{\Sigma,\alpha}(\gamma)$ is a pre-gallery from $x = \rho_{\Sigma,\alpha}(x)$ to $\rho_{\Sigma,\alpha}(y)$ whose underlying gallery is shorter than γ. $\square$

Proposition 3.19. *The subgraph spanned by a root is convex.*

Proof. Let $s = \text{refl}_\Sigma(\alpha)$, let $x, y \in \alpha$ and let $\gamma = (u_0, u_1, \ldots, u_k)$ be a minimal gallery from x to y. By 3.8, γ crosses M_α at most once. By 3.10, γ crosses M_α an even number of times. It follows that γ does not cross M_α at all. By 3.12, therefore, $u_i \in \alpha$ for all $i \in [0, k]$. $\square$

In the next few results, we begin to put roots and foldings to use.

Proposition 3.20. *Let $x, y \in \Sigma$ and let k denote the number of roots of Σ which contain the chamber x but not the chamber y. Then $\text{dist}(x, y) = k$. More precisely, if $(u_0, u_1, \ldots, u_k)$ is a minimal gallery from x to y, then the roots*

$$\Sigma_{(u_0 \backslash u_1)}, \Sigma_{(u_1 \backslash u_2)}, \ldots, \Sigma_{(u_{k-1} \backslash u_k)}$$

as defined in 3.15 are distinct, they all contain x but not y and every other root which contains x also contains y.

Proof. Let $\gamma = (u_0, u_1, \ldots, u_k)$ be a minimal gallery from x to y and let α_i denote the root $\Sigma_{(u_{i-1} \backslash u_i)}$ for all $i \in [1, k]$. Thus

$$\alpha_i = \{w \in \Sigma \mid \text{dist}(w, u_{i-1}) < \text{dist}(w, u_i)\}$$

and α_i is the unique root containing u_{i-1} but not u_i for each $i \in [1, k]$. If α is an arbitrary root containing x but not y, then α contains u_{i-1} but not u_i for some $i \in [1, k]$ and hence $\alpha = \alpha_i$. Since γ is minimal, $(u_0, \ldots, u_{i-1})$ lies in α_i and $(u_i, \ldots, u_k)$ lies in $-\alpha_i$ for each $i \in [1, k]$. Therefore the roots $\alpha_1, \ldots, \alpha_k$ are distinct. $\qquad\square$

Proposition 3.21. *Let x and y be chambers of Σ and let S be the set of roots containing x and y. (The set S might be empty.) Then a chamber u lies on an minimal gallery from x to y if and only if u is contained in every root in S. (In particular, if $S = \emptyset$, then every chamber lies on a minimal gallery from x to y.)*

Proof. By 3.19, every minimal gallery from x to y is contained in every root in S. Now let u be a chamber contained in every root in S. Let T denote the set of roots containing x but not y, let T_1 denote the set of roots containing x but not u and let T_2 denote the set of roots containing u but not y. If a root contains x and y, then it contains u. This implies that $T_1 \subset T$. If a root contains neither x nor y, then its opposite contains both x and y and hence also u. This implies that $T_2 \subset T$. It follows that T is the disjoint union of T_1 and T_2. By 3.20, therefore,

$$\begin{aligned} \text{dist}(x, y) &= |T| \\ &= |T_1| + |T_2| \\ &= \text{dist}(x, u) + \text{dist}(u, y). \end{aligned}$$

This is equivalent to the assertion that the concatenation of a minimal gallery from x to u with a minimal gallery from u to y is a minimal gallery from x to y. $\qquad\square$

The following result describes a fundamental property of Coxeter chamber systems.

Theorem 3.22. *Let x be a chamber and let R be a residue of Σ. Then there is a unique chamber w in R which is nearest x. For every chamber $y \in R$, there is a minimal gallery from x to y which passes through w, or equivalently,*

$$\text{dist}(x, y) = \text{dist}(x, w) + \text{dist}(w, y).$$

Proof. Let w be a chamber in R which is nearest x and let y be an arbitrary chamber in R. Suppose that α is a root containing x and y and let ρ denote the folding $\rho_{\Sigma,\alpha}$ as defined in 3.16. Then $\rho(y) = y$, so $y \in R \cap \rho(R)$. By 3.17, ρ is a special endomorphism of Σ. By 1.19, therefore, $\rho(R) \subset R$. Hence $\rho(w) \in R$. By 3.18 and the choice of w, it follows that $w \in \alpha$. Since α is arbitrary, it follows by 3.21 that w lies on a minimal gallery from x to y. In particular, $\text{dist}(x, w) < \text{dist}(x, y)$ if y is distinct from w, so w is unique. $\qquad\square$

Definition 3.23. For each residue R of Σ, let proj_R denote the map which sends each chamber x to the unique chamber of R which is nearest x. This map will be called the *projection from Σ to R*.

Here is our first application of the projection map.

Proposition 3.24. *All residues of Σ are convex.*

Proof. Let R be a J-residue for some $J \subset I$, let x and z be chambers of R and let γ be a minimal gallery from x to z. By 2.7, it suffices to show that every chamber of γ is contained in R. Let y be a chamber of Σ not in R and let $w = \text{proj}_R y$. By 3.22, $\text{dist}(x, w) < \text{dist}(x, y)$ and $\text{dist}(w, z) < \text{dist}(y, z)$. There are therefore galleries from x to z which pass through w which are shorter than any gallery from x to z which passes through y. Hence no minimal gallery from x to z contains y. Since y is arbitrary, it follows that $\gamma \subset R$. $\qquad\square$

Note that 3.24 says, in particular, that the distance between two chambers of a residue R is the same whether it is measured in R or in Σ.

The following observation will be needed in the proofs of 5.15 and 5.16 and 8.25.

Proposition 3.25. *Let J and J' be subsets of I, let R and R' be residues of Σ of type J and J', let $S = R \cap R'$ and suppose that $S \neq \emptyset$. Then S is a residue of type $J \cap J'$ and*

$$\text{proj}_R u = \text{proj}_S u$$

for all $u \in R'$.

Proof. By 3.24, S is $J \cap J'$-connected and hence a $J \cap J'$-residue. Let $u \in R'$ and $x \in S$. By 3.22 there exists a minimal gallery γ from u to x which contains $\text{proj}_R u$, and by 3.24, $\gamma \subset R'$. Therefore $\text{proj}_R u \in S$. It follows that $\text{proj}_R u = \text{proj}_S u$. $\qquad\square$

We close this chapter by showing how the well-known *exchange condition* for Coxeter groups follows from our results about roots and foldings. We will not, in fact, make any use of the exchange condition in this book.

Proposition 3.26 ('Exchange Condition'). *Let* $t \in W$ *be a reflection, let* $f = i_1 \cdots i_k$ *be a word in* M_I *and let* $x = r_f t$ *or* $t r_f$. *If* $\|x\| < \|r_f\|$, *then there exists* $j \in [1, k]$ *such that* $x = r_g$, *where* g *is the word obtained from* f *by deleting the factor* i_j.

Proof. Since $\|u\| = \|u^{-1}\|$ for all $u \in W$, it suffices to prove the claim for $x = t r_f$. Let $x = t r_f$ and suppose that $\|x\| < \|r_f\|$. By 2.5, there exists a gallery

$$\gamma = (x_0, \ldots, x_k)$$

in Σ of type f from 1 to r_f. Let α denote the root associated with the reflection t (so $t = \text{refl}_\Sigma(\alpha)$) which contains 1. Then α also contains x since otherwise

$$\|r_f\| = \text{dist}(1, r_f) = \text{dist}(1, \rho_{\Sigma, \alpha}(x)) < \text{dist}(1, x) = \|x\|$$

by 3.18. By 3.11, therefore, $r_f = tx \in t\alpha = -\alpha$. Hence, by 3.10, we choose $j \in [1, k]$ such that γ crosses the wall M_t at the panel $\{x_{j-1}, x_j\}$. This means that t interchanges x_{j-1} and x_j. Let $\gamma_1 = (x_0, \ldots, x_{j-1})$, let $\gamma_2 = (x_j, \ldots, x_k)$ and let g denote the word obtained from f by deleting the factor i_j. Since left multiplication by t is a special automorphism and $t x_j = x_{j-1}$,

$$(\gamma_1, t\gamma_2)$$

is a gallery of type g from 1 to $t r_f = x$. By 2.5, therefore, $x = r_g$. $\square$

The property described in 3.26 is actually the *strong* exchange condition. The exchange condition itself is the special case where the reflection t is assumed to equal r_i for some $i \in I$. By Theorem 1 in § 1.6 of Chapter 4 of [1], the exchange condition characterizes Coxeter groups.

Chapter Four

Reduced Words

In this chapter, we use residues, roots and the projection map to look deeper into the structure of a Coxeter chamber system. The main results are 4.2 and 4.3; the rest of the chapter will be devoted to some of their consequences.

We continue to assume that $[m_{ij}]$ is a Coxeter matrix with index set I, that Π is the corresponding Coxeter diagram, that (W, r) is the corresponding Coxeter system, and that $\Sigma = \Sigma_\Pi$ is the corresponding Coxeter chamber system.

Recall the definition of the map p and an elementary homotopy given in 3.1. Thus an elementary homotopy is a transformation of a word in the free monoid M_I of the form $f_1 p(i, j) f_2$ into the word $f_1 p(j, i) f_2$.

Here are the main definitions of this chapter.

Definition 4.1. Two words f and g in M_I are *homotopic* if f can be transformed into g by a sequence of elementary homotopies. We will write $f \simeq g$ to denote that f and g are homotopic. A word in M_I is *contractible* if it is of the form $f_1 i i f_2$ for some $i \in I$. A word in M_I will be called *reduced* if it is not homotopic to a contractible word. We emphasize that all of these notions depend on the given Coxeter matrix $[m_{ij}]$, or equivalently, on the given Coxeter diagram Π.

The next several results are fundamental.

Proposition 4.2. *Let x, y be two chambers of Σ, let γ and γ' be two minimal galleries from x to y and let f and g denote their types. Then $f \simeq g$.*

Proof. We proceed by induction with respect to $\text{dist}(x, y)$. If $x = y$ or if $\text{dist}(x, y) = 1$, in which case $\gamma = (x, y) = \gamma'$, there is nothing to prove. Suppose that $\text{dist}(x, y) > 1$ and let i and j be the last letters of f and g. Thus $f = f_1 i$ and $g = g_1 j$ for some $f_1, g_1 \in M_I$ and $\gamma = (\gamma_1, y)$ and $\gamma' = (\gamma'_1, y)$ for galleries γ_1 of type f_1 and γ'_1 of type g_1. Let y_1 and y'_1 denote the last chambers of γ_1 and γ'_1. If $i = j$, then y_1 and y'_1 both lie on the i-panel containing y, hence $y_1 = y'_1$, hence $f_1 \simeq g_1$ by induction and therefore $f \simeq g$. Now suppose that $i \neq j$, let R denote the $\{i, j\}$-residue containing y and let $z = \text{proj}_R x$. Let γ_0 be a minimal gallery from x to z and let γ_2 and γ'_2 be minimal galleries from z to y_1 and from z to y'_1. By 3.22, (γ_0, γ_2) and (γ_0, γ'_2)

are minimal galleries from x to y_1 and from x to y_1'. Since

$$\text{dist}(x, y_1) = \text{dist}(x, y) - 1 = \text{dist}(x, y_1'),$$

it follows that (γ_2, y) and (γ_2', y) are minimal galleries of the same length. By 3.24, both $[\gamma_2]$ and $[\gamma_2']$ are subgraphs of the $\{i, j\}$-residue R. By 2.6, it follows that $m_{ij} < \infty$, the type of (γ_2, y) is $p(j, i)$ and the type of (γ_2', y) is $p(i, j)$. There is thus an elementary homotopy from the type of (γ_0, γ_2, y) to the type of (γ_0, γ_2', y). By induction, the type of γ is homotopic to the type of (γ_0, γ_2, y) and the type of (γ_0, γ_2', y) is homotopic to the type of γ'. $\square$

Proposition 4.3. *A gallery of Σ is minimal if and only if its type is reduced.*

Proof. Let γ be a gallery of Σ, let f denote the type of γ and let x and y denote the first and last chambers of γ. Suppose first that f is not reduced, i.e. that f is homotopic to a word g such that $g = g_1 i i g_2$ for some $g_1, g_2 \in M_I$ and some $i \in I$. Then $r_f = r_g$, so by 2.5, there is a gallery γ' from x to y of type g. The galleries γ and γ' both have length $|f| = |g|$. We have

$$\gamma' = (x, \ldots, u, v, w, \ldots, y),$$

where $(x, \ldots, u)$ is of type g_1, $(w, \ldots, y)$ is of type g_2 and $u \sim_i v \sim_i w$. Since Γ is thin, $u = w$. We thus obtain a gallery from x to y which is shorter than γ' by deleting v and w. Therefore γ is not minimal.

Now suppose that f is reduced. We will show that γ is minimal by using induction with respect to the length $|f|$ of f. We can assume that $|f| > 1$ and hence that $f = gij$ for some $g \in M_I$ and some $i, j \in I$ (necessarily distinct). Let $\gamma_1 = (x, \ldots, z)$ denote the gallery of type gi obtained from γ by deleting the last chamber. By induction, γ_1 is minimal, so $\text{dist}(x, z) = |f| - 1$. Suppose that γ itself is not minimal. By 3.6, it follows that $\text{dist}(x, y) = |f| - 2$. Hence there is a minimal gallery $\gamma_2 = (x, \ldots, y)$ from x to y of length $|f| - 2$. Let h denote the type of γ_2. Thus γ_1 and (γ_2, z) are both minimal galleries from x to z, one of type gi and the other of type hj. By 4.2, $gi \simeq hj$. Therefore $f = gij \simeq hjj$. This contradicts the assumption that f is reduced. $\square$

Proposition 4.4. *Let f and g be reduced words in M_I such that $r_f = r_g$. Then $f \simeq g$.*

Proof. By 2.5, there are galleries γ and γ' in Σ of type f and g which begin at 1 and end at $r_f = r_g$. By 4.3, γ and γ' are minimal. By 4.2, therefore, $f \simeq g$. $\square$

Proposition 4.5. *Let $w = r_g$ for some word $g \in M_I$. Then $\|w\| \leqslant |g|$ with equality if and only if g is reduced.*

Proof. Let f be the type of a minimal gallery γ from 1 to w. By 2.9, $\|w\| = |f|$. By two applications of 2.5, $w = r_f$ and there is a gallery γ' of type g from 1 to w. Since γ is minimal, $|f| \leqslant |g|$ with equality if and only if γ' is also minimal. By 4.3, therefore, $|f| = |g|$ if and only if g is reduced.   □

The following important result generalizes 2.6.

Theorem 4.6. *Let J be a subset of I, let Π_J denote the subdiagram of Π spanned by the set J (i.e. the subdiagram obtained from Π by deleting all the vertices not in J and all the edges containing a vertex of J), let*

$$W_J = \langle r_i \mid i \in J \rangle,$$

and let r_J denote the restriction of r to M_J. Then (W_J, r_J) is a Coxeter system of type Π_J.

Proof. The group W_J is certainly a quotient of the Coxeter group associated with the diagram Π_J. By 3.4, therefore, it is only necessary to show that if f and g are any two words in M_J which are equivalent in M_I, then they are, in fact, equivalent in M_J, by which we mean that f can be transformed into g by a sequence of contractions, expansions and elementary homotopies in such a way that all the intermediate words lie in M_J. Suppose that f and g are two words of M_J which are equivalent in M_I, i.e. such that $r_f = r_g$. Using only elementary homotopies and contractions, we can find reduced words $f' \in M_J$ and $g' \in M_J$ such that $r_{f'} = r_f$ and $r_{g'} = r_g$. This means that f is equivalent to f' in M_J and that g is equivalent to g' in M_J. Since $r_{f'} = r_{g'}$, we have $f' \sim g'$ by 4.4. Hence f' is equivalent to g' in M_J. It follows that f is equivalent to g in M_J.   □

4.7. Not to have to assume that $J \neq \emptyset$ in 4.9, 7.18 and 7.20 below, we prefer to include explicitly the case $J = \emptyset$ in 4.6. To do this, we must allow $I = \emptyset$ in 2.2, in which case Π is the 'empty' Coxeter diagram, $M_I = \{\emptyset\}$ and the corresponding Coxeter group W is the trivial group. The corresponding Coxeter chamber system has just one chamber, no edges and no roots.

The following result generalizes 2.7, but note that 2.7, via 3.24, 4.2 and 4.4, is needed in its proof.

Proposition 4.8. *Let $f \in M_I$ be a reduced word, let $J \subset I$ and let W_J be as in 4.6. Then $r_f \in W_J$ if and only if $f \in M_J$.*

Proof. If $r_f \in W_J$, then $r_f = r_g$ for some reduced word $g \in M_J$ and hence $f \in M_J$ by 4.4. □

Proposition 4.9. *Let R be a J-residue of Σ for some $J \subset I$ and let Π_J be as in 4.6. Then there is a special isomorphism from the Coxeter chamber system Σ_{Π_J} to the residue R.*

Proof. By 4.6, the inclusion map from $W_J = \langle r_i \mid i \in J \rangle$ into W yields a special isomorphism from Σ_{Π_J} to the J-residue of Σ containing 1. By 2.8, left multiplication by an arbitrary element of R yields a special isomorphism from this residue to R. □

By 4.9, it makes sense to talk about roots of a residue R (with the understanding that R has no roots if its type is empty, i.e. if R consists of a single chamber).

Proposition 4.10. *Let R be a residue of Σ, let α be a root of Σ and let $s = \mathrm{refl}_\Sigma(\alpha)$. Suppose that neither $R \subset \alpha$ nor $R \subset -\alpha$. Then $R \cap \alpha$ is a root of R, its wall is contained in the wall M_s of α, s maps R to itself and its restriction to R is the reflection $\mathrm{refl}_R(R \cap \alpha)$.*

Proof. Since R is connected, we can choose adjacent chambers x and y such that $x \in R \cap \alpha$ and $y \in R \cap -\alpha$. By 3.15 and 3.24,

$$R \cap \alpha = \{u \in R \mid \mathrm{dist}(u, x) < \mathrm{dist}(u, y)\}$$

and hence $R \cap \alpha$ is a root of R. By 3.12, the wall of this root contains $\{x, y\}$ and is contained in the wall M_s. Since s is a special automorphism of Σ which fixes $\{x, y\}$, it maps R to itself. By 3.7, the restriction of s to R is the unique reflection of R fixing $\{x, y\}$. By 3.15 again, it follows that the restriction of s to R equals $\mathrm{refl}_R(R \cap \alpha)$. □

Proposition 4.11. *Let $f \in M_I$ and $i \in I$. If f is reduced but fi (respectively, if) is not, then f is homotopic to a word which ends (respectively, begins) with i.*

Proof. Let f be a reduced word. Suppose first that fi is not reduced. By 2.5, there is a gallery γ of type f from 1 to r_f; let k denote its length (i.e. $k = |f|$). By 4.3, γ is minimal and the gallery (γ, r_{fi}) is not. By 3.6, therefore, $\mathrm{dist}(1, r_{fi}) = k - 1$. Let γ' be a minimal gallery from 1 to r_{fi} and let g denote its type. Then (γ', r_f) is a gallery from 1 to r_f of length k and type r_{gi}. By 4.2, $f \simeq gi$. Thus if fi is not reduced, then f is homotopic to a word which ends in i.

Suppose instead that if is not reduced. Then $\bar{f}$ (where $\bar{f}$ is as defined in 3.2) is reduced but $\bar{f}i$ is not. By the conclusion of the previous paragraph, there is a word h such that $\bar{f} \simeq hi$. Therefore $f \simeq i\bar{h}$, i.e. f is homotopic to a word beginning in i. $\quad\square$

We close this chapter with a small observation which will be needed in the proofs of 6.4 and 6.13.

Proposition 4.12. *Suppose that Π is irreducible and that $|I| \geqslant 2$, let α be a root of Σ and let $x \in \partial\alpha$, where $\partial\alpha$ is as defined in 3.13. Then x is adjacent to chambers of α which are not in $\partial\alpha$.*

Proof. By 3.14, there is a unique chamber w adjacent to x which is contained in $-\alpha$. Let i denote the type of the panel containing x and w. By hypothesis, there exists a $j \in I$ such that $m_{ij} \geqslant 3$. Let y denote the unique chamber which is j-adjacent to x. Since $j \neq i$, we have $y \in \alpha$. It will therefore suffice to show that $y \notin \partial\alpha$. Let z be any chamber adjacent to y and different from x. Then the type of the gallery (w, x, y, z) is reduced. By 4.3, therefore, this gallery is minimal, so $\text{dist}(x, z) < \text{dist}(w, z)$. Hence, by 3.15, $z \in \alpha$. Since z is arbitrary, it follows that $y \notin \partial\alpha$. $\quad\square$

Chapter Five

Opposites

In this chapter we examine some special properties of finite Coxeter chamber systems. Finite Coxeter groups were classified in 1935 by Coxeter himself [3]. It is noteworthy, however, that this classification is not required in any of the proofs given in this book. Not to be too secretive, however, and because the classification does play an essential role in the classification of thick irreducible spherical buildings (which is summarized in Chapter 12), we formulate Coxeter's result in 5.17 below.

We continue to assume that $[m_{ij}]$ is a Coxeter matrix with index set I, that Π is the corresponding Coxeter diagram, that (W, r) is the corresponding Coxeter system, and that $\Sigma = \Sigma_\Pi$ is the corresponding Coxeter chamber system. Recall that in 1.1 we defined two chambers x, y of a chamber system Δ to be opposite if $\text{dist}(x, y) = \text{diam } \Delta < \infty$. Recall, too, that we defined Π to be spherical in 2.2 if the group W (equivalently, the chamber system Σ) is finite.

Proposition 5.1. $|\Sigma| < \infty$ if and only if $\text{diam } \Sigma < \infty$.

Proof. Suppose that Σ is infinite. If $|I| < \infty$, then there are only finitely many galleries of any given length starting at any given chamber, so diam Σ is also infinite. Suppose that I is infinite. Then M_I contains words of arbitrary length which are composed of distinct letters. A word composed of distinct letters is reduced, so by 4.3, diam Σ is infinite. □

Proposition 5.2. *If x and y are opposite chambers of Σ, then*

$$|\alpha \cap \{x, y\}| = 1$$

for all roots α. In particular, no root contains a pair of opposite chambers.

Proof. Let α be a root, let x and y be arbitrary chambers of R and suppose that $|\alpha \cap \{x, y\}| \neq 1$. Replacing α by its opposite if necessary, we can assume that x and y both lie in α. Let $y' = sy$, where $s = \text{refl}_\Sigma(\alpha)$ is as defined in 3.13. By 3.11, $y' \in s\alpha = -\alpha$. Hence $y = \rho_{\Sigma,\alpha}(y')$, where $\rho_{\Sigma,\alpha}$ is as in 3.16. By 3.18, therefore, $\text{dist}(x, y) < \text{dist}(x, y')$. We conclude that the chambers x and y are not opposite. □

Proposition 5.3. *Suppose that Σ is finite. Then Σ has exactly*

$$2 \cdot \operatorname{diam} \Sigma$$

roots.

Proof. Choose opposite chambers x and y in Σ and let S be the set of roots which contain x but not y and let $T = \{-\alpha \mid \alpha \in S\}$. Then $|S| = |T|$ and T is the set of roots containing y but not x (so S and T are, in particular, disjoint). By 3.20,

$$\operatorname{diam} \Sigma = \operatorname{dist}(x, y) = |S|.$$

By 5.2, every root of Σ lies in S or T. $\square$

Proposition 5.4. *If x, y are opposite chambers of Σ, then every chamber lies on a minimal gallery from x to y, or equivalently,*

$$\operatorname{dist}(x, u) + \operatorname{dist}(u, y) = d$$

for all $u \in \Sigma$, where $d = \operatorname{dist}(x, y) = \operatorname{diam} \Sigma$.

Proof. This holds by 3.21 and 5.2. $\square$

Proposition 5.5. *Suppose that Σ is finite. Then for each chamber of Σ there is a unique chamber which is opposite.*

Proof. Since Σ is finite, there exist pairs of opposite chambers. By 2.8, $\operatorname{Aut}(\Sigma)$ acts transitively on Σ. Therefore every chamber is opposite at least one chamber. If x, y, z are chambers such that x and y are opposite, then by 5.4, either $\operatorname{dist}(x, z) < \operatorname{dist}(x, y)$ or $y = z$. $\square$

Definition 5.6. Let J be a subset of I such that W_J is finite and let R be a J-residue of Σ (so $R = \Sigma$ if $J = I$). By 2.8, $\operatorname{diam} R$ depends only on J and not on R. By 3.24, $\operatorname{diam} R$ is the same whether it is measured in R or in Δ. By 4.9 and 5.5, therefore, for each chamber u of R, there is a unique chamber $\operatorname{op}_R u$ of R such that

$$\operatorname{dist}(u, \operatorname{op}_R u) = \operatorname{diam} R,$$

i.e. such that u and $\operatorname{op}_R u$ are opposite chambers of R. Let $w_J = \operatorname{op}_R 1$, where now R is the unique J-residue of Σ containing 1. By 2.9, $\|w_J\| = \operatorname{diam} R$, w_J is the unique longest element of W_J with respect to $\| \cdot \|$ and $w_J = w_J^{-1}$ (since $\|x\| = \|x^{-1}\|$ for all $x \in W$).

Proposition 5.7. *Suppose that Σ is finite and let w_I be as in 5.6. Then*

$$\|u\| + \|w_I u\| = \operatorname{diam} \Sigma$$

for all $u \in W$. In particular,

$$\|u\| < \|v\| \text{ if and only if } \|w_I u\| > \|w_I v\|$$

for all $u, v \in W$.

Proof. Let $u \in W$. By 5.6, 1 and w_I are opposite, so by 5.4 there is a minimal gallery in Σ from 1 to w_I which contains u. Thus

$$\operatorname{dist}(1, u) + \operatorname{dist}(u, w_I) = \operatorname{diam} \Sigma.$$

By 2.8, $\operatorname{dist}(u, w_I) = \operatorname{dist}(w_I u, w_I w_I) = \operatorname{dist}(w_I u, 1)$ since $w_I = w_I^{-1}$. By 2.9, $\operatorname{dist}(1, u) = \|u\|$ and $\operatorname{dist}(w_I u, 1) = \|w_I u\|$. $\qquad\square$

Proposition 5.8. *Let Σ be finite, let J be a proper subset of I and let w_J and w_I be as defined in 5.6. Then $\|w_J r_i\| > \|w_J\|$ for all $i \in I \backslash J$. In particular, $w_J \neq w_I$.*

Proof. Choose a reduced word f in M_J such that $r_f = w_J$. By 4.11, fi is reduced and hence $\|w_J r_i\| = |fi| > |f| = \|w_J\|$ by 4.5 for every $i \in I \backslash J$. By 5.6, on the other hand, there is no element in W longer than w_I (with respect to $\|\cdot\|$). Thus $w_J \neq w_I$. $\qquad\square$

5.9. Let R and R' be finite residues of Σ and suppose that there is an automorphism ϕ (not necessarily special) of Σ mapping R to R'. Then both $\operatorname{op}_{R'}$ and the composition

$$\phi|_R \cdot \operatorname{op}_R \cdot \phi|_R^{-1}$$

(where $\phi|_R$ denotes the restriction of ϕ to R) map each chamber of R' to its opposite in R'. Hence these two maps are equal.

Proposition 5.10. *Suppose that Σ is finite and let op_Σ and w_I be as in 5.6. Then $\operatorname{op}_\Sigma x = x w_I$ for all chambers x.*

Proof. Let $d = \operatorname{diam} \Sigma$ and choose a reduced word $f \in M_I$ such that $w_I = r_f$. By 4.5 and 5.6, $d = \|w_I\| = |f|$. Let $x \in \Sigma$. By 2.5, there is a gallery of type f from x to $x w_I$. By 4.3, this gallery is minimal. Hence $\operatorname{dist}(x, x w_I) = |f| = d$, i.e. x and $x w_I$ are opposite. $\qquad\square$

Proposition 5.11. *Suppose that Σ is finite and let op_Σ and w_I be as in 5.6. Then there is a unique permutation σ of I such that $r_{\sigma(i)} = w_I r_i w_I$. The map op_Σ is a σ-automorphism of Σ.*

Proof. Let $d = \text{diam } \Sigma$. Choose $i \in I$, let x and x' be i-adjacent chambers of Σ and let $y = \text{op}_\Sigma x$ and $y' = \text{op}_\Sigma x'$. By two applications of 5.4,

$$\text{dist}(x', x) + \text{dist}(x, y') = d,$$

so $\text{dist}(x, y') = d - 1$, and

$$\text{dist}(x, y') + \text{dist}(y', y) = d.$$

It follows that $\text{dist}(y', y) = 1$, i.e. that y' is j-adjacent to y for some $j \in I$. By 2.4, $x' = xr_i$ and $y' = yr_j$, and by 5.10, $y = xw_I$ and $y' = x'w_I$. Therefore

$$xr_iw_I = x'w_I = y' = yr_j = xw_Ir_j.$$

Hence $r_j = w_I^{-1}r_iw_I = w_Ir_iw_I$. Thus, in particular, j depends on i but not on the i-panel $\{x, x'\}$. We conclude that there is a map σ from I to itself such that op_Σ maps i-adjacent chambers to $\sigma(i)$-adjacent chambers and $r_{\sigma(j)} = w_Ir_iw_I$ for all $i \in I$. Since the composition

$$\text{op}_\Sigma \cdot \text{op}_\Sigma$$

is the identity map on Σ, the composition $\sigma \cdot \sigma$ is the identity map on I. It follows that op_Σ and σ are both bijective and two chambers are i-adjacent (for each $i \in I$) if and only if their images under op_Σ are $\sigma(i)$-adjacent. $\qquad\square$

Definition 5.12. Suppose that R is a finite residue of type J for some $J \subset I$ (which might equal I) and let w_J and op_R be as in 5.6 (so $w_J = w_J^{-1}$). By 5.11 with R in place of Σ, there is a unique permutation of J, which we will denote by op_J, such that

$$r_{\text{op}_J(i)} = w_Jr_iw_J$$

for all $i \in J$, and the map op_R is an op_J-automorphism of R. In particular, op_Σ is an op_I-automorphism of Σ.

The maps op_J and op_I defined in 5.12 should, more properly, be called op_{Π_J} and op_Π. We call them op_J and op_I only to avoid double subscripts.

Definition 5.13. Suppose that Σ is finite, let R be a J-residue and R' a J'-residue for two subsets J and J' of I. The residues R and R' are *opposite* if $\text{op}_\Sigma(R) = R'$, in which case, by 5.11, $\text{op}_I(J) = J'$ and op_Σ restricted to R is an op_I-isomorphism from R to R'. If x is any chamber of R, then $\text{op}_\Sigma(R)$ is precisely the $\text{op}_I(J)$-residue containing $\text{op}_\Sigma(x)$.

The following result is needed in the proof of 9.11, which will, in turn, play a crucial role in the proof of the results about extensions of isometries in Chapter 10.

Proposition 5.14. *Suppose that Σ is finite, let R be a residue of Σ and let $R' = \mathrm{op}_\Sigma(R)$, let J denote the type of R, let $J' = \mathrm{op}_I(J)$ (so R' is a residue and J' is its type), let σ denote the map $\mathrm{op}_J \cdot \mathrm{op}_I|_{J'}$ from J' to J and let σ' denote the map $\mathrm{op}_{J'} \cdot \mathrm{op}_I|_J$ from J to J'. Then the following hold.*

(i) *The restriction of proj_R to R' is a σ-isomorphism from R' to R, the restriction of $\mathrm{proj}_{R'}$ to R is a σ'-isomorphism from R to R', and these two maps are inverses of each other (and hence $\sigma' = \sigma^{-1}$).*

(ii) *$\mathrm{proj}_R x$ and $\mathrm{op}_\Sigma x$ are opposite chambers of R for all $x \in R'$.*

(iii) *$\mathrm{proj}_R x = x w_I w_J$ for all $x \in R'$.*

Proof. Let $\pi = \mathrm{op}_R \cdot \mathrm{op}_\Sigma|_{R'}$ and $\pi' = \mathrm{op}_{R'} \cdot \mathrm{op}_\Sigma|_R$. By 5.10, $\pi(x) = x w_I w_J$ for every $x \in R'$. By 5.12, π is a σ-isomorphism from R' to R and π' is a σ'-isomorphism from R to R'. By 5.9,

$$\mathrm{op}_R = \mathrm{op}_\Sigma|_R \cdot \mathrm{op}_{R'} \cdot \mathrm{op}_\Sigma|_R$$

and

$$\mathrm{op}_{R'} = \mathrm{op}_\Sigma|_{R'} \cdot \mathrm{op}_R \cdot \mathrm{op}_\Sigma|_{R'}.$$

It follows that the maps π and π' are inverses of each other. Now choose $x \in R'$. Let $y = \mathrm{proj}_R x$ and $z = \mathrm{op}_\Sigma x$. By 5.4,

$$\mathrm{dist}(x, z) = \mathrm{dist}(x, w) + \mathrm{dist}(w, z)$$

for all chambers w. Thus

$$\mathrm{dist}(x, y) + \mathrm{dist}(y, z) = \mathrm{dist}(x, \pi(x)) + \mathrm{dist}(\pi(x), z).$$

By 3.23, $\mathrm{dist}(x, y) \leqslant \mathrm{dist}(x, \pi(x))$ (since $\pi(x) \in R$). Therefore

$$\mathrm{dist}(\pi(x), z) \leqslant \mathrm{dist}(y, z).$$

By 3.24, we have $\mathrm{dist}(\pi(x), z) = \mathrm{diam}\, R$ (since $z \in R$ and $\pi(x) = \mathrm{op}_R(\mathrm{op}_\Sigma x) = \mathrm{op}_R z$). Therefore $\mathrm{dist}(y, z) = \mathrm{diam}\, R$ (since also $y \in R$). By 5.5, it follows that $\pi(x) = y$. Thus proj_R restricted to R' coincides with π. By symmetry, $\mathrm{proj}_{R'}$ restricted to R coincides with π'. $\qquad\square$

The next two results will be needed in the proof of 9.13.

Lemma 5.15. *Let J_1 and J_2 be disjoint subsets of I and let $W_i = W_{J_i}$ for $i = 1$ and 2 be as defined in 4.6. Suppose that W_2 is finite and let w_{J_2} be as defined in 5.6. Then for each $w_1 \in W_1$ and each non-trivial $w_2 \in W_2$, $\|w_1 w_{J_2} w_2\| < \|w_1 w_{J_2}\|$.*

Proof. Let R_i denote the J_i-residue containing 1 for $i = 1$ and 2. Thus $R_i = W_i$ for $i = 1$ and 2. Choose $w_1 \in W_1$ and $u \in W_2$. By 3.25, $R_1 \cap R_2 = \{1\}$ and $\text{proj}_{R_2} w_1^{-1} = 1$. By 3.22, therefore,

$$\text{dist}(w_1^{-1}, 1) + \text{dist}(1, u) = \text{dist}(w_1^{-1}, u).$$

By 2.9, $\text{dist}(w_1^{-1}, 1) = \|w_1\|$, $\text{dist}(1, u) = \|u\|$ and

$$\text{dist}(w_1^{-1}, u) = \text{dist}(1, w_1 u) = \|w_1 u\|,$$

so $\|w_1\| + \|u\| = \|w_1 u\|$. It follows that if u, v are two elements of W_2, then $\|u\| < \|v\|$ if and only if $\|w_1 u\| < \|w_1 v\|$. It remains only to observe that, since w_{J_2} is the unique longest element of W_2, $\|w_{J_2} w_2\| < \|w_{J_2}\|$ for all non-trivial $w_2 \in W_2$. $\qquad\square$

Lemma 5.16. *Let J_1 and J_2 be subsets of I such that $J_1 \cap J_2 = \{i\}$ for some $i \in I$ and let $W_i = W_{J_i}$ for $i = 1$ and 2 be as defined in 4.6. Suppose that W_2 is finite and let w_{J_2} be as defined in 5.6. Then for each $w_1 \in W_1$ and each $w_2 \in W_2$, $\|w_1 w_{J_2} w_2\| \leqslant \|w_1 w_{J_2}\|$ unless $w_2 = r_j$, where $j = \text{op}_{J_2} i$.*

Proof. Let R_i denote the J_i-residue containing 1 for $i = 1$ and 2 and let S denote their intersection. Choose $w_1 \in W_1$. By 3.25, $S = \{1, r_i\}$ and $\text{proj}_{R_2} w_1^{-1} = \text{proj}_S w_1^{-1}$. Suppose that $\text{proj}_{R_2} w_1^{-1} = 1$. By 3.22,

$$\text{dist}(w_1^{-1}, 1) + \text{dist}(1, u) = \text{dist}(w_1^{-1}, u)$$

and hence $\|w_1\| + \|u\| = \|w_1 u\|$ for all $u \in W_2$. Therefore,

$$\|w_1 u\| < \|w_1 v\| \text{ if and only if } \|u\| < \|v\|$$

for $u, v \in W_2$, and hence $\|w_1 w_{J_2} w_2\| < \|w_1 w_{J_2}\|$ for all non-trivial $w_2 \in W_2$ exactly as in the proof of 5.15.

Now suppose that $\text{proj}_{R_2} w_1^{-1} = r_i$. By 3.22,

$$\text{dist}(w_1^{-1}, r_i) + \text{dist}(r_i, u) = \text{dist}(w_1^{-1}, u)$$

and hence $\|w_1 r_i\| + \|r_i u\| = \|w_1 u\|$ for all $u \in W_2$. It follows that

$$\|w_1 u\| - \|r_i u\| = \|w_1 v\| - \|r_i v\|$$

and hence

$$\|w_1 u\| - \|w_1 v\| = \|r_i u\| - \|r_i v\|$$

for all $u, v \in W_2$. Suppose now that $\|w_1 w_{J_2} w_2\| > \|w_1 w_{J_2}\|$ for some $w_2 \in W_2$. Letting $u = w_{J_2} w_2$ and $v = w_{J_2}$, we deduce that $\|r_i w_{J_2} w_2\| > \|r_i w_{J_2}\|$. Hence $\|w_{J_2} r_j w_2\| > \|w_{J_2} r_j\|$ for $j = \mathrm{op}_{J_2} i$ since $r_i w_{J_2} = w_{J_2} r_j$ by 5.12. By 5.7 with R_2 in place of Σ, it follows that $\|r_j w_2\| < \|r_j\| = 1$. Therefore $w_2 = r_j$. □

We come now to Coxeter's classification of finite Coxeter groups. Note that by 4.6, an arbitrary Coxeter group is the direct sum of the Coxeter groups corresponding to the connected components of its Coxeter diagram.

Theorem 5.17. *Let Π be an irreducible spherical Coxeter diagram. Then Π is either a single vertex, the diagram*

for some $n \geqslant 3$, one of the diagrams A_ℓ or C_ℓ for $\ell \geqslant 3$, D_ℓ for $\ell \geqslant 4$, E_ℓ for $\ell = 6$, 7 or 8, or F_4 illustrated in 12.13–12.19 or one of the diagrams

$$H_3 = \bullet\!\!\!\!\!\!\!\!-\!\!\!\!\!\!\!\!\bullet\!\!\!\!\overset{5}{-\!\!\!\!\!\!\!\!}\bullet$$

or

$$H_4 = \bullet\!\!\!\!\!\!-\!\!\!\!\!\!\bullet\!\!\!\!\!\!-\!\!\!\!\!\!\bullet\!\!\!\overset{5}{-\!\!\!\!\!\!}\bullet.$$

Proof. This famous result was first proved in [3]. □

In the proof of 6.13, we will require one small consequence of 5.17 for which, however, we can give an easy proof.

Proposition 5.18. *If W is finite, Π irreducible and $|I| > 2$, then there are no entries in the Coxeter matrix $[m_{ij}]$ greater than 5.*

Proof. This holds by 5.17, but we can also reason as follows. Suppose that Π is irreducible, $|I| > 2$ and $m_{ij} > 5$ for some $i, j \in I$. Since Π is irreducible and $|I| > 2$, there exists $k \in I \backslash \{i, j\}$ such that $m_{jk} \geqslant 3$ (after relabeling i and j if necessary). For each $p \geqslant 1$, the word $(jijijk)^p$ is reduced, as is easily checked since its homotopy class is small. By 4.4, the map from $[1, \infty)$ to W which sends p to the image in W of $(jijijk)^p$ is injective (since homotopic words must have the same length). Hence W is infinite. □

As observed in [13] and in the exercises on pp. 25 and 26 of [7], it is possible, at least in principle, to deduce the entire classification of finite Coxeter groups from 4.4 by generalizing the proof of 5.18. It would be difficult, however, to work out all the details.

Example 5.19. Let (W, r) be the Coxeter system of type A_ℓ. We number the vertex set I of A_ℓ as in 12.13. By 2.2, there is a surjective homomorphism from W to the symmetric group $S_{\ell+1}$ which maps r_i to the transposition $(i, i + 1)$ for all $i \in I$. This homomorphism is, in fact, an isomorphism. To see this, it suffices to show that $|W| \leqslant |S_{\ell+1}|$. To prove this inequality, it suffices, by induction, to show that the subgroup $\langle r_1, r_2, \ldots, r_{\ell-1} \rangle$ of W, which we denote by H, has index at most $\ell + 1$ in W. This follows from the observation (whose verification we leave to the reader) that for all $i \in I$, left multiplication by r_i maps the set of left cosets

$$\{x_k H \mid k \in [1, \ell + 1]\}$$

to itself, where $x_k = r_k r_{k+1} \cdots r_\ell$ for all $k \in [1, \ell]$ and $x_{\ell+1} = 1$.

Chapter Six

2-Interiors

Our goal in this chapter is to prove 6.13. This result will be needed in the proof of 11.6. The proof we give is due to Bernhard Mühlherr.

For the rest of this chapter, we assume that Π is an irreducible spherical Coxeter diagram of rank at least three and we let I, $[m_{ij}]$, (W, r) and $\Sigma = \Sigma_\Pi$ have their usual meanings. We continue to identify W with $\text{Aut}^\circ(\Sigma)$ as described in 2.8. Thus if $s \in W$ and $x \in \Sigma$ (so really both s and x lie in W), then sx denotes both their product in W and the image of x under the special automorphism s.

Choose a root α of Σ and let $\text{refl}_\Sigma(\alpha)$ and $\partial\alpha$ be as in 3.13. We set $t = \text{refl}_\Sigma(\alpha)$ and

$$\text{dist}(v, \partial\alpha) = \min\{\text{dist}(v, x) \mid x \in \partial\alpha\}$$

for all $v \in \alpha$.

Lemma 6.1. $\text{dist}(v, \partial\alpha) + \text{dist}(w, \partial\alpha) < \text{dist}(v, tw)$ *for all* $v, w \in \alpha$.

Proof. Let $v, w \in \alpha$ and let $\gamma = (u_0, \ldots, u_k)$ be a minimal gallery from v to tw. By 3.11, $tw \in -\alpha$. Therefore $u_{i-1} \in \alpha$ and $u_i \in -\alpha$ for some $i \in [1, k]$. By 3.12, $u_{i-1} \in \partial\alpha$ and t exchanges u_{i-1} and u_i. Hence

$$\text{dist}(w, \partial\alpha) \leqslant \text{dist}(w, u_{i-1})$$
$$= \text{dist}(t \cdot tw, tu_i) = \text{dist}(tw, u_i) = k - i.$$

Since

$$\text{dist}(v, \partial\alpha) \leqslant \text{dist}(v, u_{i-1}) = i - 1,$$

we conclude that $\text{dist}(v, \partial\alpha) + \text{dist}(w, \partial\alpha) \leqslant k - 1$. $\qquad\square$

Lemma 6.2. *Let* $v \in \alpha$ *and let* $k = \text{dist}(v, \partial\alpha)$. *Then* $\text{dist}(v, tv) = 2k + 1$ *and every gallery of length k from v to a chamber in $\partial\alpha$ extends to a minimal gallery from v to tv.*

Proof. Let γ be a gallery of length k from v to some chamber x in $\partial\alpha$. By 3.13, tx is adjacent to x. Hence $(\gamma, t\bar\gamma)$ is a gallery of length $2k + 1$ from v to tv, where $\bar\gamma$ denotes the gallery γ in reverse and $t\bar\gamma$ denotes the image of this gallery under left multiplication by t. On the other hand, $\text{dist}(v, tv) \geqslant 2k + 1$ by 6.1. Therefore $\text{dist}(v, tv) = 2k + 1$ and the gallery $(\gamma, t\bar\gamma)$ is minimal. $\qquad\square$

Lemma 6.3. *Let v and w be adjacent chambers of α such that*

$$\text{dist}(v, \partial\alpha) = \text{dist}(w, \partial\alpha)$$

and let s denote the reflection which interchanges v and w. Then s and t commute, and s maps both α to itself and $\partial\alpha$ to itself.

Proof. Let $k = \text{dist}(v, \partial\alpha)$ and let β denote the root $\Sigma_{(v\setminus w)}$ as defined in 3.15. Thus $s = \text{refl}_\Sigma(\beta)$ as defined in 3.13. By 6.1, $2k + 1 \leqslant \text{dist}(tv, w)$, and by 6.2, $\text{dist}(tv, v) = 2k + 1$. By 3.6, therefore,

$$\text{dist}(tv, w) > \text{dist}(tv, v).$$

Thus, by 3.15, $tv \in \beta$. Interchanging v and w in this argument, we obtain

$$\text{dist}(tw, w) < \text{dist}(tw, v)$$

and therefore $tw \in -\beta$. Since v and w are adjacent, so are tv and tw. By 3.12, therefore, $\{tv, tw\}$ is a panel in M_s, i.e. s interchanges tv and tw. Since s also interchanges v and w, we thus have

$$st \cdot s(tv) = st \cdot tw = s \cdot t^2 w = sw = v$$

and therefore $stst = 1$. i.e. s and t commute. Hence M_α, the set of panels fixed by t, is mapped to itself by s. By 3.10, it follows that s maps α to itself or to $-\alpha$. Since $sv = w$ and both v and w are contained in α, the reflection s must, in fact, map α to itself. Hence s also maps $\partial\alpha$ to itself. $\qquad\square$

Definition 6.4. Let A_α denote the set of all chambers x in α such that

$$\text{dist}(y, \partial\alpha) \leqslant \text{dist}(x, \partial\alpha)$$

for all chambers $y \in \alpha$ which are adjacent to x.

Since $|W| < \infty$, we can choose $u \in \alpha$ such that $\text{dist}(u, \partial\alpha)$ is maximal. The chamber u is contained in A_α. Thus $A_\alpha \neq \emptyset$.

Notation 6.5. Choose $c \in A_\alpha$ such that $\text{dist}(c, \partial\alpha)$ is minimal and let $m = \text{dist}(c, \partial\alpha)$.

By 4.12, $A_\alpha \cap \partial\alpha = \emptyset$, so $c \notin \partial\alpha$ and $m > 0$. For each $i \in I$, let c_i denote the unique chamber of Σ which is i-adjacent to c. Since $c \notin \partial\alpha$, $c_i \in \alpha$ for all $i \in I$. Let

$$J = \{j \in I \mid \text{dist}(c_j, \partial\alpha) = \text{dist}(c, \partial\alpha)\},$$

let s_j denote the unique reflection interchanging c with c_j for all $j \in J$, let

$$V = \langle s_j \mid j \in J \rangle,$$

and let R denote the J-residue containing c. (If $J = \emptyset$, then $V = 1$ and $R = \{c\}$.)

Lemma 6.6. *The group V acts transitively on R and maps α to itself, every element of V commutes with t, $\mathrm{dist}(x, \partial\alpha) = m$ for all $x \in R$ and $R \subset A_\alpha$, where A_α is as in 6.4.*

Proof. The group V contains an element mapping c to c_j for all $j \in J$ and the residue R is connected. Hence V acts transitively on R. By 6.3 applied to the generators s_j for all $j \in J$, every element of V commutes with t and fixes both α and $\partial\alpha$ and thus also A_α (setwise). It follows that $\mathrm{dist}(x, \partial\alpha) = m$ and $x \in A_\alpha$ for all $x \in R$ (since $\mathrm{dist}(c, \partial\alpha) = m$ and $c \in A_\alpha$). $\square$

Lemma 6.7. *For each $x \in R$, $x = \mathrm{proj}_R tx$.*

Proof. Let $x \in R$. By 6.6, $\mathrm{dist}(y, \partial\alpha) = m$ for all $y \in R$. Therefore $\mathrm{dist}(y, tx) \geqslant 2m + 1$ for all $y \in R$ by 6.1 and $\mathrm{dist}(x, tx) = 2m + 1$ by 6.2. By 3.23, therefore, $x = \mathrm{proj}_R tx$. $\square$

Lemma 6.8. *Let $x, y \in R$ be opposite in R. Then y is opposite tx in Σ and*

$$\mathrm{diam}\, \Sigma = \mathrm{diam}\, R + 2m + 1.$$

Proof. Let $d = \mathrm{diam}\, R + 2m + 1$. By 6.6, we can assume that $y = c$. Let j be an arbitrary element of J. By 3.24, 4.9 and 5.4, c_j lies on a minimal gallery γ_1 from c to x (whose length is $\mathrm{diam}\, R$). By 6.2 and 6.6, there is a minimal gallery γ_2 from x to tx of length $2m + 1$. By 3.22 and 6.7, (γ_1, γ_2) is a minimal gallery from c to tx. Thus, in particular, $\mathrm{dist}(c, tx) = d$. Now let i be an arbitrary element of I not in J. By 6.4 and the choice of J, $\mathrm{dist}(c_i, \partial\alpha) = m - 1$. By 6.2, therefore, c_i lies on a gallery of length $2m + 1$ from c to tc. This gallery extends to a gallery of length d from c to tx. We conclude that every chamber adjacent to c lies on a minimal gallery from c to tx, i.e.

$$\mathrm{dist}(tx, c_i) < \mathrm{dist}(tx, c) = d$$

for all $i \in I$. By 5.4, on the other hand, there is a minimal gallery from tx to $\mathrm{op}_\Sigma tx$ which contains c. It follows that $c = \mathrm{op}_\Sigma tx$. Therefore $d = \mathrm{diam}\, \Sigma$. $\square$

Lemma 6.9. *$A_\alpha = R$. In particular, A_α is connected.*

Proof. By 6.6, $R \subset A_\alpha$. Let $x \in A_\alpha$, let $v = \text{proj}_R tx$ and let $w = \text{op}_R v$. By 3.24, $\text{dist}(v, w) = \text{diam } R$. By 6.5, $\text{dist}(x, \partial\alpha)$ and $\text{dist}(v, \partial\alpha)$ are both at least m. By 6.1, therefore, $\text{dist}(tx, v) \geqslant 2m + 1$. By 3.22, $\text{dist}(tx, w) = \text{dist}(tx, v) + \text{dist}(v, w)$. Thus

$$\text{dist}(tx, w) \geqslant 2m + 1 + \text{diam } R.$$

By 6.8, $2m + 1 + \text{diam } R = \text{diam } \Sigma$. Hence tx and w are opposite in Σ. By 6.8, we also know that w is opposite tv in Σ. By 5.5, therefore, $tx = tv$. Thus $x = v \in R$. Since x is arbitrary, we conclude that $A_\alpha = R$. $\square$

Definition 6.10. Let $\alpha^{(k)}$ (for $k \geqslant 1$) denote the set of chambers x in α such that α contains every residue of rank k containing x. Thus $\alpha^{(1)} = \alpha \backslash \partial\alpha$. The set $\alpha^{(k)}$ is called the *k-interior* of α.

Lemma 6.11. *Let $x \in \alpha$. If $\text{dist}(x, \partial\alpha) = 1$, then x is adjacent to a chamber in $\alpha^{(2)}$, where $\alpha^{(2)}$ is as defined in 6.10.*

Proof. Suppose that $\text{dist}(x, \partial\alpha) = 1$. Let u be a chamber in $\partial\alpha$ adjacent to x and let $v = tu$. By 3.14, v is adjacent to u and lies in $-\alpha$. Let ij denote the type of the gallery (v, u, x). By 4.3, this gallery is minimal. Let T denote the $\{i, j\}$-residue containing v, u and x. By 2.6, T contains $2m_{ij}$ chambers, and by 4.10, m_{ij} of them lie in α. Since $T \cap \alpha$ contains u, x and the chamber which is i-adjacent to x, we have $m_{ij} > 2$. By assumption, Π is irreducible and has at least three vertices. We can choose $k \in I \backslash \{i, j\}$, therefore, such that the subdiagram of Π spanned by $\{i, j, k\}$ is irreducible. Let y denote the chamber k-adjacent to x. We claim that $y \in \alpha^{(2)}$. Let S be a residue of rank two containing y. We need to show that $S \subset \alpha$. By 3.22, there is a unique chamber p in S nearest v and a minimal gallery γ from v to y which contains p. Let f denote the type of γ and let γ_1 denote the subgallery of γ which starts at v and ends at p. Since the word ijk is reduced, it follows by 4.2 and 4.3 that f and ijk are homotopic. The word ijk is homotopic only to itself or (but only if $m_{jk} = 2$, in which case $m_{ik} > 2$ by the choice of k) ikj. Thus f begins with i, so γ passes through u, and f involves all three colors i, j and k, so $[\gamma]$ is not contained in S (since S is of rank two). By 3.24, therefore, $v \notin S$. Thus $p \neq v$. We conclude that u is contained in the subgallery γ_1. Now let $w \in S$ be arbitrary. By 3.22 again, γ_1 extends to a minimal gallery from v to w. Hence

$$\text{dist}(u, w) < \text{dist}(v, w).$$

By 3.15, it follows that $w \in \alpha$. Therefore $S \subset \alpha$. Since S is arbitrary, it follows that $y \in \alpha^{(2)}$. $\square$

Lemma 6.12. *Let* $x \in \alpha$. *If* $\mathrm{dist}(x, \partial\alpha) \geqslant 3$, *then* $x \in \alpha^{(2)}$.

Proof. Let S be a residue of rank two containing chambers in both α and $-\alpha$. By 5.18, $m_{ij} \leqslant 5$, where $\{i, j\}$ is the type of S. By 2.6, S contains $2m_{ij}$ chambers, and by 4.10, $S \cap \alpha$ is a root of S. Thus $|S \cap \alpha| = m_{ij} \leqslant 5$ and $|S \cap \partial\alpha| = 2$. It follows that $\mathrm{dist}(x, \partial\alpha) \leqslant 2$ for all $x \in S \cap \alpha$.   □

We have now reached our goal (first proved in (39.34) of [20]).

Theorem 6.13. *Let* $\Sigma = \Sigma_\Pi$ *for some Coxeter diagram* Π *which is spherical, irreducible and has at least three vertices, let* α *be a root of* Σ, *and let* $\alpha^{(2)}$ *denote the 2-interior of* α *as defined in 6.10. Then the following hold.*

(i) $\alpha^{(2)}$ *is non-empty.*

(ii) *The subgraph spanned by* $\alpha^{(2)}$ *is connected.*

(iii) *Every panel contained in* α *lies in a residue* S *of rank two such that* $S \subset \alpha$ *and* S *contains a chamber adjacent to a chamber in* $\alpha^{(2)}$.

Proof. By 4.12, the set $\{w \in \alpha \mid \mathrm{dist}(w, \partial\alpha) = 1\}$ is non-empty. By 6.11, therefore, (i) holds. Let $x \in \alpha^{(2)}$. By 6.10, $\mathrm{dist}(x, \partial\alpha) \geqslant 2$. If $x \notin A_\alpha$, then by 6.4, x is adjacent to a chamber $y \in \alpha$ such that $\mathrm{dist}(y, \partial\alpha) = \mathrm{dist}(x, \partial\alpha) + 1 \geqslant 3$. By 6.12, $y \in \alpha^{(2)}$. By repeating this observation as many times as is necessary, we conclude that for each $x \in \alpha^{(2)}$, there exists a gallery $(x, \ldots, z)$ contained in $\alpha^{(2)}$ such that $z \in A_\alpha$. By 6.9, $A_\alpha = R$. By 6.6, the group V maps $\alpha^{(2)}$ to itself and acts transitively on R. Hence $R \subset \alpha^{(2)}$. Since R is connected, it follows that (ii) holds.

We turn now to (iii). Let P be a panel contained in α and let u, v denote the two chambers in P. Suppose that $\mathrm{dist}(w, \partial\alpha) \geqslant 1$ for $w = u$ or v. By 6.11 and 6.12, it follows that P lies in a residue S of rank two which contains a chamber in $\alpha^{(2)}$. By 6.10, $S \subset \alpha$. We can suppose, therefore, that u and v both lie in $\partial\alpha$. By 4.12, we can choose a chamber z in α adjacent to u such that $\mathrm{dist}(z, \partial\alpha) = 1$. Let ij denote the type of the gallery (z, u, v), let S denote the residue of type $\{i, j\}$ containing z, u and v and let s denote the reflection interchanging u and v. By 2.6, S contains $2m_{ij}$ chambers, and by 4.10, either $S \subset \alpha$ or $|S \cap \alpha| = m_{ij}$. Suppose that $|S \cap \alpha| = m_{ij}$. Since $z, u, v \in S \cap \alpha$, we have $m_{ij} \geqslant 3$. By 6.3, s fixes both α and $\partial\alpha$ (setwise). Therefore $sz \in \alpha$ and $\mathrm{dist}(sz, \partial\alpha) = 1$. The chambers sz and $su = v$ are i-adjacent. Thus $sz \in S$. Since $m_{ij} \geqslant 3$, the word iji is reduced. By 4.3, therefore, the gallery (z, u, v, sz) is minimal. Thus $S \cap \alpha$ contains, in addition to the chambers z and sz, four distinct chambers adjacent to z or sz, i.e. $m_{ij} = |S \cap \alpha| \geqslant 6$. By 5.18, however, $m_{ij} \leqslant 5$. With this contradiction, we conclude that $S \subset \alpha$. By 6.11, z is adjacent to a chamber in $\alpha^{(2)}$. Hence (iii) holds.   □

We have now finished assembling all the results about Coxeter chamber systems we will need.

Chapter Seven

Buildings

Here, finally, is our protagonist.

Definition 7.1. Let Π be a Coxeter diagram with vertex set I and let (W, r) be the Coxeter system of type Π. A *building of type Π* is a pair (Δ, δ), where Δ is a chamber system whose index set is I and δ is a function from $\Delta \times \Delta$ to W, such that for each reduced word f in the free monoid M_I (reduced with respect to the Coxeter diagram Π) and for each ordered pair (x, y) of chambers, $\delta(x, y) = r_f$ if and only if there is a gallery in Δ of type f from x to y.

Let (Δ, δ) be a building of type Π with index set I and let (W, r) be the Coxeter system corresponding to Π. We call the group W the *Weyl group* and the map δ the *Weyl-distance function* of Δ. By 7.22 below, the type Π and the Weyl-distance function δ are uniquely determined by the chamber system Δ alone. We will often denote the building (Δ, δ) simply by Δ. The Weyl distance $\delta(x, y)$ from x to y should not be confused with the distance $\text{dist}(x, y)$ from x to y in the sense of 1.1 (see 7.8 below). Since the empty word is reduced, $\delta(x, y) = 1$ if and only if $x = y$. We will sometimes refer to the type Π of Δ as the *Coxeter diagram of Δ*.

Proposition 7.2. *Let (Δ, δ) be a building. Then δ is surjective and Δ is connected.*

Proof. Let I denote the index set of Δ. By 1.4, for each chamber x and each $i \in I$, there exist chambers i-adjacent to x. Hence for each chamber x and each word f in M_I, there exist galleries in Δ of type f which begins at x. By 7.1 ('$\delta(x, y) = r_f$ if there is a gallery of type f from x to y'), therefore, the map δ is surjective. By 7.1 ('$\delta(x, y) = r_f$ only if there is a gallery of type f from x to y'), Δ is connected. $\qquad\square$

Proposition 7.3. $\delta(x, y) = \delta(y, x)^{-1}$ *for all chambers x, y of a building (Δ, δ).*

Proof. A gallery of type f from x to y read in reverse order is a gallery of type $\bar{f}$ from y to x, and if f is reduced, so is $\bar{f}$. Here $\bar{f}$ is as in 3.2. Moreover, $r_{\bar{f}} = r_f^{-1}$. The claim holds, therefore, by 7.1. $\qquad\square$

A *complex* over a set I is a triple (V, τ, S), where V is a set, τ is a map from V to I and S is a set of subsets of V such that every subset of V consisting of a single element lies in S, every subset of an element of S lies in S and the restriction of τ to any element of S is injective. Originally (for instance, in 3.1 of [14]), buildings were defined as certain complexes. For discussions of the equivalence between 'buildings as complexes' and 'buildings as chamber systems,' see [10], 3.7 of [14] and 2.2 of [16].

Example 7.4. Let X be a right vector space over a field or skew-field K of dimension $\ell + 1$ for some $\ell \geqslant 1$, let V denote the set of all proper subspaces of X, let $I = [1, \ell]$, let $\tau(Y) = \dim_K Y$ for all $Y \in V$, and let S be the set of all non-empty subsets $\{Y_1, Y_2, \ldots, Y_m\}$ of V (so the subspaces $Y_1, \ldots, Y_m$ are, in particular, distinct) such that

$$Y_1 \subset Y_2 \subset \cdots \subset Y_m$$

(so $m \leqslant \ell$). We write $(Y_1, \ldots, Y_m)$ in place of $\{Y_1, \ldots, Y_m\}$ to indicate the natural ordering of the Y_i by inclusion. The complex (V, τ, S) is a building of type A_ℓ (as defined in [14]), where A_ℓ is the Coxeter diagram pictured in 12.13 below. See, for example, p. 84 in [2] for a sketch of the proof of this. The corresponding chamber system Δ has the maximal elements of S as its chambers, its index set is the interval $[1, \ell]$ and two chambers $(Y_1, \ldots, Y_\ell)$ and $(Y_1', \ldots, Y_\ell')$ are i-adjacent for some $i \in [1, \ell]$ if $Y_i \neq Y_i'$ and $Y_j = Y_j'$ for all $j \in [1, \ell]$ distinct from i. By 5.19, the Coxeter group W corresponding to A_ℓ is the symmetric group $S_{\ell+1}$. The Weyl-distance map δ associated with Δ is calculated as follows. Let $y = (Y_1, \ldots, Y_\ell)$ and $y' = (Y_1', \ldots, Y_\ell')$ be two chambers of Δ (so $\dim_K Y_i = \dim_K Y_i' = i$ for all $i \in [1, \ell]$), let $Y_0 = Y_0' = \{0\}$, let $Y_{\ell+1} = Y_{\ell+1}' = X$ and let

$$\sigma(i) = \min\{j \in [1, \ell + 1] \mid Y_i \subset Y_{i-1} + Y_j'\}$$

for all $i \in [1, \ell + 1]$. Then σ is a permutation of the interval $[1, \ell + 1]$[1] and $\delta(y, y') = \sigma$ (under the convention that products in $S_{\ell+1}$ are composed from left to right). A direct proof that the pair (Δ, δ) is a building as defined in 7.1 can be derived from the observation that $\delta(y, y') = \sigma$ (for y, y' as above) if

---

[1] Suppose that $\sigma(i) = \sigma(k)$ for $i, k \in [1, \ell + 1]$ and let $j = \sigma(i)$. Then $Y_i = Y_{i-1} + \langle v \rangle$ and $Y_k = Y_{k-1} + \langle w \rangle$ for vectors v and w both in $Y_j' \backslash Y_{j-1}'$. Thus $w = v\lambda + u$ for some $\lambda \in K^*$ and some $u \in Y_{j-1}'$. Then $k \leqslant i$ since otherwise $v \in Y_i \subset Y_{k-1}$, which would imply that

$$Y_k = Y_{k-1} + \langle w \rangle = Y_{k-1} + \langle u \rangle \subset Y_{k-1} + Y_{j-1}'.$$

Similarly, $i \leqslant k$. Thus σ is injective and hence a permutation of $[1, \ell + 1]$.

and only if there is a basis $x_1, \ldots x_{\ell+1}$ of X such that

$$Y_i = \langle x_{\sigma(1)}, \ldots, x_{\sigma(i)} \rangle$$

and

$$Y'_i = \langle x_1, \ldots, x_i \rangle$$

(where $\langle \cdot \rangle$ denotes the subspace spanned by the given vectors) for all $i \in [1, \ell]$. We leave the numerous details to the reader. The building (Δ, δ) described here will be encountered again (in another guise) in 12.13.

Example 7.5. Let Π be a Coxeter diagram, let (W, r) denote the corresponding Coxeter system, let $\Sigma = \Sigma_\Pi$ denote the corresponding Coxeter chamber system, and let $\delta_W : \Sigma \times \Sigma \to W$ be given by

$$\delta_W(x, y) = x^{-1} y$$

for all $x, y \in \Sigma$. By 2.5, (Σ, δ_W) is a building of type Π. By 8.11 below, it is, in fact, the only thin building of type Π (up to a special isomorphism). This example will assume a central role in the next chapter.

We turn now to the first few basic properties of buildings. These results generalize results of Chapter 4. We begin with a definition.

Definition 7.6. Let Δ be a building of type Π and let I denote its index set. An *elementary homotopy* of galleries of Δ is a transformation of a gallery of the form $(\gamma_1, \gamma_2, \gamma_3)$, where γ_2 is a gallery of type $p(i, j)$ for some $i, j \in I$ (distinct) which starts at the last chamber of γ_1 and ends at the first chamber of γ_3, into a gallery $(\gamma_1, \gamma'_2, \gamma_3)$, where γ'_2 is a gallery of type $p(j, i)$ having the same first and last chambers as γ_2. Two galleries are *homotopic* if one can be transformed into the other by a finite sequence of elementary homotopies.

Proposition 7.7. *Let Δ be a building of type Π and let I denote the index set of Δ. Let $x, y \in \Delta$, let γ be a gallery in Δ from x to y and let f denote the type of γ. Then the following hold.*

(i) *If $g \in M_I$ is a word homotopic to f, then there exists a gallery from x to y of type g which is homotopic to γ as defined in 7.6.*

(ii) *The gallery γ is minimal if and only if its type f is reduced.*

(iii) *If γ is a minimal gallery, then it is the unique gallery of type f from x to y.*

Proof. Let (W, r) denote the Coxeter system of type Π. The words $p(i, j)$ and $p(j, i)$ are reduced and have the same image under r for all distinct $i, j \in I$. By 7.1, therefore, if γ_2 is a gallery in Δ of type $p(i, j)$ for some distinct $i, j \in I$, then there always exists a gallery of type $p(j, i)$ with the same first and last chambers as γ_2. Hence if g is a word obtained from f by an elementary homotopy, then there exists an elementary homotopy which transforms γ into a gallery of type g. Therefore (i) holds.

If f is not reduced, then, by (i), we can assume that f is of the form $f_1 i i f_2$ for some $i \in I$ and thus contains a subgallery (p, w, q) of type ii. By 1.4, either p is i-adjacent to q or $p = q$. It follows that we can delete either one or two chambers from γ to obtain a gallery of type $f_1 i f_2$ or $f_1 f_2$ from x to y. Hence γ is not minimal. Suppose, instead, that f is reduced. Let h denote the type of a minimal gallery from x to y. As we have just seen, this implies that h is reduced. By 7.1, therefore, $r_h = r_f$. By 4.4, it follows that $f \simeq h$; in particular, f and h have the same length. Hence γ is minimal. Therefore (ii) holds.

We prove (iii) by induction with respect to the length k of γ. Suppose that γ is minimal. We can assume that $k \geqslant 2$. By (ii), f is reduced. Let

$$\gamma = (x, \ldots, u, v, y)$$

and suppose that

$$\gamma' = (x, \ldots, u', v', y)$$

is another gallery of type f from x to y. The chambers v and v' are both i-adjacent to y, where i is the last letter of f. By 1.4, therefore, they are i-equivalent to each other. Suppose that $v \neq v'$. Then $(x, \ldots, u', v', v)$ and $(x, \ldots, u, v)$ are galleries of length k and $k - 1$ from x to v. Hence the first of these two galleries is not minimal. Its type, however, is f and by (ii) again, every gallery of type f is minimal. With this contradiction, we conclude that $v = v'$. By induction, therefore, $\gamma = \gamma'$. Thus (iii) holds.   □

Proposition 7.8. *Let (Δ, δ) be a building. Then*

$$\text{dist}(x, y) = \|\delta(x, y)\|$$

for all $x, y \in \Delta$, where $\| \cdot \|$ is as defined in 2.9.

Proof. Let $x, y \in \Delta$, let γ be a minimal gallery from x to y, and let f denote the type of γ. Since γ is minimal, we have $\text{dist}(x, y) = |f|$. By 7.7 (ii), f is reduced. By 7.1, therefore, $\delta(x, y) = r_f$, and by 4.5, $\|r_f\| = |f|$. Thus $\text{dist}(x, y) = \|\delta(x, y)\|$.   □

Proposition 7.9. *Let x and y be two chambers of a building Δ of type Π and let γ and γ' be two minimal galleries from x to y. Then γ and γ' are homotopic as defined in 7.6.*

Proof. Let f denote the type of γ and g the type of γ'. By 7.7 (ii), f and g are both reduced. Hence, by 7.1, $r_f = r_g$, where (W, r) denotes the Coxeter system of type Π. By 4.4, therefore, $f \simeq g$. Hence, by 7.7 (i), γ is homotopic to a gallery γ'' of type g. By 7.7 (iii), $\gamma'' = \gamma'$. $\qquad\square$

Definition 7.10. Let Δ be a building of type Π. The building Δ is called *spherical* if Π is spherical (i.e. if its Weyl group W is finite) and Δ is called *irreducible* if Π is irreducible (i.e. if the underlying graph of Π is connected).

A building of rank one is just a connected chamber system of rank one, i.e. a complete graph all of whose edges have the same color.

We now consider buildings of rank two. These play a special role in the general theory of buildings. To begin, we note a few basic terms from the theory of graphs (without edge colorings).

Definition 7.11. Let $\Gamma = (V, E)$ be a graph. We will sometimes say 'u is adjacent to v' (for $u, v \in V$) or 'u is joined to v by an edge' to express that $\{u, v\} \in E$. An automorphism of Γ is a permutation g of V such that for all $u, v \in V$, u and v are adjacent if and only if u^g and v^g are. The set of all automorphisms of Γ forms a group (under composition of functions) which we denote by $\mathrm{Aut}(\Gamma)$. For each subgroup G of $\mathrm{Aut}(\Gamma)$ and for each $u \in V$, we denote by Γ_u the set of vertices of Γ adjacent to u and by $G_u^{(1)}$ the pointwise stabilizer of $\{u\} \cup \Gamma_u$ in G. A *path of length k* in Γ is a sequence

$$(x_0, x_1, \ldots, x_k)$$

of vertices $x_0, x_1, \ldots, x_k$ such that x_i is adjacent to x_{i-1} for all $i \in [1, k]$ and x_i is different from x_{i-2} for all $i \in [2, k]$. (The latter condition is absent in the definition of a gallery.) A *circuit* is a path of positive length whose first and last vertices are the same. The *girth* of a graph is the length of a shortest circuit (or ∞ if there are no circuits). As noted already in 1.8, a graph is *bipartite* if there exists a partition of its vertex set into two subsets such that each edge joins a vertex of the one subset to a vertex of the other, and if a bipartite graph is connected, then this partition is unique. A graph (V, E) is called a *complete bipartite graph* if V has a partition into two non-empty subsets such that E consists of *all* two-element subsets of V containing one element from each of the two subsets.

Definition 7.12. A *generalized polygon* is a bipartite graph of finite diameter whose girth equals twice its diameter. A *generalized n-gon* (for any $n \geqslant 2$) is a generalized polygon of diameter n. An *apartment* of a generalized n-gon is the subgraph spanned by the vertices contained in a circuit of length $2n$.

Note that a generalized polygon, being of finite diameter, is, in particular, connected.

Proposition 7.13. *Let Γ be a generalized n-gon for some $n \geqslant 2$. Then*

(i) *every path of length $n + 1$ in Γ lies on a unique apartment;*

(ii) *every vertex of Γ has at least two neighbors.*

Proof. Let $\gamma = (x_0, x_1, \ldots, x_n, x_{n+1})$ be a path of length $n + 1$ in Γ. Since the girth of Γ is $2n$, the subpath $(x_0, \ldots, x_n)$ is a minimal path from x_0 to x_n, i.e. the distance from x_0 to x_n is n. Since Γ is bipartite and of diameter n, the distance from x_0 to x_{n+1} must be $n - 1$. This implies (again, since the girth of Γ is $2n$) that γ lies on a unique apartment. Thus (i) holds.

Now let u be a vertex of Γ. Choose an apartment Σ of Γ and a vertex v on Σ. Since the diameter of Γ is n, there exists a path γ_1 from u to v of length at most n. There is an extension γ_2 of γ_1 along Σ whose length is exactly $n+1$. By the conclusion of the previous paragraph, γ_2 lies on an apartment. The vertex u lies on this apartment and hence has at least two neighbors. Thus (ii) holds. $\square$

In the next two paragraphs we will show that there is a canonical correspondence between generalized polygons and spherical buildings of rank two—more precisely, between generalized n-gons (for $n \geqslant 2$) and buildings of type $\bullet\!\!\xrightarrow{\ n\ }\!\!\bullet$ up to a relabeling of the index set, where $\bullet\!\!\xrightarrow{\ 2\ }\!\!\bullet$ is to be interpreted as $\bullet \quad \bullet$.

7.14. Let Γ be a generalized n-gon for some $n \geqslant 2$, so every vertex of Γ has at least two neighbors by 7.13 (ii), and let Δ_Γ denote the chamber system with index set $I = \{1, 2\}$ constructed from Γ as in 1.8. The chamber system Δ_Γ is unique up to a relabeling of I. Let $\Delta = \Delta_\Gamma$, let $\Pi = \bullet\!\!\xrightarrow{\ n\ }\!\!\bullet$, and let (W, r) denote the Coxeter system of type Π. By 2.6, $|W| = 2n$. It follows that the words $p(1, 2)$ and $p(2, 1)$ as defined in 3.1 are the only words in M_I of length n which are reduced (with respect to Π), and every other reduced word in M_I is of length less than n and homotopic only to itself. Let $x, y \in \Delta$ (so x and y are edges of Γ). It follows by 7.12 that either $\mathrm{dist}(x, y) < n$ and there is a unique minimal gallery from x to y in Δ or $\mathrm{dist}(x, y) = n$ and there are exactly two minimal galleries from x to y, one of type $p(1, 2)$ and the other of type $p(2, 1)$. We can thus define a map $\delta : \Delta \times \Delta \to W$ by setting $\delta(x, y) = r_f$ if $\mathrm{dist}(x, y) < n$, where f is the type of the unique minimal gallery from x to

y, and $\delta(x, y) = r_{p(1,2)}$ if $\text{dist}(x, y) = n$. Then (Δ, δ) is a building of type Π. It is thick in the sense of 1.7 if and only if every vertex of Γ has at least three neighbors, and it is irreducible as defined in 7.10 if and only if $n \geqslant 3$.

7.15. Let Δ be a building of type $\Pi = \bullet\!\!\overset{n}{-\!\!-\!\!}\!\!\bullet$ for some $n \geqslant 2$, let 1 and 2 denote the two elements of its index set and let Γ_Δ denote the bipartite graph constructed from Δ as in 1.9. By 7.1, 7.7 (ii) and the properties of the Coxeter system of type Π given in 7.14, $\text{diam}\,\Delta = n$, and for all $x, y \in \Delta$, there are just two minimal galleries from x to y—one of type $p(1, 2)$ and one of type $p(2, 1)$—if $\text{dist}(x, y) = n$, and a unique minimal gallery from x to y if $\text{dist}(x, y) < n$. It follows that Γ_Δ is a generalized n-gon.

Let (Δ, δ) be the building of type A_ℓ described in 7.4 and suppose that $\ell = 2$. The vertex set of the corresponding bipartite graph Γ_Δ is the set of proper subspaces of the three-dimensional vector space X and the edge set of Γ_Δ is the set of pairs of proper subspaces of X such that one is a proper subspace of the other. The reader can verify directly that this graph is a thick generalized 3-gon.

7.16. Let Δ be a spherical building of rank two with index set I, let $\Gamma_\Delta = (V, E)$ denote the corresponding generalized polygon and let V_1 and V_2 be as in 1.8. If $g \in \text{Aut}(\Delta)$, then for some permutation σ of I (there are only two) depending only on g, g maps each panel of type i to a panel of type $\sigma(i)$, and two panels have a non-trivial intersection if and only if their images under g do. If $g \in \text{Aut}(\Gamma_\Delta)$, then g permutes the set E of chambers of Δ and (since the partition of V into V_1 and V_2 is unique) there is a permutation σ of I depending only on g such that two chambers are i-adjacent for each $i \in I$ if and only if their images under g are $\sigma(i)$-adjacent. It follows that $\text{Aut}(\Delta)$ and $\text{Aut}(\Gamma_\Delta)$ are really the same group.

7.17. A bipartite graph having diameter two must be a complete bipartite graph as defined in 7.11. By 7.13 (ii), therefore, a generalized 2-gon is a complete bipartite graph such that each vertex has at least two neighbors. Conversely, every complete bipartite graph such that each vertex has at least two neighbors is a generalized 2-gon.

We return now to buildings of arbitrary rank and consider subbuildings, residues and convexity. In 7.18–7.20, we explicitly allow $J = \emptyset$ with the understanding that a building of empty type is just a graph consisting of a single chamber; this is consistent with 4.7.

Proposition 7.18. *Let (Δ, δ) be a building of type Π with index set I, let Δ_0 be a sub-chamber system of Δ (see 1.5) with index set $J \subset I$ and let δ_0 denote* *the restriction of* δ *to* $\Delta_0 \times \Delta_0$. *Then* Δ_0 *is convex as defined in 1.12 if and only if* (Δ_0, δ_0) *is a building of type* Π_J *(and, in particular,* $\delta(\Delta_0 \times \Delta_0) \subset W_J$*), where* Π_J *and* W_J *are as in 4.6.*

Proof. Suppose that Δ_0 is convex. Let $x, y \in \Delta_0$ and let γ be a minimal gallery from x to y. Let f denote the type of γ. By 7.7 (ii), f is reduced. Since Δ_0 is convex, $[\gamma] \subset \Delta_0$. Since the index set of Δ_0 is J, this means that the word f lies in M_J. By 7.1, therefore, $\delta(x, y) = r_f \in W_J$. Thus $\delta(\Delta_0 \times \Delta_0) \subset W_J$. Suppose now that $\delta(x, y) = r_g$ for some other reduced word $g \in M_J$. By 7.1, there is a gallery γ' of type g in Δ from x to y. By 7.7 (ii), γ' is minimal. Hence $[\gamma'] \subset \Delta_0$, again since Δ_0 is convex. It follows that (Δ_0, δ_0) is a building of type Π_J.

Now suppose that (Δ_0, δ_0) is a building of type Π_J and let $\gamma = (x, \dots, y)$ be a minimal gallery of Δ such that x and y both lie in Δ_0. Let f denote the type of γ. By 7.7 (ii), f is reduced, hence by 7.1, $r_f = \delta(x, y) \in \delta(\Delta_0, \Delta_0) \subset W_J$ and thus $f \in M_J$ by 4.8. By 7.1 applied to (Δ_0, δ_0), therefore, there is a gallery γ_0 in Δ_0 from x to y of type f. By 7.7 (iii), $\gamma = \gamma_0$ and hence $[\gamma] \subset \Delta_0$. Thus Δ_0 is convex. $\qquad\square$

Definition 7.19. A *subbuilding* of a building is a sub-chamber system having the two properties shown to be equivalent in 7.18. If Δ, Δ_0, Π, J, etc., are as in 7.18 and Δ_0 is a subbuilding, then we will say that Δ_0 is a *subbuilding of type* Π_J.

The following fundamental result makes it possible in many situations to prove things about buildings by using induction on the rank.

Theorem 7.20. *Let* (Δ, δ) *be a building of type* Π *with index set* I. *Let* $J \subset I$, *let* Π_J *be as in 4.6 and let* R *be a* J-*residue of* Δ. *Then* R *is a subbuilding of* Δ. *More precisely,* R *is convex and* (R, δ_R) *is a subbuilding of type* Π_J, *where* δ_R *denotes the restriction of* δ *to* $R \times R$.

Proof. Every residue is a sub-chamber system. Let (W, r) denote the Coxeter system of type Π, let W_J be as in 4.6, let u, v be chambers of R, let γ be a J-gallery from u to v and let f denote its type. Suppose that f is not reduced. Then f is homotopic to a word g of the form f_1iif_2 in M_J. By 7.7 (i), there is a gallery γ_1 from u to v of type g (and hence of the same length as γ). Since we can delete one or two chambers from γ_1 to obtain a shorter J-gallery from u to v, it follows that γ is not a J-gallery from u to v of minimal length.

We now assume that γ is a J-gallery from u to v of minimal length. By the conclusion of the previous paragraph, its type f is reduced. By 7.1, therefore,

$\delta(u, v) = r_f$. Now let γ_2 be a minimal I-gallery from u to v and let h denote its type. By 7.7 (ii), h is reduced, hence $r_h = r_f \in W_J$ by 7.1 and hence $h \in M_J$ by 4.8. Thus $[\gamma_2] \subset R$. We conclude that R is convex. By 7.19, it follows that R is a subbuilding of type Π_J. $\qquad\square$

Corollary 7.21. *Residues of a building are convex.*

Proof. This holds by 7.20. $\qquad\square$

By 7.21, every residue of a building equals the subgraph spanned by its chambers. It should thus not cause any confusion if we occasionally (for instance, in 8.13 and 8.21) let the same letter refer to the set of chambers of a residue of a building and to the residue itself (as we did in earlier chapters with the residues of Coxeter chamber systems).

Let Δ be a building of type Π with index set I and let R be a J-residue of Δ for some $J \subset I$. Then J is the type of R as defined in 1.6. By 7.20, however, R is a subbuilding of Δ and as a building, its type is Π_J. We hope that this ambiguous use of the term 'type' does not cause any confusion.

The following result justifies talking about the type (or Coxeter diagram) of a building.

Proposition 7.22. *Suppose that (Δ, δ) and $(\hat{\Delta}, \hat{\delta})$ are buildings of type Π and $\hat{\Pi}$ with index sets I and $\hat{I}$ and Weyl groups W and $\hat{W}$ and that ϕ is a σ-isomorphism from Δ to $\hat{\Delta}$ (as chamber systems) for some bijection σ from I to $\hat{I}$ (i.e. from the vertex set of Π to the vertex set of $\hat{\Pi}$) as defined in 1.14. Then the following hold.*

(i) *σ is an isomorphism from Π to $\hat{\Pi}$ (i.e. an isomorphism of graphs which maps edges with a given label to edges with the same label). Hence there exists an isomorphism ψ from W to $\hat{W}$ such that $r_i^{\psi} = r_{\sigma(i)}$ for all $i \in I$.*

(ii) *$\delta(x, y)^{\psi} = \hat{\delta}(x^{\phi}, y^{\phi})$ for all $x, y \in \Delta$, where ψ is as in (i).*

Proof. Let $[m_{ij}]$ denote the Coxeter matrix corresponding to Π and let $\{i, j\}$ be a two-element subset of I. By 7.15 and 7.21, every $\{i, j\}$-residue of Δ is of diameter m_{ij} and every $\{\sigma(i), \sigma(j)\}$-residue of $\hat{\Delta}$ is of diameter $m_{\sigma(i),\sigma(j)}$. Since ϕ maps $\{i, j\}$-residues of Δ to $\{\sigma(i), \sigma(j)\}$-residues of $\hat{\Delta}$, it follows that $m_{ij} = m_{\sigma(i),\sigma(j)}$. In particular, $\{i, j\}$ is an edge of Π if and only if $\{\sigma(i), \sigma(j)\}$ is an edge of $\hat{\Pi}$. Since the subset $\{i, j\}$ is arbitrary, this means that σ is an isomorphism from Π to $\hat{\Pi}$ which maps edges with a given label to edges with the same label. Hence, by 2.2, there exists an isomorphism ψ from W to $\hat{W}$ such that $r_i^{\psi} = r_{\sigma(i)}$ for all $i \in I$. Thus (i) holds.

Let $x, y \in \Delta$, choose a minimal gallery γ from x to y, let $f = i_1 \cdots i_k$ denote its type and let $\sigma(f) = \sigma(i_1) \cdots \sigma(i_k)$. Thus $r_{\sigma(f)} = r_f^{\psi}$, where ψ is as above. Since γ^{ϕ} is a minimal gallery of type $\sigma(f)$ from x^{ϕ} to y^{ϕ}, we have $\delta(x, y) = r_f$ and $\hat{\delta}(x^{\phi}, y^{\phi}) = r_{\sigma(f)}$ by 7.1 and 7.7 (ii). Thus (ii) holds. $\qquad\square$

Thus, by 7.22, the type Π of a building (Δ, δ) (and therefore also the corresponding Coxeter system (W, r)) as well as the Weyl-distance function δ are uniquely determined by the underlying chamber system Δ.

Corollary 7.23. *Let Δ be a building of type Π. Then the map which sends a σ-automorphism of Δ to σ is an injective homomorphism from $\mathrm{Aut}(\Delta) / \mathrm{Aut}^{\circ}(\Delta)$ to the group of (edge-label-preserving) automorphisms of the Coxeter diagram Π.*

Proof. This holds by 1.15 and 7.22 (i). $\qquad\square$

7.24. Suppose that Π is an irreducible spherical Coxeter diagram. Thus Π is one of the diagrams described in 5.17. Let I denote the vertex set of Π and let $\Sigma = \Sigma_{\Pi}$. By 7.5, Σ is a building of type Π and by 5.12, op_{Σ} is an op_I-automorphism of Σ. By 7.22 (i), therefore, op_I is an automorphism of Π, i.e. a graph automorphism which maps edges with a given label to edges with the same label. We could, of course, have proved this special case of 7.22 (i) in Chapter 5. It can be shown that op_I is the unique non-trivial automorphism of Π if $\Pi = \bullet\!\!\overset{n}{\rule{1.5em}{0.4pt}}\!\!\bullet$ with $n \geqslant 3$ odd, if $\Pi = \mathsf{A}_{\ell}$ with $\ell \geqslant 2$ arbitrary, if $\Pi = \mathsf{D}_{\ell}$ with $\ell \geqslant 5$ odd, or if $\Pi = \mathsf{E}_6$, and that op_I is the identity in every other case.

Proposition 7.25. *Let R and R' be residues of type J and J' of a building Δ, let $S = R \cap R'$ and suppose that $S \neq \emptyset$. Then S is a residue of type $J \cap J'$.*

Proof. By 7.21, S is $J \cap J'$-connected and hence a $J \cap J'$-residue. $\qquad\square$

Proposition 7.26. *Let R be a residue of type J and P a panel of type i of a building (Δ, δ) and suppose that $|R \cap P| > 1$. Then $i \in J$ and $P \subset R$.*

Proof. This is a special case of 7.25. $\qquad\square$

The following little observation and its corollary 7.28 will play a big role in the next chapter.

Proposition 7.27. *Let x be a chamber of a building (Δ, δ) of type Π. Then the map*

$$u \mapsto \delta(x, u)$$

is a special homomorphism (as defined in 1.16) from Δ to the Coxeter chamber system Σ_Π mapping adjacent chambers to distinct chambers if and only if one of them lies on a minimal gallery from x to the other.

Proof. Let (W, r) denote the Coxeter system of type Π. Let $y, z \in \Delta$, suppose that y and z are i-adjacent for some $i \in I$ and choose a reduced word f such that $\delta(x, y) = r_f$. By 7.1, we can choose a gallery γ from x to y of type f. Then (γ, z) is a gallery from x to z of type fi. If fi is reduced, then by 7.1 again, $\delta(x, z) = r_{fi} = \delta(x, y)r_i$. In this case, (γ, z) is minimal by 7.7 (ii). Suppose that fi is not reduced. By 4.11, there exists a word g ending in i (so $g = hi$ for some $h \in M_I$) which is homotopic to f (and hence also reduced). Then $\delta(x, y) = r_f = r_g$, so by 7.1, we can choose a gallery $(x, \ldots, w, y)$ from x to y whose type is g. This gallery is minimal by 7.7 (ii) and either $w = z$ or $(x, \ldots, w, z)$ is a gallery whose type is also g (and hence $\text{dist}(x, y) = |g| = \text{dist}(x, z)$). By 7.1,

$$\delta(x, z) = r_h = r_g r_i = \delta(x, y)r_i$$

in the first case and $\delta(x, y) = r_g = \delta(x, z)$ in the second. $\square$

Corollary 7.28. *Let (Δ, δ) be a building of type Π with index set I, let (W, r) denote the Coxeter system of type Π, let $x, y, z \in \Delta$ and suppose that y and z are i-adjacent for some $i \in I$. Then either $\delta(y, x) = \delta(z, x)$ or $\delta(y, x) = r_i \delta(z, x)$.*

Proof. This holds by 7.3 and 7.27. $\square$

The following definition will be important in Chapters 8 and 10.

Definition 7.29. Let Δ and $\hat{\Delta}$ be two buildings of the same type Π (and hence having the same index set). A map from a subset X of Δ to $\hat{\Delta}$ will be called *full* if it maps every panel of Δ which is contained in X bijectively to a panel of $\hat{\Delta}$ of the same type. Thus a map π from a subset X of Δ is full if for each panel P of Δ contained in X, its image P^π is a panel of $\hat{\Delta}$ of the same type as P and π restricted to P is injective.

Proposition 7.30. *Let Δ and $\hat{\Delta}$ be two buildings of the same type and let π be a map from Δ to $\hat{\Delta}$. Then π is a special isomorphism from Δ to $\hat{\Delta}$ (and, in particular, surjective) if and only if it is full as defined in 7.29.*

Proof. Suppose first that π is full. Then π maps every gallery of Δ to a gallery of $\hat{\Delta}$ of the same type. By 7.7 (ii), therefore, π maps every minimal gallery of Δ to a minimal gallery of $\hat{\Delta}$. This implies that π is injective. Since π is full, we also know that every gallery of $\hat{\Delta}$ which starts at a chamber in the image of

π lies completely in the image of π. Since $\hat{\Delta}$ is connected (by 7.2), it follows that π is surjective. We conclude that π is a special isomorphism.

Now suppose that π is a special isomorphism from Δ to $\hat{\Delta}$. Then both π and π^{-1} map i-adjacent chambers to i-adjacent chambers for all $i \in I$. It follows that π is full. $\square$

Proposition 7.31. *Let* (Δ, δ) *and* $(\hat{\Delta}, \hat{\delta})$ *be two buildings of the same type* Π, *let* π *be a full map from some subset* X *of* Δ *to* $\hat{\Delta}$ *and let* R *be a residue of* Δ *contained in* X. *Then* R^{π} *is a residue of* $\hat{\Delta}$ *of the same type as* R *and the restriction* $\pi|_R$ *is a special isomorphism from* R *to* R^{π}.

Proof. Since π is full, it maps galleries of type f (for arbitrary $f \in M_I$) to galleries of type f. It follows that R^{π} is contained in a residue $\hat{R}$ of $\hat{\Delta}$ of the same type as R. Hence the restriction $\pi|_R$ is a full map from R to $\hat{R}$. By 7.20 and 7.30, therefore, $\pi|_R$ is a special isomorphism from R to $\hat{R}$. $\square$

When we come to classification results for spherical buildings in Chapters 10–12, we always assume that the buildings in question are irreducible. By the next two results, arbitrary spherical buildings are obtained from irreducible ones by taking direct products.

Proposition 7.32. *Let* $(\Delta_1, \delta_1), \ldots, (\Delta_k, \delta_k)$ *be a finite set of buildings whose index sets are pairwise disjoint, let* $W_1, \ldots, W_k$ *denote their Weyl groups, and let* Δ *denote the direct product (of chamber systems)*

$$\Delta_1 \times \cdots \times \Delta_k$$

as defined in 1.10. Let Π *be the disjoint union[2] of the Coxeter diagrams (i.e. of the types) of* $\Delta_1, \ldots, \Delta_k$ *and let* W *denote the corresponding Coxeter group which, by 4.6, is isomorphic to* $W_1 \times \cdots \times W_k$. *Then* (Δ, δ) *is a building of type* Π, *where* $\delta \colon \Delta \times \Delta \to W$ *is given by*

$$\delta((x_1, \ldots, x_k), (y_1, \ldots, y_k)) = \delta_1(x_1, y_1) \cdots \delta_k(x_k, y_k)$$

for all $(x_1, \ldots, x_k), (y_1, \ldots, y_k) \in \Delta$.

Proof. Let I_p denote the index set of Δ_p for each $p \in [1, k]$ and let I denote the index set of Δ, or equivalently, the vertex set of Π (so I is the disjoint union

---

[2] The *disjoint union* of a set $\{\Pi_p \mid p \in M\}$ of Coxeter diagrams is the Coxeter diagram whose vertex set is the disjoint union I of the vertex sets of the Π_p and whose edge set is the union of the edge sets of the Π_p with labels unchanged. Thus if i and j are distinct elements of I, and p and q are the unique elements of M such that i is a vertex of Π_p and j is a vertex of Π_q, then $\{i, j\}$ is an edge of Π with label m_{ij} if and only if $p = q$ and $\{x, y\}$ is an edge of Π_p with label m_{ij}.

of the I_p). We say that an elementary homotopy is trivial if it transforms a word $fijg$ of M_I into the word $fjig$ for i and j in distinct subsets I_p and I_q, and we say that two words are trivially homotopic if one can be transformed into the other by a finite sequence of trivial elementary homotopies. Then every word f of M_I is trivially homotopic to a unique product $f_1 \cdots f_k$, where $f_t \in M_{I_t}$ for all $t \in [1, k]$, and, by 1.10, if there is gallery in Δ of type f from a chamber x to a chamber y, then there is also a gallery from x to y of any type trivially homotopic to f. It follows from the definitions 1.10 and 7.1 and these observations that (Δ, δ) is a building. □

Proposition 7.33. *Let (Δ, δ) be a building of type Π with index set I and Coxeter matrix $[m_{ij}]$. Suppose that there is a partition of I into a finite number of disjoint subsets $I_1, \ldots, I_k$ such that $m_{ij} = 2$ whenever i and j lie in distinct subsets. Let x be a chamber of Δ and let Δ_t denote the I_t-residue of Δ containing x for all $t \in [1, k]$. Then there is a special isomorphism from Δ to the direct product $\Delta_1 \times \cdots \times \Delta_k$.*

Proof. By induction, it suffices to assume that $k = 2$. Let R_1 and R_2 be arbitrary I_1- and I_2-residues. Choose $u \in R_1$ and $v \in R_2$. Then $\delta(u, v) = r_{f_1 f_2}$, where $f_1 \in M_{I_1}$, $f_2 \in M_{I_2}$ and $f_1 f_2$ is reduced. By 7.1, there is a chamber w and galleries γ from u to w of type f_1 and γ' from w to v of type f_2. It follows that $w \in R_1 \cap R_2$. By 7.25, therefore, every I_1-residue intersects every I_2-residue in a unique chamber.

Let R be an arbitrary I_t-residue for $t = 1$ or 2, let $a \in R$, let b be a chamber i-adjacent to a for some $i \notin I_t$ and let R' denote the I_t-residue containing b. By 7.21, $R' \neq R$. Choose $c \in R$. Let γ be a minimal gallery from a to c and let f denote its type. By 7.7 (ii) and 7.21, f is a reduced word in M_{I_t}. By 4.11, if and fi are also reduced words. By 7.1, therefore, $\delta(b, c) = r_{if}$ since (b, γ) is a gallery from b to c of type if. Since $i \notin I_t$, we have $r_{if} = r_{fi}$. By 7.1 again, therefore, there is also a gallery $(x_0, \ldots, x_{m-1}, x_m)$ of type fi from b to c. Thus c is i-adjacent to the chamber x_{m-1} and, since $(x_0, \ldots, x_{m-1})$ is a gallery of type $f \in M_{I_t}$, $x_{m-1} \in R'$. We conclude that if R and R' are two I_t-residue (for $t = 1$ or 2) and there exists a chamber in R which is i-adjacent to a chamber in R' for some $i \notin I_t$, then every chamber of R is i-adjacent to some chamber in R'.

For each chamber $u \in \Delta$ and for $t = 1$ and 2, we denote by R_t^u the unique I_t-residue containing u. Thus $\Delta_t = R_t^x$ for $t = 1$ and 2. As we observed above, every I_1-residue intersects every I_2-residue in a unique chamber. Let ϕ denote the map from Δ to $\Delta_1 \times \Delta_2$ given by $\phi(y) = (y_1, y_2)$, where y_1 is the unique chamber in $\Delta_1 \cap R_2^y$ and y_2 is the unique chamber in $R_1^y \cap \Delta_2$. Let ψ denote the map from $\Delta_1 \times \Delta_2$ to Δ given by $\psi(y_1, y_2) = y$, where y is the unique chamber in $R_1^{y_2} \cap R_2^{y_1}$. The maps ϕ and ψ are inverses of each other. By the conclusion of the previous paragraph, ϕ and ψ both map i-adjacent chambers to i-adjacent chambers for all $i \in I$. Hence ϕ is a special isomorphism from Δ to $\Delta_1 \times \Delta_2$. $\qquad\qquad\square$

By 7.33, a building of type $\bullet \quad \bullet$ is the direct product of two buildings of rank one. This little observation follows also from 7.17.

Chapter Eight

Apartments

We begin this chapter by introducing isometries. Isometries will play a central role from now on.

Definition 8.1. Let (Δ, δ) and $(\hat{\Delta}, \hat{\delta})$ be two buildings of the same type (and thus having the same index set and the same Weyl group). A map π from a subset X of Δ to $\hat{\Delta}$ will be called an *isometry* from X to $\hat{\Delta}$ if

$$\hat{\delta}(x^\pi, y^\pi) = \delta(x, y)$$

for all $x, y \in X$.

Proposition 8.2. *Let (Δ, δ) and $(\hat{\Delta}, \hat{\delta})$ be two buildings of the same type Π and let π be a map from Δ to $\hat{\Delta}$. Then π is an isometry from Δ to $\hat{\Delta}$ if and only if π is a special isomorphism from Δ to Δ^π. If π is an isometry, then Δ^π is a subbuilding of type Π of $\hat{\Delta}$ as defined in 7.19 and $\Delta^\pi = \hat{\Delta}$ if and only if π is full as defined in 7.29.*

Proof. Let I denote the vertex set if Π (i.e. the index set of both Δ and $\hat{\Delta}$) and let (W, r) denote the Coxeter system corresponding to Π. Suppose first that π is a special isomorphism from Δ to Δ^π and let $\hat{\delta}_0$ denote the restriction of $\hat{\delta}$ to $\Delta^\pi \times \Delta^\pi$. Choose $x, y \in \Delta$ and let f be a reduced word in M_I such that $\delta(x, y) = r_f$. Then by 7.1, there is a gallery γ in Δ of type f from x to y. Again by 7.1,

$$\hat{\delta}_0(x^\pi, y^\pi) = \hat{\delta}(x^\pi, y^\pi) = r_f,$$

since γ^π is a gallery in Δ^π of type f from x^π to y^π. Therefore π is an isometry and $(\Delta^\pi, \hat{\delta}_0)$ is just the building (Δ, δ) with its chambers relabeled via the map π. Therefore $(\Delta^\pi, \hat{\delta}_0)$ is a subbuilding of $\hat{\Delta}$ of type Π.

Suppose, conversely, that π is an isometry. Choose $x, y \in \Delta$ and $i \in I$. By 8.1, $\delta(x, y) = \hat{\delta}(x^\pi, y^\pi)$. By 7.1, $x \sim_i y$ if and only if $\delta(x, y) = r_i$ and $x^\pi \sim_i y^\pi$ if and only if $\hat{\delta}(x^\pi, y^\pi) = r_i$. Hence x and y are i-adjacent if and only if x^π and y^π are. We have $x = y$ if and only if $\delta(x, y) = 1$ and $x^\pi = y^\pi$ if and only if $\hat{\delta}(x^\pi, y^\pi) = 1$. Hence π is injective. We conclude that π is a special isomorphism from Δ to Δ^π. By 7.30, $\Delta^\pi = \hat{\Delta}$ if and only if π is full. $\square$

Here now is the main definition of this chapter.

Definition 8.3. Let (Δ, δ) be a building of type Π. By 7.5 and 8.1, Σ_Π is a building of type Π, and an isometry from a subset X of Σ_Π to Δ is a map π from X to Δ such that

$$\delta(x^\pi, y^\pi) = x^{-1}y$$

for all $x, y \in X$. An *apartment* of Δ is a subgraph of Δ whose chamber and edge sets are the images of the chamber and edge sets of the building Σ_Π under an isometry π from Σ_Π to Δ.

8.4. Let Π be a Coxeter diagram. By 8.2, an isometry π from Σ_Π to a building of type Π is a special isomorphism from Σ_Π to the image of π. Thus *apartments of a building of type Π are Coxeter chamber systems of type Π* as defined in 2.4. This observation is crucial since it tells us (in conjunction with the next result) that we can apply all the results of Chapters 2–6 to the study of buildings.

The following important theorem (3.7.4 in [16]) tells us, in particular, that apartments exist (and, in fact, that there are lots of them).

Theorem 8.5. *Let Δ be a building of type Π. Then every isometry from a subset of Σ_Π to Δ extends to an isometry from Σ_Π to Δ.*

Proof. Let π be an isometry from a proper subset X of Σ_Π to Δ and let (W, r) denote the Coxeter system corresponding to Π. By Zorn's Lemma, it suffices to extend π to an isometry from X' to Δ for some subset X' of Σ_Π which contains X properly.[1] We can assume that $X \neq \emptyset$. Since Σ_Π is connected, we can find adjacent chambers $u \in X$ and $v \notin X$. Let ζ denote the special automorphism of Σ_Π given by left multiplication (in W) by u as described in 2.8. By 8.3, the

---

[1] Here are the details. Let M denote the set of ordered pairs (Y, π_Y) such that Y is a subset of Σ_Π containing X and π_Y is an isometry from Y to Δ extending π. Let $(Y_1, \pi_{Y_1}) \leqslant (Y_2, \pi_{Y_2})$ for (Y_1, π_{Y_1}) and (Y_2, π_{Y_2}) in M whenever $Y_1 \subset Y_2$ and π_{Y_2} is an extension of π_{Y_1}. Then

(i) $y \leqslant y$ for all $y \in M$;

(ii) if $y_1 \leqslant y_2$ and $y_2 \leqslant y_1$ (for $y_1, y_2 \in M$), then $y_1 = y_2$; and

(iii) if $y_1 \leqslant y_2$ and $y_2 \leqslant y_3$ (for $y_1, y_2, y_3 \in M$), then $y_1 \leqslant y_3$.

In other words, $\leqslant$ is a *partial ordering* of M. Let $C \subset M$ be a *chain* of M (with respect to $\leqslant$). This means that for any two element y_1 and y_2 in C, either $y_1 \leqslant y_2$ or $y_2 \leqslant y_1$. Let $A \subset \Sigma_\Pi$ denote the set of chambers contained in the first coordinate of some element of C and let π_A denote the map from A to Σ_Π defined as follows. For each $y \in A$, choose $(Y, \pi_Y) \in C$ such that $y \in Y$ and let $\pi_A(y) = \pi_Y(y)$. Since C is a chain, π_A is well defined and $(A, \pi_A) \in M$. Moreover, $(Y, \pi_Y) \leqslant (A, \pi_A)$ for all $(Y, \pi_Y) \in C$, i.e. (A, π_A) is an *upper bound* of C in M. Thus M has the property that every chain in M has an upper bound in M. Zorn's Lemma says that partially ordered sets with this property contain a *maximal element*, i.e. an element which is greater than every other element. It suffices, therefore, to show that $X \neq \Sigma_\Pi$ implies that (X, π) is not a maximal element of M.

composition $\pi \cdot \zeta$ is an isometry from $u^{-1}X$ to Δ. Replacing π by $\pi \cdot \zeta$ and X by $u^{-1}X$, we can thus assume that $u = 1$. Since v is adjacent to $u = 1$, we have $v = r_i$ for some $i \in I$. Let $X' = X \cup \{r_i\}$.

Suppose that ig is reduced for every reduced word g such that $r_g \in X$. Let w be any chamber of Δ which is i-adjacent to 1^π. We extend π to X' by setting $r_i^\pi = w$. Choose $x \in X$ and then choose a reduced word g such that $x = r_g$. By 8.3, $\delta(1^\pi, x^\pi) = x = r_g$. By 7.1, therefore, there is a gallery of type g in Δ from 1^π to x^π. Hence there is a gallery of type ig from w to x^π. By assumption, ig is reduced. Hence $\delta(r_i^\pi, x^\pi) = \delta(w, x^\pi) = r_{ig} = r_i x = r_i^{-1}x$ by 7.1. Since x is arbitrary, we conclude that the extension of π is an isometry from X' to Δ.

Now suppose that ig is not reduced for some reduced word g such that $r_g \in X$. By 4.11, g is homotopic to a reduced word f which begins with i. Thus $f = ih$ for some reduced word h. By 2.5, there is a gallery from 1 to $r_f = r_g$ in Σ_Π of type f. By 4.3, this gallery is minimal. It follows that

$$\mathrm{dist}(r_i, r_g) < \mathrm{dist}(1, r_g)$$

in Σ_Π. (We will use 'dist' only to refer to distance in Σ_Π, not in Δ, in this proof.) By 8.3, $\delta(1^\pi, r_g^\pi) = r_g = r_f$. By 7.1, therefore, there is a gallery

$$(w_0, w_1, \ldots, w_k)$$

of type f in Δ from 1^π to r_g^π. We extend π to X' by setting $r_i^\pi = w_1$. To show that this extension of π is an isometry from X' to Δ, we just need to show that $\delta(w_1, x^\pi) = r_i^{-1}x$ for all $x \in X$, i.e. that the map

$$\beta(x) = r_i \delta(w_1, x^\pi)$$

from X to Σ_Π fixes every element of X. Since $\delta(1^\pi, x^\pi) = x$ for all $x \in X$ and w_1 is i-adjacent to 1^π, it follows by 7.28 that $\beta(x) = r_i x$ for every $x \in X$ which is not fixed by β. Note, too, that β fixes 1 since $(w_1, 1^\pi)$ is a gallery of type i and hence $\delta(w_1, 1^\pi) = r_i^{-1}$ by 7.1, and β fixes r_g since $(w_1, \ldots, w_k)$ is a gallery of type h from w_1 to r_g^π and hence $\delta(w_1, r_g^\pi) = r_h = r_i^{-1}r_g$, again by 7.1.

By 2.9 and 8.3,

$$\|\delta(y_1^\pi, y_2^\pi)\| = \|y_1^{-1}y_2\| = \mathrm{dist}(y_1, y_2)$$

for all $y_1, y_2 \in \Sigma_\Pi$. By 1.18, 7.8 and 7.27, therefore,

$$\mathrm{dist}(\delta(w_1, y_1^\pi), \delta(w_1, y_2^\pi)) \leqslant \mathrm{dist}(y_1, y_2)$$

for all $y_1, y_2 \in \Sigma_\Pi$. By 2.8, left multiplication by r_i preserve distances in Σ_Π. Therefore,

$$\text{dist}(\beta(y_1), \beta(y_2)) \leqslant \text{dist}(y_1, y_2)$$

for all $y_1, y_2 \in \Sigma_\Pi$. By the conclusions of the previous paragraph, it follows that

$$\text{dist}(1, r_i x) = \text{dist}(\beta(1), \beta(x)) \leqslant \text{dist}(1, x)$$

and

$$\text{dist}(r_g, r_i x) = \text{dist}(\beta(r_g), \beta(x)) \leqslant \text{dist}(r_g, x)$$

for all $x \in X$ which are not fixed by β.

Let α denote the root $\Sigma_{(1 \backslash r_i)}$ of Σ_Π. Thus, by 3.15,

$$\alpha = \{v \in \Sigma_\Pi \mid \text{dist}(v, 1) < \text{dist}(v, r_i)\}$$

and $\text{refl}_\Sigma(\alpha) = r_i$. As we observed above,

$$\text{dist}(r_i, r_g) < \text{dist}(1, r_g).$$

Therefore $1 \in \alpha$ but $r_g \in -\alpha$. By 3.11, $r_i x \in -\alpha$ if $x \in \alpha$ and $r_i x \in \alpha$ if $x \in -\alpha$. Thus $\rho_{\Sigma_\Pi, \alpha}(r_i x) = x$ if $x \in \alpha$ and $\rho_{\Sigma_\Pi, -\alpha}(r_i x) = x$ if $x \in -\alpha$, where $\rho_{\Sigma_\Pi, \alpha}$ and $\rho_{\Sigma_\Pi, -\alpha}$ are as defined in 3.16. By 3.18, therefore,

$$\text{dist}(1, x) = \text{dist}(1, \rho_{\Sigma_\Pi, \alpha}(r_i x)) < \text{dist}(1, r_i x)$$

if $x \in \alpha$ and

$$\text{dist}(r_g, x) = \text{dist}(r_g, \rho_{\Sigma_\Pi, -\alpha}(r_i x)) < \text{dist}(r_g, r_i x)$$

if $x \in -\alpha$. Thus β fixes every element of X by the conclusions of the previous paragraph.   □

The following simple consequence of 8.5 will be useful.

Corollary 8.6. *Every two chambers of a building are contained in a common apartment.*

Proof. Let x and y be chambers of a building (Δ, δ) of type Π. Then the map from $\{1, \delta(x, y)\}$ to Δ which sends 1 to x and $\delta(x, y)$ to y is an isometry from the subset $\{1, \delta(x, y)\}$ of Σ_Π to Δ. It follows by 8.5 that there is an apartment containing x and y.   □

Here is one way to characterize apartments.

Proposition 8.7. *Let Δ be a building, let Π denote the type of Δ and let Σ be a subgraph of Δ. Then Σ is an apartment if and only if Σ is a thin subbuilding of type Π.*

Proof. Suppose that Σ is an apartment. By 8.3, Σ is the image of an isometry π from Σ_Π to Δ. By 8.2, therefore, Σ is a subbuilding of type Π and π is a special isomorphism from Σ_Π to Σ. Since Σ_Π is thin, it follows that Σ is also thin. Suppose, conversely, that Σ is a thin subbuilding of type Π. By 8.5 with Σ in place of Δ, there is an isometry π from Σ_Π to Σ. Since Σ is thin, the isometry π is full. By 7.30, therefore, π is surjective. Thus Σ is an apartment of Δ. $\qquad\square$

Proposition 8.8. *Let Δ be a building, let I denote the index set of Δ and let Σ be a subgraph of Δ. Then Σ is an apartment if and only if Σ is a thin, convex sub-chamber system whose index set is I.*

Proof. This holds by 7.19 and 8.7. $\qquad\square$

We thus have one more important result about convexity.

Corollary 8.9. *Apartments are convex.*

Proof. This holds by 8.8. $\qquad\square$

By 8.9, an apartment is the same as the subgraph spanned by its set of chambers.

Corollary 8.10. *Let Δ and $\hat{\Delta}$ be two buildings and let π be an isomorphism from Δ to $\hat{\Delta}$. Then π maps apartments of Δ to apartments of $\hat{\Delta}$.*

Proof. This follows from 8.8. $\qquad\square$

Proposition 8.11. *For each Coxeter diagram Π, Σ_Π is (up to a special isomorphism) the only thin building of type Π.*

Proof. Let Δ be a thin building of type Π. By 8.7, Δ is an apartment (of itself). By 8.3, there is thus an isometry π from Σ_Π onto Δ. By 8.2, π is a special isomorphism. $\qquad\square$

Proposition 8.12. *Let Δ be a building with index set I, let Σ be an apartment of Δ and let R be a J-residue of Δ for some $J \subset I$. Then $\Sigma \cap R$ is either empty or a J-residue of Σ.*

Proof. It suffices to observe that by 7.21 and 8.9, the subgraph $\Sigma \cap R$ is convex and therefore J-connected. □

Recall that by 7.20, residues of a building are themselves buildings so that it makes sense to speak of apartments of a residue, as we do in the next result.

Proposition 8.13. *Let (Δ, δ) be a building and let R be a residue of Δ. Then the following hold.*

(i) *If Σ is an apartment of Δ such that $\Sigma \cap R \neq \emptyset$ and α is a root of Σ, then $\Sigma \cap R$ is an apartment of R and either $\alpha \cap R$ is a root of $\Sigma \cap R$ or $\Sigma \cap R \subset \alpha$ or $\Sigma \cap R \subset \Sigma \backslash \alpha$.*

(ii) *If Σ_0 is an apartment of R, then $\Sigma_0 = \Sigma \cap R$ for some apartment Σ of Δ, and for each such apartment Σ and for each root α_0 of Σ_0, there is a unique root α of Σ such that $\alpha_0 = \alpha \cap R$.*

Proof. Suppose that Σ is an arbitrary apartment of Δ such that $\Sigma \cap R \neq \emptyset$. By 7.21 and 8.9, $\Sigma \cap R$ is convex. By 8.8, therefore, $\Sigma \cap R$ is an apartment of R. Suppose that α is a root of Σ such that $\Sigma \cap R$ contains both chambers in α and chambers not in α. Since $\Sigma \cap R$ is connected, it thus contains adjacent chambers u and v such that $u \in \alpha$ and $v \notin \alpha$. By 3.15, therefore,

$$\alpha \cap R = \{ z \in \Sigma \cap R \mid \text{dist}(u, z) < \text{dist}(v, z) \}$$

and hence $\alpha \cap R$ is a root of $\Sigma \cap R$. Thus (i) holds.

Let Σ_0 be an apartment of R, let W denote the Weyl group of Δ and let W_J be as in 4.6, where J denotes the type of R. By 8.3, Σ_0 is the image of an isometry π from W_J to R. By 8.5, π extends to an isometry from Σ_Π to Δ, where Π denotes the type of Δ. Let Σ denote its image. If $y^\pi \in R$ for some $y \in \Sigma_\Pi$, then

$$y = \delta(1^\pi, y^\pi) \in \delta(R, R) \subset W_J$$

by 7.20 and 8.3 and hence $y^\pi \in \Sigma_0$. Thus $\Sigma_0 = \Sigma \cap R$. Suppose now that α_0 is a root of Σ_0. Choose adjacent chambers u and v such that $u \in \alpha_0$ and $v \in \Sigma_0 \backslash \alpha_0$. By 3.15, the set

$$\alpha = \{ z \in \Sigma \mid \text{dist}(z, u) < \text{dist}(z, v) \}$$

is the unique root of Σ such that $\alpha_0 = \alpha \cap \Sigma_0 = \alpha \cap R$. Hence (ii) holds. □

The following little fact will be used in the proof of 10.6.

Proposition 8.14. *Let Δ be a building, let R be a residue of Δ, and let Σ_0 be an apartment of R. Suppose that Σ is an apartment of Δ containing Σ_0. Then $\Sigma_0 = \Sigma \cap R$.*

Proof. Let J denote the type of R. By 8.13 (i), $\Sigma \cap R$ is an apartment of R. By 8.8, $\Sigma \cap R$ and Σ_0 are both thin chamber systems with index set J. Since $\Sigma_0 \subset \Sigma \cap R$, it follows that for all $x \in \Sigma_0$, every chamber of $\Sigma \cap R$ adjacent to x is contained in Σ_0. By 8.9, or by 8.12, $\Sigma \cap R$ is connected. Therefore $\Sigma_0 = \Sigma \cap R$. □

We now introduce retractions. First we observe the following.

8.15. Let Δ be a building of type Π, let Σ be an apartment of Δ, and let x be a chamber of Σ. Then by 2.8, 8.2 and 8.3, there is a unique isometry from Σ_Π onto Σ mapping 1 to x.

Definition 8.16. Let (Δ, δ) be a building of type Π, let Σ be an apartment of Δ, and let x be a chamber of Σ. By 8.15, there is a unique isometry π from Σ_Π onto Σ mapping 1 to x. The Weyl group W of Δ, i.e. the image of δ, is precisely the set of chambers of Σ_Π. We can thus set

$$\text{retr}_{\Sigma,x}(y) = \delta(x, y)^\pi$$

for all $y \in \Delta$. The map $\text{retr}_{\Sigma,x}$ is called the *retraction* of Δ to Σ with *center* x.

Proposition 8.17. *Let (Δ, δ) be a building of type Π, let Σ be an apartment, let $x \in \Sigma$ and let $y \in \Delta$. Then $\text{retr}_{\Sigma,x}(y)$ is the unique chamber of Σ such that*

$$\delta(x, \text{retr}_{\Sigma,x}(y)) = \delta(x, y).$$

In particular, $\text{retr}_{\Sigma,x}(y) = y$ for all $y \in \Sigma$.

Proof. Let $\rho = \text{retr}_{\Sigma,x}$, let π be the unique isometry from Σ_Π to Σ mapping 1 to x and let f be a reduced word such that $\delta(x, y) = r_f$. By 2.5, there exists a gallery of type f in Σ_Π from 1 to r_f. By 8.2, the image of this gallery under π is a gallery of type f from x to $r_f^\pi = \delta(x, y)^\pi = \rho(y)$, which we denote by γ. By 7.1, therefore, $\delta(x, \rho(y)) = r_f$. Now suppose that z is an arbitrary chamber of Σ such that $\delta(x, z) = r_f$. By 7.1 again, there is a gallery γ' in Δ of type f from x to z. By 7.7 (ii), γ' is minimal. By 8.9, therefore, $\gamma' \subset \Sigma$. By 2.5, there is only one gallery in Σ of type f beginning at x. Hence $\gamma' = \gamma$ and thus $z = \rho(y)$. □

Proposition 8.18. *Let Δ be a building. Then* retr $_{\Sigma,x}$ *is a special homomorphism from Δ to Σ for each apartment Σ and each chamber $x \in \Sigma$.*

Proof. This holds by 7.27, 8.2 and 8.16.   □

Proposition 8.19. *Let Σ and Σ_1 be two apartments of a building Δ both containing a chamber x. Then* retr $_{\Sigma,x}$ *restricted to Σ_1 is a special isomorphism from Σ_1 to Σ.*

Proof. By 8.17, retr $_{\Sigma,x}$ restricted to Σ_1 and retr $_{\Sigma_1,x}$ restricted to Σ are inverses of each other. By 8.18, retr $_{\Sigma,x}$ restricted to Σ_1 is therefore a special isomorphism from Σ_1 to Σ.   □

Here is our first application of retractions. We will need this result in 9.8.

Proposition 8.20. *Let Σ_1 and Σ_2 be two apartments of a building Δ and let R_1 and R_2 be two residues such that $R_i \cap \Sigma_j \neq \emptyset$ for all $i, j = 1, 2$. Then there is a special isomorphism from Σ_1 to Σ_2 which maps $\Sigma_1 \cap R_j$ to $\Sigma_2 \cap R_j$ for $j = 1$ and 2.*

Proof. Let I denote the index set of Δ. By 8.12, it will suffice to show that there is a special isomorphism from Σ_1 to Σ_2 mapping some chamber of $\Sigma_1 \cap R_j$ to a chamber of $\Sigma_2 \cap R_j$ for $j = 1$ and 2. We first assume that $\Sigma_1 \cap \Sigma_2 \cap R_1 \neq \emptyset$ and that $\Sigma_1 \cap R_2$ contains chambers which are adjacent to chambers in $\Sigma_2 \cap R_2$. Choose $x \in \Sigma_1 \cap \Sigma_2 \cap R_1$ and adjacent chambers $y \in \Sigma_1 \cap R_2$ and $z \in \Sigma_2 \cap R_2$. By 7.21, y and z are, in fact, i-adjacent for some $i \in J_2$, where J_2 denotes the type of R_2. If $\delta(x, y) = \delta(x, z)$, then by 8.17 and 8.19, there is a special isomorphism from Σ_1 to Σ_2 which fixes x and maps y to z. We can assume, therefore, that $\delta(x, y) \neq \delta(x, z)$. By 7.27, we can assume that there is a minimal gallery $\gamma = (x, \ldots, y, z)$ from x to z containing y. Let f denote the type of γ. Then $f = gi$ for some $g \in M_I$. Let u denote the unique chamber of Σ_1 which is i-adjacent to y. Then $u \in \Sigma_1 \cap R_2$ (since $i \in J_2$) and $(x, \ldots, y, u)$ is a gallery also of type f. By 7.7 (ii), f is reduced. Thus, by 7.1, $\delta(x, u) = \delta(x, z)$. Again by 8.17 and 8.19, it follows that there is a special isomorphism from Σ_1 to Σ_2 which fixes x and maps u to z.

We now turn to the general case. Since residues are connected, we can choose galleries $\gamma_i = (x_i, \ldots, y_i)$ in R_i for $i = 1, 2$ which start in Σ_1 and end in Σ_2. By 8.6, for each chamber in γ_2 we can choose an apartment containing it as well as x_1; let Σ' denote the last of these apartments. By repeated application of the conclusion of the previous paragraph, we obtain a special isomorphism from Σ_1 to Σ' which maps $R_i \cap \Sigma_1$ to $R_i \cap \Sigma'$ for $i = 1$ and 2. By more repeated application of the conclusion of the previous paragraph, we then obtain a special isomorphism from Σ' to Σ_2 which maps $R_i \cap \Sigma'$ to $R_i \cap \Sigma_2$ for $i = 1$ and 2. $\square$

Using retractions and our results about apartments, we can extend the result 3.22 about projection maps in Coxeter chamber systems to buildings. The result we obtain describes a fundamental property of buildings.

Theorem 8.21. *Let* (Δ, δ) *be a building, let R be a residue of Δ and let x be a chamber of Δ. Then there is a unique chamber w in R nearest x,*

$$\text{dist}(x, y) = \text{dist}(x, w) + \text{dist}(w, y),$$

for every $y \in R$, and w is contained in every apartment containing x and some chamber in R.

Proof. Let w be any chamber of R at minimal distance from x. Choose $y \in R$. By 8.6, we can choose an apartment Σ containing x and y. Suppose that $w \notin \Sigma$. Let $\gamma = (x_0, \ldots, x_k)$ be a minimal gallery from x to w. There exists $i \in [1, k]$ such that $x_{i-1} \in \Sigma$ but $x_i \notin \Sigma$. Let P denote the panel containing these two chambers, let b denote the unique chamber in $P \cap \Sigma$ different from x_{i-1} and let $\rho = \text{retr}_{\Sigma, b}$. By 8.18, ρ is a special homomorphism from Δ to Σ. By 1.18, therefore, $\rho(\gamma)$ is a pre-gallery. By 8.17, $\rho(x_i) = x_{i-1}$ since

$$\delta(b, x_{i-1}) = r_j = \delta(b, x_i),$$

where j denotes the type of the panel P. Thus the gallery underlying $\rho(\gamma)$, which we denote by γ_1, is shorter than γ. By 8.17 again, $\rho(x) = x$ and $\rho(y) = y$ since $x, y \in \Sigma$. Therefore γ_1 starts at x and $y \in R \cap \rho(R)$. Thus, by 1.19, $\rho(R) \subset R$. Since γ_1 ends at $\rho(w)$ and $\rho(w) \in \rho(R)$, we conclude that $\rho(w)$ is a chamber of R nearer to x than w is. This contradicts the choice of w. Therefore $w \in \Sigma$. By 8.12, $\Sigma \cap R$ is a residue of Σ. Hence, by 3.22 and 8.9,

$$\text{dist}(x, y) = \text{dist}(x, w) + \text{dist}(w, y).$$

In particular, $\text{dist}(x, w) < \text{dist}(x, y)$ if y is distinct from w, so the chamber w is unique. $\square$

Corollary 8.22. *Let Δ be a building, let x be a chamber and let P be a panel of Δ. Then there is a unique chamber $w \in P$ such that*

$$\text{dist}(x, z) = \text{dist}(x, w) + 1$$

for all $z \in P \backslash \{w\}$.

Proof. This is just a (very important) special case of 8.21. $\square$

Definition 8.23. Let Δ be a building, let $x \in \Delta$ and let R be a residue of Δ. Let proj_R denote the map from Δ to R which sends each chamber x to the unique chamber in R which is nearest x. This map is called the *projection map* from Δ to R. By 8.21, $\text{proj}_R x$ is contained in every apartment containing x and some chamber of R. In other words, if Σ is an apartment containing x and $\Sigma \cap R \neq \emptyset$ (so $\Sigma \cap R$ is a residue of Σ by 8.12), then $\text{proj}_R x = \text{proj}_{\Sigma \cap R} x$.

The following version of 8.21 will play an important role in Chapter 10.

Proposition 8.24. *Let R be a residue of a building (Δ, δ), let x be a chamber of Δ and let y be a chamber of R. Then*

$$\delta(x, y) = \delta(x, \text{proj}_R x) \cdot \delta(\text{proj}_R x, y).$$

Proof. Let $u = \text{proj}_R x$ and choose a minimal gallery γ_1 from x to u and a minimal gallery γ_2 from u to y. Let f_i denote the type of γ_i for $i = 1$ and 2. By 8.21, the concatenation (γ_1, γ_2) is a minimal gallery from x to y. By 7.7 (ii), therefore, the words f_1, f_2 and $f_1 f_2$ are all reduced. Thus

$$\delta(x, y) = r_{f_1 f_2} = r_{f_1} r_{f_2} = \delta(x, u) \cdot \delta(u, y)$$

by 7.1. $\square$

Recall that by 7.25, the intersection of two residues of a building is either a residue or is empty.

Proposition 8.25. *Let S denote the intersection of two residues R and R' of a building Δ and suppose that S is not empty. Then $\text{proj}_R y = \text{proj}_S y$ for every $y \in R'$.*

Proof. Let $y \in R'$. By 8.6, there exists an apartment Σ containing y and some chamber of S. By 8.23, $\text{proj}_R y = \text{proj}_{\Sigma \cap R} y$, and by 3.25, $\text{proj}_{\Sigma \cap R} y \in \Sigma \cap S$. In particular, $\text{proj}_R y \in S$. This implies that $\text{proj}_R y = \text{proj}_S y$. $\square$

Proposition 8.26. *Suppose that R and R' are two residues of a building Δ whose intersection is not empty, let $x \in R$ and let $z \in R'$. Let $y = \text{proj}_R z$, let γ be a minimal gallery from x to y and let γ' be a minimal gallery from y to z. Then $[\gamma] \subset R$, $[\gamma'] \subset R'$ and the concatenation (γ, γ') is a minimal gallery from x to z.*

Proof. By 8.25, $y \in R \cap R'$. By two applications of 7.21, therefore, $[\gamma] \subset R$ and $[\gamma'] \subset R'$. By 8.21, (γ, γ') is a minimal gallery from x to z. $\square$

Proposition 8.27. *Suppose that R and R' are two residues of a building Δ such that $R \cap R' \neq \emptyset$ and let P be a panel containing at least two chambers in $R \cup R'$. Then $P \subset R$ or $P \subset R'$.*

Proof. Let x and z be distinct chambers of P which are contained in $R \cup R'$. Suppose that $x \in R$ and $z \in R'$. Since x and z are both contained in P, we have $\text{dist}(x, z) = 1$. Let y, γ and γ' be as in 8.26. Since (γ, γ') is a minimal gallery from x to z, its length must be one. It follows that $x = y \in R'$ or $z = y \in R$. We conclude that x and z are both in R or both in R'. Thus $|P \cap R| > 1$ or $|P \cap R'| > 1$. By 7.26, therefore, $P \subset R$ or $P \subset R'$. $\qquad\square$

The next definition and the results 8.29–8.31 which follow will be needed in Chapter 10.

Definition 8.28. Let Δ be a building. For all subsets $\{x, y, \ldots, z\}$ of Δ and all $k \geqslant 1$, let $\text{Res}^{(k)}_{\Delta,x,y,\ldots,z}$ denote the set of residues of Δ of rank k which contain all the chambers $x, y, \ldots, z$ and let $\Delta^{(k)}_{x,y,\ldots,z}$ denote the set of all chambers contained in some residue in $\text{Res}^{(k)}_{\Delta,x,y,\ldots,z}$. Thus $\Delta^{(k)}_c$ for $c \in \Delta$ is what is called $E_k(c)$ in [14]. We denote by $\Delta \circ \Delta$ the set of ordered pairs (x, z) such that x and z are opposite chambers of Δ (so $\Delta \circ \Delta = \emptyset$ unless Δ is spherical).

Lemma 8.29. *Let Δ be a thick building, let $(x, z) \in \Delta \circ \Delta$ and let P be a panel of Δ contained in $\Delta^{(2)}_x \cup \Delta^{(2)}_z$. Then P is contained in some residue of $\text{Res}^{(2)}_{\Delta,x}$ or $\text{Res}^{(2)}_{\Delta,z}$.*

Proof. Since Δ is thick, $|P \cap \Delta^{(2)}_u| \geqslant 2$ for $u = x$ or z. By 8.27, it follows that $P \subset R$ for some $R \in \text{Res}^{(2)}_{\Delta,u}$. $\qquad\square$

Proposition 8.30. *Let Δ and $\hat{\Delta}$ be two buildings of the same type Π (so Δ and $\hat{\Delta}$ have the same index set), let $x \in \Delta$, let π be a map from $\Delta^{(2)}_x$ to $\hat{\Delta}$, and let $\hat{x} = x^\pi$. Then the following are equivalent.*

(i) *π is a full isometry from $\Delta^{(2)}_x$ to $\hat{\Delta}$.*

(ii) *The restriction of π to each residue R in $\text{Res}^{(2)}_{\Delta,x}$ is full.*

(iii) *The restriction of π to each residue R in $\text{Res}^{(2)}_{\Delta,x}$ is a special isomorphism from R to the residue in $\text{Res}^{(2)}_{\hat{\Delta},\hat{x}}$ of the same type.*

Proof. By 7.29, (i) implies (ii), and by 7.31, (ii) implies (iii). Suppose that (iii) holds. By 8.2, the restriction of π to each residue $R \in \text{Res}^{(2)}_{\Delta,x}$ is a full isometry from R to the residue in $\text{Res}^{(2)}_{\hat{\Delta},\hat{x}}$ of the same type. Let R and R' be distinct residues in $\text{Res}^{(2)}_{\Delta,x}$ and choose $u \in R$ and $v \in R'$. By 8.26, there exist galleries γ in R from u to a chamber $z \in R \cap R'$ and γ' in R' from z to v such that (γ, γ')

is a minimal gallery from u to v. Let f denote the type of γ and let g denote the type of γ'. Then $(\gamma, \gamma')^\pi$ is a gallery of type fg in $\hat{\Delta}$ from u^π to v^π. By 7.7 (ii), the word fg is reduced. We conclude that $\delta(u, v) = r_{fg} = \hat{\delta}(u^\pi, v^\pi)$. Thus π is an isometry from $\Delta_x^{(2)}$ to $\hat{\Delta}$. By 8.27, every panel contained in $\Delta_x^{(2)}$ is contained in some residue R in $\mathrm{Res}_{\Delta,x}^{(2)}$. Hence π is full. Thus (i) holds. $\qquad\square$

Corollary 8.31. *Let Δ and $\hat{\Delta}$ be as in 8.30, $x \in \Delta$ and let π be a full isometry from $\Delta_x^{(2)}$ to $\hat{\Delta}$. Then π maps $\Delta_x^{(2)}$ bijectively to $\hat{\Delta}_{\hat{x}}^{(2)}$, where $\hat{x} = x^\pi$, and there is a full isometry $\hat{\pi}$ from $\hat{\Delta}_{\hat{x}}^{(2)}$ to Δ whose image is $\Delta_x^{(2)}$ such that $\hat{\pi} \cdot \pi$ is the identity on $\Delta_x^{(2)}$ and $\pi \cdot \hat{\pi}$ is the identity on $\hat{\Delta}_{\hat{x}}^{(2)}$.*

Proof. This holds by 8.30. $\qquad\square$

We close this chapter with an observation which will be needed in the proof of 11.43.

Proposition 8.32. *Let Δ be a building with index set I, let c, x, y be chambers of Δ and let $i \in I$. Then $x \sim_i y$ if and only if there exists a minimal gallery $\gamma = (x_0, \ldots, x_s)$ from c to x whose type we denote by f and a minimal gallery $\gamma' = (y_0, \ldots, y_t)$ from c to y whose type we denote by g such that either*

(i) $s = t - 1, \gamma = (y_1, \ldots, y_s)$ *and g ends in i, or*

(ii) $s = t, (x_1, \ldots, x_{s-1}) = (y_1, \ldots, y_{t-1})$ *but $x_s \ne y_t$ and both f and g end in i, or*

(iii) $t = s - 1, (x_1, \ldots, x_t) = \gamma'$ *and f ends in i.*

Proof. Suppose $x \sim_i y$. If $\mathrm{dist}(c, x) \ne \mathrm{dist}(c, y)$, then (i) or (iii) holds. If $\mathrm{dist}(c, x) = \mathrm{dist}(c, y)$, then (ii) holds by 8.22. The converse holds by 1.4. $\qquad\square$

Chapter Nine

Spherical Buildings

From now on, we focus on spherical buildings. A building, we recall, is *spherical* if its Coxeter diagram is spherical, or equivalently, if its Weyl group is finite. We prove three fundamental results about apartments in spherical buildings in 9.2, 9.3 and 9.7. The rest of this chapter is devoted to proving important properties of the residues in a spherical building.

We first observe that spherical buildings, like spherical Coxeter systems, have finite diameter.

Proposition 9.1. *Let* (Δ, δ) *be a spherical building of type* Π *with index set* I *and with Weyl group* W, *let* $w_I \in W$ *be as in 5.6 and let* $d = \|w_I\|$. *Then* Δ *and all of its apartments have diameter* d *(so two chambers of an apartment* Σ *are opposite in* Σ *if and only if they are opposite in* Δ) *and* $\delta(x, y) = w_I$ *for* $x, y \in \Delta$ *if and only if* x *and* y *are opposite.*

Proof. By 7.2, δ is surjective. By 5.6 and 7.8, therefore, diam $\Delta = d$ and the Weyl distance between two chambers is w_I if and only if they are opposite. By 8.3 and 8.9, therefore, every apartment of Δ also has diameter d. $\qquad\square$

Theorem 9.2. *Let* Δ *be a spherical building of type* Π. *Then each pair of opposite chambers* x, y *is contained in a unique apartment. This apartment consists of all the chambers of* Δ *which lie on some minimal gallery from* x *to* y.

Proof. Let x, y be opposite chambers of Δ. By 8.6, there exists an apartment Σ containing them both. By 8.4, there is a special isomorphism from Σ_Π to Σ. By 5.4 and 8.9, therefore, a chamber is contained in Σ if and only if it is contained in some minimal gallery from x to y. This implies that Σ is the unique apartment containing x and y. $\qquad\square$

The following result will play an important role in Chapter 11.

Theorem 9.3. *Let* Δ *be a spherical building, let* Σ *be an apartment of* Δ, *let* α *be a root of* Σ *and let* P *be a panel of* Δ *such that* $|P \cap \alpha| = 1$. *For each* $v \in P \backslash P \cap \alpha$, *there exists a unique apartment* Σ_v *of* Δ *which contains* α *and*

v, the root α is also a root of Σ_v, there exists a special isomorphism ϕ from Σ to Σ_v which is the identity on α and either $\Sigma \cap \Sigma_v = \alpha$ or $\Sigma = \Sigma_v$.

Proof. Let $d = \operatorname{diam} \Delta$, let x denote the unique chamber in $\alpha \cap P$, let y denote the other chamber in $\Sigma \cap P$, let $z = \operatorname{op}_\Sigma y$ and choose $v \in P \backslash P \cap \alpha$. By 5.2, $z \in \alpha$. By 3.6 and 8.9,

$$\operatorname{dist}(x, z) = \operatorname{dist}(y, z) - 1 = d - 1.$$

By 3.20, therefore, there are $2(d - 1)$ roots of Σ which contain x or z but not both. By 5.3, therefore, α is the only root of Σ which contains them both (and $-\alpha$ is the only root which contains neither). Choose $w \in \alpha$. By 3.21 and 8.9, there exists a minimal gallery γ from z to x containing w. Since y and z are opposite, (γ, y) is a minimal gallery. The sequence (γ, v) is a gallery of the same type. By 7.7 (ii), it is also minimal. Hence z and v are opposite. By 9.2, therefore, there is a unique apartment Σ_v containing z and v, and this apartment contains γ. Since w is arbitrary, we conclude that $\alpha \subset \Sigma_v$. Let ϕ denote the restriction of $\operatorname{retr}_{\Sigma_v, x}$ to Σ. By 8.19, ϕ is a special isomorphism from Σ to Σ_v. In particular, $\phi(\alpha)$ is a root of Σ_v. By 8.17, ϕ is the identity on α. Suppose, finally, that u is an arbitrary chamber of $\Sigma \cap \Sigma_v$. If $u \notin \alpha$, then $\operatorname{op}_\Sigma u \in \alpha \subset \Sigma \cap \Sigma_v$ by 5.2 and hence $\Sigma = \Sigma_v$ by 9.2. $\qquad \square$

The next result will be needed in the proof of 10.15.

Proposition 9.4. *Let Δ be a spherical building with index set I, let Σ be an apartment of Δ, let $x \in \Sigma$ and let*

$$\omega = \operatorname{op}_\Sigma \cdot \operatorname{retr}_{\Sigma, x} .$$

Then ω is an op_I-homomorphism from Δ to Σ such that $\omega(y)$ is opposite y for all $y \in \Delta$.

Proof. By 5.11 and 5.12, op_Σ is an op_I-automorphism of Σ. By 8.18, therefore, ω is an op_I-homomorphism from Δ to Σ. Let $\rho = \operatorname{retr}_{\Sigma, x}$ and choose $y \in \Delta$. Then $\rho(y)$ and $\omega(y)$ are opposite in Σ and hence, by 9.1, they are opposite in Δ. By 8.17, ρ acts trivially on Σ. In particular, $\rho(\omega(y)) = \omega(y)$. Thus

$$\begin{aligned}
\operatorname{diam} \Delta &= \operatorname{dist}(\rho(y), \omega(y)) \\
&= \operatorname{dist}(\rho(y), \rho(\omega(y))) \\
&\leqslant \operatorname{dist}(y, \omega(y))
\end{aligned}$$

by 1.18. Therefore y is opposite $\omega(y)$. $\qquad \square$

The following result will be needed in the proof of 11.22.

Lemma 9.5. *Let Δ be a spherical building, let Σ be an apartment of Δ, let x_1 and x_2 be adjacent chambers of Σ and let $x_i' = \mathrm{op}_\Sigma x_i$ for $i = 1$ and 2. Let Q denote the panel of Δ containing x_1' and x_2' (which exists since op_Σ is an automorphism of Σ by 5.11). Then Σ is the only apartment of Δ which contains x_1, x_2 and some chamber in Q.*

Proof. Let $d = \mathrm{diam}\, \Delta$. Then

$$\mathrm{dist}(x_1, x_2') = \mathrm{dist}(x_1', x_2) = d - 1$$

by 3.6 and 8.9. By 8.22, therefore, x_1 and x_2 are both opposite every chamber in $Q \backslash \{x_1', x_2'\}$. Hence, by 5.5, there is no apartment containing x_1 and x_2 which also contains a chamber of $Q \backslash \{x_1', x_2'\}$. By 9.2, Σ is the only apartment containing x_1 and x_2 which is not disjoint from $\{x_1', x_2'\}$. $\qquad\square$

The next result will be needed in the proof of 9.7.

Lemma 9.6. *Let Δ be a spherical building and let $G = \mathrm{Aut}(\Delta)$. For each $x \in \Delta$, let $G_x^{(1)}$ denote the pointwise stabilizer in G of the set of chambers equal to or adjacent to x. (This is consistent with the notation in 7.11.) Then*

$$G_u^{(1)} \cap G_v \subset G_v^{(1)}$$

for all ordered pairs (u, v) of opposite chambers of Δ.

Proof. Let u, v be opposite chambers, let $g \in G_u^{(1)} \cap G_v$ and let P be an arbitrary panel containing v. By 1.15, $G_u^{(1)}$ is contained in $\mathrm{Aut}^\circ(\Delta)$. Since the element g fixes v, it therefore maps the panel P to itself. By 9.2, there is a unique apartment Σ containing both u and v. Let z denote the chamber in $P \cap \Sigma$ other than v and let $w = \mathrm{op}_\Sigma z$. By 5.11, w is adjacent to u and by 5.5, w is not opposite v. Let Q denote the panel containing w and u. By 8.22, v is the unique chamber of P not opposite w and w is the unique chamber of Q not opposite v. Choose $x \in P \backslash \{v\}$. Then x and w are opposite. By 8.22 again, there is a unique $y \in Q \backslash \{w\}$ not opposite x. Since $y \neq w$, the chamber y is opposite v. By a final application of 8.22, x is thus the unique chamber of P not opposite y. Since g is contained in $G_u^{(1)}$, it fixes y. Since g maps P to itself, it therefore fixes x. Since x is arbitrary, it follows that g acts trivially on P. Since P is arbitrary, we conclude that $g \in G_v^{(1)}$. $\qquad\square$

The following result describes a fundamental rigidity property of spherical buildings. It is a restatement of Theorem 4.1.1 of [14].

Theorem 9.7. *Let Δ be a thick spherical building, let $G = \mathrm{Aut}(\Delta)$ and let $G_x^{(1)}$ be as in 9.6 for each chamber x. Then*

$$G_u^{(1)} \cap G_v = 1$$

for all ordered pairs of opposite chambers (u, v). Equivalently,

$$G_x^{(1)} \cap G_\Sigma = 1$$

for each apartment Σ and each $x \in \Sigma$.

Proof. By 5.5 and 9.1, for each chamber x of an apartment Σ there is a chamber in Σ opposite x. Thus, the first assertion implies the second. By 9.2, the second assertion implies the first.

Let (u, v) be an ordered pair of opposite chambers and let x be an arbitrary chamber adjacent to v. To prove the first assertion, it will suffice, since Δ is connected, to show that

$$G_u^{(1)} \cap G_v \subset G_w^{(1)} \cap G_x$$

for some w opposite x. By 9.6, this holds with $w = u$ if x is opposite u. We can assume, therefore, that x is not opposite u. There is thus a minimal gallery from u to v which contains x. By 9.2, there is a unique apartment Σ containing u, x and v. Let $y = \mathrm{op}_\Sigma\, x$. By 5.11, y is adjacent to u, and by 5.5, y is not opposite v. Let P denote the panel containing u and y. By 8.22, v is opposite every chamber in $P\backslash\{y\}$ and x is opposite every chamber in $P\backslash\{u\}$. Since Δ is thick, we can choose a chamber w in P distinct from u and y and hence opposite both x and v. By two applications of 9.6, we have

$$G_u^{(1)} \cap G_v \subset G_v^{(1)} \cap G_w \subset G_w^{(1)} \cap G_x.$$

$\square$

Our next goal is to extend the results of Chapter 5 about opposite residues in a finite Coxeter chamber system to spherical buildings.

Definition 9.8. Let R and R' be residues of a spherical building Δ. Then R and R' are *opposite* if there is an apartment Σ such that $\Sigma \cap R$ and $\Sigma \cap R'$ are opposite residues of Σ as defined in 5.13. By 8.20, R and R' are opposite if and only if $\Sigma \cap R$ and $\Sigma \cap R'$ are opposite residues in *every* apartment Σ such that $\Sigma \cap R$ and $\Sigma \cap R'$ are non-empty.

Proposition 9.9. *Let R and R' be opposite residues of a spherical building Δ. Then for every $x \in R$, there exist chambers in R' opposite x in Δ.*

Proof. Choose $x \in R$ and $y \in R'$. By 8.6, we can choose an apartment Σ containing both x and y. By 9.8, $R \cap \Sigma$ and $R' \cap \Sigma$ are opposite residues of Σ. By 5.13, $\mathrm{op}_{\Sigma} x$ is a chamber of $R' \cap \Sigma$ which is opposite x. □

It is useful to think of opposite residues as follows.

Proposition 9.10. *Let Δ be a spherical building with index set I, let R be a J-residue of Δ for some $J \subset I$, let y be any chamber of Δ opposite some chamber in R, and let R' denote the $\mathrm{op}_I(J)$-residue of Δ containing y. Then R' is the unique residue opposite R which contains the chamber y.*

Proof. Choose $x \in R$ opposite y. By 8.6, there is an apartment Σ containing x and y. By 8.12, $\Sigma \cap R$ is a J-residue and $\Sigma \cap R'$ is an op_I J-residue of Σ. By 5.13, therefore, $\Sigma \cap R'$ is the unique residue of Σ which is opposite $\Sigma \cap R$. Thus R and R' are opposite residues and if R'' is an arbitrary residue opposite R which contains y, then $\Sigma \cap R'' = \Sigma \cap R'$, thus R'' is also of type $\mathrm{op}_I J$ and therefore $R'' = R'$. □

The following result will play a crucial role in the next chapter.

Proposition 9.11. *Let R and R' be opposite residues of a spherical building Δ with index set I, let J denote the type of R and $J' = \mathrm{op}_I(J)$ (so J' is the type of R'), let σ denote the map $\mathrm{op}_J \cdot \mathrm{op}_I |_{J'}$ from J' to J, and let σ' denote the map $\mathrm{op}_{J'} \cdot \mathrm{op}_I |_J$ from J to J'. Then the following hold.*

(i) *The restriction of proj_R to R' is a σ-isomorphism from R' to R, the restriction of $\mathrm{proj}_{R'}$ to R is a σ'-isomorphism from R to R' and these two maps are inverses of each other.*

(ii) *If z is a chamber of R which is opposite a chamber x of R' in Δ, then z is opposite $\mathrm{proj}_R x$ in R.*

(iii) *$\delta(x, \mathrm{proj}_R x) = w_I w_J$ for every $x \in R'$, where w_I and w_J are as in 5.6.*

Proof. Let $x \in R'$. By 9.9, we can choose $z \in R$ opposite x in Δ. By 8.6, we can choose an apartment Σ containing x and z. By 8.23, $\mathrm{proj}_R x = \mathrm{proj}_{\Sigma \cap R} x \in \Sigma \cap R$ and $\mathrm{proj}_{R'} p = \mathrm{proj}_{\Sigma \cap R'} p$ for all $p \in \Sigma \cap R$. By 9.8, $\Sigma \cap R$ and $\Sigma \cap R'$ are opposite residues of Σ. By 5.14 (i), therefore,

$$\mathrm{proj}_{R'}(\mathrm{proj}_R x) = \mathrm{proj}_{\Sigma \cap R'}(\mathrm{proj}_{\Sigma \cap R} x) = x.$$

We conclude that the composition $\mathrm{proj}_{R'} \cdot \mathrm{proj}_R$ restricted to R' is the identity. By symmetry, the composition $\mathrm{proj}_R \cdot \mathrm{proj}_{R'}$ restricted to R is the identity.

Suppose now that u is a chamber of R' which is i-adjacent to x for some $i \in J'$. Let $y = \text{proj}_R x$ and $v = \text{proj}_R u$. By 8.6, there is an apartment Σ_1 containing u and y. By the conclusion of the previous paragraph, $\text{proj}_{R'} y = x$. By 8.23, therefore, both v and x lie in Σ_1, $v = \text{proj}_{\Sigma_1 \cap R} u$ and $y = \text{proj}_{\Sigma_1 \cap R} x$. By 5.14 (i), it follows that v and y are $\sigma(i)$-adjacent. Thus proj_R restricted to R' maps i-adjacent chambers to $\sigma(i)$-adjacent chambers of R for all $i \in J'$. By symmetry, $\text{proj}_{R'}$ restricted to R maps i-adjacent chambers to $\sigma'(i)$-adjacent chambers for all $i \in J$. Thus (i) holds.

By 9.1, $z = \text{op}_\Sigma x$, where z and Σ are as above. By 5.14 (ii), therefore, the chambers $\text{proj}_R x = \text{proj}_{\Sigma \cap R} x$ and z are opposite in $\Sigma \cap R$. By 8.13 (i), $\Sigma \cap R$ is an apartment of R. By 9.1, therefore, $\text{proj}_R x$ and z are opposite in R itself. Thus (ii) holds.

Choose an isometry π from Σ_Π to Δ whose image is Σ (equivalently, a special isomorphism from Σ_Π to Σ), where Π denotes the Coxeter diagram of Δ, let a denote the preimage of x and let S denote the preimage of $R \cap \Sigma$ with respect to π. Then S is a residue of Σ_Π and π maps $\text{proj}_S a$ to $\text{proj}_{R \cap \Sigma} x$. Hence, by 5.14 (iii) and 8.3,

$$
\begin{aligned}
\delta(x, \text{proj}_R x) &= \delta(x, \text{proj}_{R \cap \Sigma} x) \\
&= \delta(a^\pi, (\text{proj}_S a)^\pi) \\
&= a^{-1} \text{proj}_S a \\
&= w_I w_J.
\end{aligned}
$$

Thus (iii) holds.   □

Proposition 9.12. *Let R and R' be opposite residues of a spherical building. Then either $R \cap R' = \emptyset$ or $R = R' = \Delta$.*

Proof. Suppose there exists $y \in R \cap R'$. Then $\text{proj}_R y = y$. By 9.11 (iii), therefore, $w_I^{-1} w_J = w_I w_J = \delta(y, \text{proj}_R y) = \delta(y, y) = 1$, where J denotes the type of R. By 5.8, therefore, $J = I$.   □

We conclude this chapter with the following result which (with $|J| = |K| = 2$) will be needed in the proof of 10.9.

Lemma 9.13. *Let x and z be opposite chambers of a spherical building (Δ, δ) with index set I and let J and K be subsets of I such that either $J \cap \text{op}_I K = \emptyset$ or $J \cap \text{op}_I K = \{i\}$ for some $i \in I$. Let R be the J-residue containing x, let S be the K-residue containing z and let w_J be as in 5.6. If $J \cap \text{op}_I K = \emptyset$, then* for each chamber $y \in S$,

(i) $\text{proj}_R y = \text{proj}_R z$, and

(ii) $\delta(y, \text{proj}_R y) = \delta(y, x)w_J$.

If $J \cap \text{op}_I K = \{i\}$, then for each chamber $y \in S$,

(iii) $\text{proj}_R y = \text{proj}_P y$, where P denotes the panel of type $\text{op}_J i$ containing $\text{proj}_R z$,

(iv)

$$\delta(y, \text{proj}_R y) = \begin{cases} \delta(y, x)r_i w_J & \text{if } \|\delta(y, x)r_i\| > \|\delta(y, x)\|, \\ \delta(y, x)w_J & \text{otherwise;} \end{cases}$$

and

(v) $\text{proj}_Q y = \text{proj}_Q(\text{proj}_R y)$, where Q denotes the i-panel containing the chamber x.

Proof. Let $u = \text{proj}_R z$, let $K' = \text{op}_I K$ and let $j = \text{op}_J i$ if $J \cap K' = \{i\}$. Choose $y \in S$. By 9.10, z is contained in a residue opposite R. By 9.11 (iii), therefore, $\delta(z, u) = w_I w_J$. There exists a K-gallery from z to y. Hence, by 7.28, $\delta(y, u) = a\delta(z, u)$ for some $a \in W_K$ (where W_K is as in 4.6). Let $b = w_I^{-1}aw_I$. Then

$$\delta(y, u) = aw_I w_J = w_I b w_J$$

and, by 5.12, $b \in W_{K'}$. By 8.24, $\delta(y, u) = \delta(y, v)c$, where $v = \text{proj}_R y$ and $c = \delta(v, u)$. Thus $\delta(y, v) = w_I b w_J c^{-1}$. By 7.20, $c \in W_J$. By 7.8 and 8.23, either $u = v$ or $\|\delta(y, v)\| < \|\delta(y, u)\|$. Suppose that $u \neq v$ (i.e. $c \neq 1$). Then $\|w_I b w_J c^{-1}\| < \|w_I b w_J\|$. By 5.7, therefore, $\|b w_J c^{-1}\| > \|b w_J\|$. Hence, by 5.15 and 5.16, $J \cap K' = \{i\}$ and $c = r_j$ (for $j = \text{op}_J i$). Thus u and v are j-adjacent by 7.1. We conclude that either $u = v$ or $J \cap K' = \{i\}$ and u and v are $\text{op}_J i$-adjacent. Thus (i) and (iii) hold.

By 9.11 (ii), u and x are opposite in R. By 9.1, therefore, $\delta(u, x) = w_J = w_J^{-1}$. If $J \cap K' = \emptyset$, then by (i), $u = v$, so by 8.24,

$$\delta(y, x) = \delta(y, v) \cdot \delta(u, x) = \delta(y, v)w_J^{-1}.$$

Thus (ii) holds. Suppose (from now on) that $J \cap K' = \{i\}$. Let Q be the i-panel containing x. By 8.22, we can choose a minimal gallery γ from y to x which passes through $\text{proj}_Q y$, and the gallery (γ, q) is minimal for all $q \in Q$ different from $\text{proj}_Q y$. Let f denote the type of γ (so f is reduced by 7.7 (ii)). Thus f ends in i if $\text{proj}_Q y \neq x$, and if $\text{proj}_Q y = x$, the gallery (γ, q) is minimal

for all chambers $q \in Q \setminus \{x\}$. Hence, by 7.7 (ii), $\mathrm{proj}_Q \, y = x$ if and only if fi
is also reduced. By 4.5, fi is reduced if and only if $\|r_{fi}\| > \|r_f\|$. By 7.1,
$\delta(y, x) = r_f$. Thus

$$\mathrm{proj}_Q \, y = x \text{ if and only if } \|\delta(y, x)r_i\| > \|\delta(y, x)\|.$$

Let γ_1 be a minimal gallery from y to $v = \mathrm{proj}_R \, y$. By 8.21, for every minimal
gallery γ_2 from v to a chamber in R, the gallery (γ_1, γ_2) is also minimal. In
particular, the chamber of Q which is nearest v is also the chamber of Q
nearest y. Thus (v) holds. As observed above, u and x are opposite chambers
of R. By 9.10, it follows that P and Q are opposite residues of R, where P is
as in (iii). Hence, by 9.11 (i), $\mathrm{proj}_Q \, v = x$ if and only if $\mathrm{proj}_P \, x = v$. By (v)
and the conclusion of the previous paragraph, therefore,

$$\mathrm{proj}_P \, x = v \text{ if and only if } \|\delta(y, x)r_i\| > \|\delta(y, x)\|.$$

The chambers x and u are opposite in R and, by (iii), u and v both lie in P
(i.e. u and v are j-equivalent, where $j = \mathrm{op}_J \, i$ is the type of P). By 8.22, v lies
on a minimal gallery from x to u if $v = \mathrm{proj}_P \, x$ and x and v are also opposite in R
if $v \neq \mathrm{proj}_P \, x$. By 7.27, therefore, $\delta(x, v) = \delta(x, u)r_j = w_J r_j$ if $\mathrm{proj}_P \, x = v$
and $\delta(x, v) = \delta(x, u) = w_J$ if $\mathrm{proj}_P \, x \neq v$. By 5.12, $w_J r_j = r_i w_J$. Hence

$$\delta(v, x)^{-1} = \delta(x, v) = \begin{cases} r_i w_J & \text{if } \mathrm{proj}_P \, x = v, \\ w_J & \text{otherwise.} \end{cases}$$

By 8.24, $\delta(y, v) = \delta(y, x) \cdot \delta(v, x)^{-1}$. By the conclusion of the previous
paragraph, it follows that (iv) holds. $\qquad\qquad\qquad\qquad\qquad\qquad\qquad\square$

Chapter Ten

Extensions of Isometries

We come now to the central results of this book. Our goal is to prove the following two fundamental theorems, which are the translations of Proposition 4.16 and Theorem 4.1.2 of [14] into the language of chamber systems and isometries.

Theorem 10.1. *Let Δ and $\hat{\Delta}$ be thick irreducible spherical buildings of rank at least three having the same type, let $(x, z) \in \Delta \circ \Delta$, and let π be a full isometry from $\Delta_x^{(2)} \cup \{z\}$ to $\hat{\Delta}$ (where $\Delta \circ \Delta$ and $\Delta_x^{(2)}$ are as defined in 8.28). Then π has a unique extension to a special isomorphism from Δ to $\hat{\Delta}$.*

Theorem 10.2. *Let Δ and $\hat{\Delta}$ be thick irreducible spherical buildings of rank at least three having the same type and let $x \in \Delta$. Then every full isometry from $\Delta_x^{(2)}$ to $\hat{\Delta}$ can be extended to a special isomorphism from Δ to $\hat{\Delta}$.*

(Recall that in 8.30 we gave equivalent ways of saying that a map is a full isometry from $\Delta_x^{(2)}$ to $\hat{\Delta}$.)

The proof of 10.1 that we give, a modification of Tits's original proof, is due to Mark Ronan [8]. It will be given in a series of steps which will occupy us for the rest of this chapter. The result 10.2 will follow from 10.1 and 10.6.

We fix an irreducible spherical Coxeter diagram Π of rank at least three and two thick buildings (Δ, δ) and $(\hat{\Delta}, \hat{\delta})$ both of type Π for the remainder of this chapter. Let I denote the vertex set of Π (i.e. the index set of both Δ and $\hat{\Delta}$) and let (W, r) denote the Coxeter system corresponding to Π.

Lemma 10.3. *Let $z \in \Delta$ and $\hat{z} \in \hat{\Delta}$, let R be a residue of Δ, let π be a full isometry from R to $\hat{\Delta}$, and let $\hat{R} = R^\pi$ (so by 7.31, $\hat{R}$ is a residue of $\hat{\Delta}$ of the same type as R). Then the extension of π to $R \cup \{z\}$ which sends z to $\hat{z}$ is an isometry if and only if*

(i) $\delta(z, \operatorname{proj}_R z) = \hat{\delta}(\hat{z}, \operatorname{proj}_{\hat{R}} \hat{z})$, *and*

(ii) π *maps* $\operatorname{proj}_R z$ *to* $\operatorname{proj}_{\hat{R}} \hat{z}$.

Proof. We denote the extension of π to $R \cup \{z\}$ which sends z to $\hat{z}$ by θ. It follows from 8.24 that if (i) and (ii) hold, then θ is an isometry. Now assume that θ is an isometry. Under this assumption, (ii) implies (i). By 7.8 and 8.23, (ii) holds. $\qquad\square$

Lemma 10.4. *Let R be a residue of Δ, let π be a full isometry from R to $\hat{\Delta}$, let $\hat{R} = R^\pi$ and let $z \in \Delta$ and $\hat{z} \in \hat{\Delta}$ be chambers such that z is opposite some chamber of R and $\hat{z}$ is opposite some chamber of $\hat{R}$. Suppose, too, that π maps $\mathrm{proj}_R z$ to $\mathrm{proj}_{\hat{R}} \hat{z}$. Then the extension of π to $R \cup \{z\}$ which sends z to $\hat{z}$ is an isometry.*

Proof. By 9.10, z lies in a residue opposite R. By 9.11 (iii), therefore, $\delta(z, \mathrm{proj}_R z) = w_I w_J$ and $\hat{\delta}(\hat{z}, \mathrm{proj}_{\hat{R}} \hat{z}) = w_I w_J$, where J denotes the type of R (which is also the type of $\hat{R}$) and w_J and w_I are as in 5.6. Hence $\delta(z, \mathrm{proj}_R z) = \hat{\delta}(\hat{z}, \mathrm{proj}_{\hat{R}} \hat{z})$. The claim holds, therefore, by 10.3. $\qquad\square$

Proposition 10.5. *Let $(x, z) \in \Delta \circ \Delta$. Then every full isometry from $\Delta_x^{(2)} \cup \{z\}$ to $\hat{\Delta}$ is uniquely determined by its action on $\Delta_x^{(1)} \cup \{z\}$.*

Proof. By 8.31, it will suffice to show that a full isometry from $\Delta_x^{(2)} \cup \{z\}$ to Δ which fixes z and acts trivially on $\Delta_x^{(1)}$ must, in fact, act trivially on $\Delta_x^{(2)}$. Let π be such an isometry and choose $R \in \mathrm{Res}_{\Delta,x}^{(2)}$. By 10.3 (ii), π maps $\mathrm{proj}_R z$ to itself. By 9.10, z lies in a residue opposite R. By 9.11 (ii), therefore, $\mathrm{proj}_R z$ is opposite x in R. Hence, by 9.7, π acts trivially on R since it acts trivially on $\Delta_x^{(1)}$. Since R is arbitrary, we conclude that π acts trivially on $\Delta_x^{(2)}$. $\qquad\square$

Proposition 10.6. *Let π be a full isometry from $\Delta_x^{(2)}$ to $\hat{\Delta}$. Then for each $z \in \Delta$ opposite x, π can be extended to a full isometry from $\Delta_x^{(2)} \cup \{z\}$ to $\hat{\Delta}$.*

Proof. Let $\hat{x} = x^\pi$ and choose $z \in \Delta$ opposite x. By 9.2, there is a unique apartment Σ of Δ containing x and z. By 8.15, Σ is the image of an isometry ξ from Σ_Π to Δ mapping 1 to x. Let X denote the preimage under ξ of $\Delta_x^{(2)} \cap \Sigma$. Then $\pi \cdot \xi$ is an isometry from X to $\hat{\Delta}$. By 8.5, we can choose an apartment $\hat{\Sigma}$ of $\hat{\Delta}$ containing the image of $\pi \cdot \xi$. Thus $\hat{\Sigma}$ contains $(\Sigma \cap R)^\pi$ for all $R \in \mathrm{Res}_{\Delta,x}^{(2)}$. Let $\hat{z} = \mathrm{op}_{\hat{\Sigma}} \hat{x}$ and let θ denote the extension of π to $\Delta_x^{(2)} \cup \{z\}$ which sends z to $\hat{z}$.

Choose $R \in \mathrm{Res}_{\Delta,x}^{(2)}$ and let $\hat{R} = R^\pi$. By 8.30, $\hat{R} \in \mathrm{Res}_{\hat{\Delta},\hat{x}}^{(2)}$ and $\pi|_R$ is a special isomorphism from R to $\hat{R}$, and by 8.13 (i), $\Sigma \cap R$ is an apartment of R. By 8.10, therefore, $(\Sigma \cap R)^\pi$ is an apartment of $\hat{R}$. Thus, by 8.14, $\hat{\Sigma} \cap \hat{R} = (\Sigma \cap R)^\pi$. Therefore π maps $\mathrm{op}_{\Sigma \cap R} x$ to $\mathrm{op}_{\hat{\Sigma} \cap \hat{R}} \hat{x}$. By 8.23,

$$\mathrm{proj}_R z = \mathrm{proj}_{\Sigma \cap R} z \quad \text{and} \quad \mathrm{proj}_{\hat{R}} \hat{z} = \mathrm{proj}_{\hat{\Sigma} \cap \hat{R}} \hat{z}.$$

By 5.14 (ii), therefore,

$$\mathrm{proj}_R z = \mathrm{op}_{\Sigma \cap R} x \quad \text{and} \quad \mathrm{proj}_{\hat{R}} \hat{z} = \mathrm{op}_{\hat{\Sigma} \cap \hat{R}} \hat{x}$$

(since $x = \mathrm{op}_{\Sigma} z$ and $\hat{x} = \mathrm{op}_{\hat{\Sigma}} \hat{z}$). We conclude that π maps $\mathrm{proj}_R z$ to $\mathrm{proj}_{\hat{R}} \hat{z}$. By 10.4, the restriction of the map θ defined above to $R \cup \{z\}$ is an isometry from $R \cup \{z\}$ to $\hat{\Delta}$. Since R is arbitrary, it follows that θ is an isometry from $\Delta_x^{(2)} \cup \{z\}$ to $\hat{\Delta}$. By thickness and 8.27, every panel contained in $\Delta_x^{(2)} \cup \{z\}$ is contained in some residue in $\mathrm{Res}_{\Delta,x}^{(2)}$. Therefore θ is full. $\square$

We observe that 10.2 will follow from 10.6 once we have proved 10.1. We now focus on 10.1.

Lemma 10.7. *Let R and S be opposite residues of Δ, let π be a full isometry from R to $\hat{\Delta}$ (so R^{π} is a residue of $\hat{\Delta}$ of the same type as R by 7.31) and let $\hat{S}$ be a residue opposite R^{π}. Then π has a unique extension to a full isometry from $R \cup S$ to $\hat{\Delta}$ mapping S to $\hat{S}$. This extension coincides with the composition $\mathrm{proj}_{\hat{S}} \cdot \pi \cdot \mathrm{proj}_R$ on S.*

Proof. Let $\hat{R} = R^{\pi}$ and suppose that θ is a full isometry from $R \cup S$ to $\hat{\Delta}$ mapping S to $\hat{S}$ which extends π. Choose $y \in S$. By 10.3 (ii), $(\mathrm{proj}_R y)^{\pi} = \mathrm{proj}_{\hat{R}}(y^{\theta})$. Hence, by 9.11 (i),

$$y^{\theta} = \mathrm{proj}_{\hat{S}}(\mathrm{proj}_{\hat{R}}(y^{\theta}))$$
$$= \mathrm{proj}_{\hat{S}}((\mathrm{proj}_R y)^{\pi}).$$

In particular, θ is uniquely determined by π. It only remains to show that a full isometry from $R \cup S$ to $\hat{\Delta}$ extending π and mapping S to $\hat{S}$ exists.

Let ξ denote the composition $\mathrm{proj}_{\hat{S}} \cdot \pi \cdot \mathrm{proj}_R$ restricted to S. By 8.2, $\pi|_R$ is a special isomorphism from R to $\hat{R}$. Thus, by 9.11 (i), ξ is a special isomorphism from S to $\hat{S}$. Hence, by 8.2 again, ξ is a full isometry from S to $\hat{S}$. Choose $y \in S$. By 9.9, y is opposite some chamber in R and $y^{\xi} \in \hat{S}$ is opposite some chamber in $\hat{R}$. By 9.11 (i) again,

$$\mathrm{proj}_{\hat{R}}(y^{\xi}) = (\mathrm{proj}_R y)^{\pi}.$$

By 10.4, therefore, $\delta(u, y) = \hat{\delta}(u^{\pi}, y^{\xi})$ for all $u \in R$. In particular, $y^{\xi} = y^{\pi}$ if $y \in R \cap S$. It follows that there exists an isometry from $R \cup S$ to $\hat{\Delta}$ whose restriction to R is π and to S is ξ. By 8.29, this isometry is full. $\square$

Notice that by 9.12, $R \cap S$ (at the end of the previous proof) is, in fact, empty (unless $R = S$).

Lemma 10.8. *Let P and Q be opposite panels of Δ and let Σ be an apartment such that $P \cap \Sigma$ and $Q \cap \Sigma$ are both non-empty. Let π be a full isometry from $P \cup Q$ to $\hat{\Delta}$. Then there is a unique apartment $\hat{\Sigma}$ of $\hat{\Delta}$ which contains both $(P \cap \Sigma)^{\pi}$ and $(Q \cap \Sigma)^{\pi}$.*

Proof. Let x and y denote the two chambers in $P \cap \Sigma$, let $z = \mathrm{op}_\Sigma \, x$ and let $u = \mathrm{op}_\Sigma \, y$. By 9.1, z^π and x^π are opposite in $\hat{\Delta}$ as are u^π and y^π. By 9.2, there is a unique apartment $\hat{\Sigma}$ of $\hat{\Delta}$ containing x^π and z^π. By 5.13 and 9.8, $Q \cap \Sigma = \{z, u\}$. Let $\hat{P} = P^\pi$ and $\hat{Q} = Q^\pi$. By 7.31 and 9.10, $\hat{P}$ and $\hat{Q}$ are opposite panels of $\hat{\Delta}$. By 10.7, therefore,

$$y^\pi = \mathrm{proj}_{\hat{P}}((\mathrm{proj}_Q \, y)^\pi)$$

and

$$u^\pi = \mathrm{proj}_{\hat{Q}}((\mathrm{proj}_P \, u)^\pi).$$

By 5.5 and 9.1, y is not opposite z and x is not opposite u in Δ. By 8.22, it follows that $\mathrm{proj}_Q \, y = z$ and $\mathrm{proj}_P \, u = x$. Thus $y^\pi = \mathrm{proj}_{\hat{P}}(z^\pi)$ and $u^\pi = \mathrm{proj}_{\hat{Q}}(x^\pi)$. We have $x^\pi \in \hat{P} \cap \hat{\Sigma}$ and $z^\pi \in \hat{Q} \cap \hat{\Sigma}$. In particular, $\hat{P} \cap \hat{\Sigma} \neq \emptyset$ and $\hat{Q} \cap \hat{\Sigma} \neq \emptyset$. Hence, by 8.23, y^π and u^π both lie in $\hat{\Sigma}$.   □

The next result is a particularly important step in the proof of 10.1.

Lemma 10.9. *Let π be a full isometry from $\Delta_x^{(2)} \cup \{z\}$ to $\hat{\Delta}$ for some $(x, z) \in \Delta \circ \Delta$. Then there is a unique extension of π to a full isometry from $\Delta_x^{(2)} \cup \Delta_z^{(2)}$ to $\hat{\Delta}$.*

Proof. Let $\hat{z} = z^\pi$. By 9.10, to each residue R in $\mathrm{Res}_{\Delta,x}^{(2)}$ there is a unique residue S in $\mathrm{Res}_{\Delta,z}^{(2)}$ which is opposite R (namely, the residue of type $\mathrm{op}_I \, J$, where J denotes the type of R) and a unique residue $\hat{S}$ in $\mathrm{Res}_{\hat{\Delta},\hat{z}}^{(2)}$ which is opposite R^π (i.e. the residue of type $\mathrm{op}_I \, J$), and by 10.7, there is a unique extension π_R of $\pi|_R$ to a full isometry from $R \cup S$ to $\hat{\Delta}$ mapping S to $\hat{S}$. This implies (by 8.30) that a full isometry from $\Delta_x^{(2)} \cup \Delta_z^{(2)}$ to $\hat{\Delta}$ which extends π is, if it exists, unique.

Let R_1 and R_2 be two residues in $\mathrm{Res}_{\Delta,x}^{(2)}$ whose types intersect in a single element $i \in I$, and let S_1, S_2 denote their opposites in $\mathrm{Res}_{\Delta,z}^{(2)}$ (whose types intersect in $\{j\}$, where $j = \mathrm{op}_I \, i$). By 7.25, $R_1 \cap R_2$ and $S_1 \cap S_2$ are panels, and by 9.10, these two panels are opposite. The restrictions of π_{R_1} and of π_{R_2} to the union of $R_1 \cap R_2$ and $S_1 \cap S_2$ are full isometries which agree on $R_1 \cap R_2$. By 10.7 again, π_{R_1} and π_{R_2} also agree on $S_1 \cap S_2$. There is thus a unique map ξ from $\Delta_z^{(2)}$ to $\hat{\Delta}$ such that for every $R \in \mathrm{Res}_{\Delta,x}^{(2)}$, ξ coincides with π_R on the residue in $\mathrm{Res}_{\Delta,z}^{(2)}$ opposite R. By 8.30, ξ is a full isometry from $\Delta_z^{(2)}$ to $\hat{\Delta}$.

Suppose now that u is a chamber of some residue R in $\mathrm{Res}_{\Delta,x}^{(2)}$ and that y is a chamber of an arbitrary residue S in $\mathrm{Res}_{\Delta,z}^{(2)}$ (i.e. S is not necessarily opposite R).

Let $\hat{u} = u^\pi$ and $\hat{y} = y^\xi$. We claim that

$$\delta(u, y) = \hat{\delta}(\hat{u}, \hat{y}).$$

Let J denote the type of R, let K denote the type of S, and let R_0 denote the residue in $\text{Res}_{\Delta,x}^{(2)}$ which is opposite S, or equivalently, the residue in $\text{Res}_{\Delta,x}^{(2)}$ of type $\text{op}_I K$. We know that π_{R_0} is an isometry from $R_0 \cup S$ to $\hat{\Delta}$. Thus if $R = R_0$ (i.e. if $J = \text{op}_I K$), then $\hat{\delta}(\hat{u}, \hat{y}) = \hat{\delta}(u^{\pi R_0}, y^{\pi R_0}) = \delta(u, y)$. Since $x \in R_0$, this implies that $\delta(x, y) = \hat{\delta}(\hat{x}, \hat{y})$ (even if $R \neq R_0$). Note, too, that by 10.3 (ii), π maps $\text{proj}_R z$ to $\text{proj}_{\hat{R}} \hat{z}$, where $\hat{R} = R^\pi$.

To finish proving our claim, we can assume that $|J \cap \text{op}_I K| < 2$. Suppose first that $J \cap \text{op}_I K = \emptyset$. By 9.13 (i), $\text{proj}_R y = \text{proj}_R z$ and $\text{proj}_{\hat{R}} \hat{y} = \text{proj}_{\hat{R}} \hat{z}$. Since π maps $\text{proj}_R z$ to $\text{proj}_{\hat{R}} \hat{z}$ (as we observed in the previous paragraph), it therefore also maps $\text{proj}_R y$ to $\text{proj}_{\hat{R}} \hat{y}$. We also observed in the previous paragraph that $\delta(x, y) = \hat{\delta}(\hat{x}, \hat{y})$. By 9.13 (ii), therefore, $\delta(y, \text{proj}_R y) = \hat{\delta}(\hat{y}, \text{proj}_{\hat{R}} \hat{y})$. Hence, by 10.3, $\delta(u, y) = \hat{\delta}(\hat{u}, \hat{y})$.

It remains to assume that $J \cap \text{op}_I K$ contains a single element i. Let $j = \text{op}_I i$, let P denote the $\text{op}_J i$-panel containing $\text{proj}_R z$, let $\hat{P}$ denote the $\text{op}_J i$-panel containing $\text{proj}_{\hat{R}} \hat{z}$, let Q denote the i-panel containing x, and let $\hat{Q}$ denote the i-panel containing $\hat{x}$. By 9.11 (ii), x and $\text{proj}_R z$ are opposite in R. By 9.10, therefore, P and Q are opposite panels of R. Similarly, $\hat{P}$ and $\hat{Q}$ are opposite panels of $\hat{R}$. Recall that R_0 is the $\text{op}_I K$-residue containing x, so also $Q \subset R_0$. By 10.3 (ii) applied to the restriction of π_{R_0} to $Q \cup \{y\}$, therefore, π maps $\text{proj}_Q y$ to $\text{proj}_{\hat{Q}} \hat{y}$. Hence, by 10.3 (ii) with R in place of Δ, P in place of R and $\text{proj}_Q y$ in place of y, the isometry π maps $\text{proj}_P(\text{proj}_Q y)$ to $\text{proj}_{\hat{P}}(\text{proj}_{\hat{Q}} \hat{y})$. By 9.13 (iii), $\text{proj}_R y \in P$ and $\text{proj}_{\hat{R}} \hat{y} \in \hat{P}$. By 9.13 (v),

$$\text{proj}_Q y = \text{proj}_Q(\text{proj}_R y) \quad \text{and} \quad \text{proj}_{\hat{Q}} \hat{y} = \text{proj}_{\hat{Q}}(\text{proj}_{\hat{R}} \hat{y}).$$

By 9.11 (i), therefore,

$$\text{proj}_P(\text{proj}_Q y) = \text{proj}_R y \quad \text{and} \quad \text{proj}_{\hat{P}}(\text{proj}_{\hat{Q}} \hat{y}) = \text{proj}_{\hat{R}} \hat{y}.$$

Thus π maps $\text{proj}_R y$ to $\text{proj}_{\hat{R}} \hat{y}$. As observed above, $\delta(y, x) = \hat{\delta}(\hat{y}, \hat{x})$. By 9.13 (iv), therefore,

$$\delta(y, \text{proj}_R y) = \hat{\delta}(\hat{y}, \text{proj}_{\hat{R}} \hat{y}).$$

Hence, by 10.3, $\delta(u, y) = \hat{\delta}(\hat{u}, \hat{y})$ also in this case. This completes the proof of our claim.

Thus $\delta(u, y) = \hat{\delta}(\hat{u}, \hat{y})$ for all $u \in \Delta_x^{(2)}$ and all $y \in \Delta_z^{(2)}$. In particular, if $u \in \Delta_x^{(2)} \cap \Delta_z^{(2)}$, then $\delta(u, u) = \hat{\delta}(u^\pi, u^\xi)$ and hence $u^\pi = u^\xi$. (One could show here that, in fact, $\Delta_x^{(2)} \cap \Delta_z^{(2)} = \emptyset$, but this would require more work.) There is thus a unique map θ from $\Delta_x^{(2)} \cup \Delta_z^{(2)}$ to $\hat{\Delta}$ which restricts to π on $\Delta_x^{(2)}$ and to ξ on $\Delta_z^{(2)}$. The map θ is an isometry and, by 8.29, it is also full. $\square$

Lemma 10.10. *Let* $z \in \Delta$ *and let* x *and* y *be adjacent chambers of* Δ *both opposite* z. *Let* π *and* ξ *be full isometries from* $\Delta_x^{(2)} \cup \Delta_z^{(2)}$ *to* $\hat{\Delta}$ *and from* $\Delta_y^{(2)} \cup \Delta_z^{(2)}$ *to* $\hat{\Delta}$ *which agree on* $\{u\} \cup \Delta_z^{(2)}$ *for* $u = x$ *or* y. *Then* π *and* ξ *agree on* $\Delta_{x,y}^{(2)}$.

Proof. Let $R \in \text{Res}_{\Delta,x,y}^{(2)}$. By 9.10, there exists a residue S in $\text{Res}_{\Delta,z}^{(2)}$ opposite R. Since π and ξ agree on $\Delta_z^{(2)}$, they agree on S. By 7.31, both π and ξ send R to the unique residue of $\hat{\Delta}$ containing u^π and having the same type as R. By 9.1, u^π and z^π are opposite chambers of $\hat{\Delta}$. Thus, by 7.31 and 9.10, R^π and S^π are opposite residues of $\hat{\Delta}$. By 10.7, therefore, π and ξ agree on R. $\square$

Lemma 10.11. *Let* $(x, z) \in \Delta \circ \Delta$, *let* $S \in \text{Res}_{\Delta,z}^{(2)}$ *and let* π *be a full isometry from* $\Delta_x^{(2)} \cup S$ *to* $\hat{\Delta}$. *Then* π *has a unique extension to a full isometry from* $\Delta_x^{(2)} \cup \Delta_z^{(2)}$ *to* $\hat{\Delta}$.

Proof. By 10.9, there is a unique full isometry ξ from $\Delta_x^{(2)} \cup \Delta_z^{(2)}$ to $\hat{\Delta}$ extending the restriction of π to $\Delta_x^{(2)} \cup \{z\}$. Let K denote the type of S. Then π and ξ agree on the unique op$_I$ K-residue R in $\text{Res}_{\Delta,x}^{(2)}$ and by 7.31, both π and ξ map S to the unique K-residue of $\hat{\Delta}$ containing z^π. By 9.1, x^π and z^π are opposite chambers and thus by 9.10, R^π and S^π are opposite residues of $\hat{\Delta}$. By 10.7, therefore, π and ξ agree on S. $\square$

Lemma 10.12. *Let* P *and* Q *be opposite panels of* Δ, *let* (x, z) *and* (y, u) *be two elements of* $\Delta \circ \Delta$ *such that* $x, y \in P$ *and* $z, u \in Q$ *and let* π *be a full isometry from* $\Delta_x^{(2)} \cup \Delta_z^{(2)}$ *to* $\hat{\Delta}$. *Then there exists a unique full isometry from* $\Delta_y^{(2)} \cup \Delta_u^{(2)}$ *to* $\hat{\Delta}$ *which agrees with* π *on* $\Delta_{x,y}^{(2)} \cup \Delta_{z,u}^{(2)}$ *(also if* $x = y$ *or* $z = u$).

Proof. By 8.22, each chamber in P is opposite all but one of the chambers in Q. Since Δ is thick, we can therefore choose $v \in Q$ which is opposite both x and y. Replace v by z if $z = u$. We now apply 10.9 three times. First we extend the restriction of π to $\Delta_x^{(2)} \cup \{v\}$ to a full isometry β from $\Delta_x^{(2)} \cup \Delta_v^{(2)}$ to $\hat{\Delta}$. Next we extend the restriction of β to $\{y\} \cup \Delta_v^{(2)}$ to a full isometry ζ from $\Delta_y^{(2)} \cup \Delta_v^{(2)}$ to $\hat{\Delta}$. Finally we extend the restriction of ζ to $\Delta_y^{(2)} \cup \{u\}$ to a full isometry ξ from $\Delta_y^{(2)} \cup \Delta_u^{(2)}$ to $\hat{\Delta}$. By construction, π and β agree on $\Delta_{x,y}^{(2)}$, as do ζ and ξ, and by 10.10 (or by the uniqueness assertion of 10.9 if $x = y$), β and ζ also agree on $\Delta_{x,y}^{(2)}$. Thus π and ξ agree on $\Delta_{x,y}^{(2)}$. By construction, β and ζ agree on $\Delta_v^{(2)}$. By the uniqueness assertion of 10.9 or by 10.10, π agrees with β and ζ agrees with ξ on $\Delta_{z,u}^{(2)}$. Since $\Delta_{z,u}^{(2)} \subset \Delta_v^{(2)}$, it follows that π and ξ agree on $\Delta_{x,y}^{(2)} \cup \Delta_{z,u}^{(2)}$. We have

$$\Delta_y^{(1)} \cup \Delta_u^{(1)} \subset \Delta_{x,y}^{(2)} \cup \Delta_{z,u}^{(2)}.$$

By two applications of 10.5, therefore, ξ is uniquely determined. $\square$

Lemma 10.13. *Let R and S be opposite residues of Δ of rank two, let $(x_0, \ldots, x_k)$ be a gallery in R and let $z \in S$ be opposite both x_0 and x_k. For $i = 0$ and k, let π_i be a full isometry from $\Delta_{x_i}^{(2)} \cup \Delta_z^{(2)}$ to $\hat{\Delta}$ and for each $i \in [1, k-1]$, let π_i be a full isometry from $\Delta_{x_i}^{(2)} \cup S$ to $\hat{\Delta}$. Suppose that π_{i-1} and π_i agree on $\Delta_{x_{i-1},x_i}^{(2)} \cup S$ for all $i \in [1, k]$. Then π_0 and π_k agree on $\Delta_z^{(2)}$.*

Proof. We use induction with respect to k. Let $k = 1$. By 10.12, there exists a full isometry ξ from $\Delta_{x_1}^{(2)} \cup \Delta_z^{(2)}$ to $\hat{\Delta}$ such that π_0 and ξ agree on $\Delta_{x_0,x_1}^{(2)} \cup \Delta_z^{(2)}$. Since $\Delta_{x_1}^{(1)} \subset \Delta_{x_0,x_1}^{(2)}$, the maps π_1 and ξ agree on $\Delta_{x_1}^{(1)} \cup \{z\}$. By 10.5, therefore, π_1 and ξ agree on $\Delta_{x_1}^{(2)} \cup \{z\}$. Thus, by 10.9, π_1 and ξ agree also on $\Delta_z^{(2)}$. Hence π_0 and π_1 agree on $\Delta_z^{(2)}$.

Now suppose that $k > 1$. Let P denote the panel containing x_{k-1} and x_k. By 7.21, $P \subset R$. By 9.10, therefore, there is a unique panel Q containing z which is opposite P and this panel Q is contained in S. By 9.9, x_{k-1} is opposite some chamber in Q. Since x_0 and x_k are both opposite z, it follows by 8.22 that the three chambers x_0, x_{k-1} and x_k are each opposite all but one of the chambers in Q. Since Δ is thick, we can therefore choose chambers $p, q \in Q$ such that p is opposite x_0 and x_{k-1} and q is opposite x_{k-1} and x_k. By 10.11, there exist full isometries

$$
\begin{aligned}
\pi_0' \quad &\text{from} \quad \Delta_{x_0}^{(2)} \cup \Delta_p^{(2)} \quad \text{to} \quad \hat{\Delta}, \\
\pi_{k-1}' \quad &\text{from} \quad \Delta_{x_{k-1}}^{(2)} \cup \Delta_p^{(2)} \quad \text{to} \quad \hat{\Delta}, \\
\pi_{k-1}'' \quad &\text{from} \quad \Delta_{x_{k-1}}^{(2)} \cup \Delta_q^{(2)} \quad \text{to} \quad \hat{\Delta}, \quad \text{and} \\
\pi_k' \quad &\text{from} \quad \Delta_{x_k}^{(2)} \cup \Delta_q^{(2)} \quad \text{to} \quad \hat{\Delta}
\end{aligned}
$$

such that π_0 and π_0' agree on $\Delta_{x_0}^{(2)} \cup S$, π_{k-1}, π_{k-1}' and π_{k-1}'' agree on $\Delta_{x_{k-1}}^{(2)} \cup S$ and π_k' and π_k agree on $\Delta_{x_k}^{(2)} \cup S$. By 10.10, π_0 and π_0' agree on $\Delta_{z,p}^{(2)}$, π_{k-1}' and π_{k-1}'' agree on $\Delta_{p,q}^{(2)}$ and π_k and π_k' agree on $\Delta_{q,z}^{(2)}$. By induction, π_0' and π_{k-1}' agree on $\Delta_p^{(2)}$ and π_{k-1}'' and π_k' agree on $\Delta_q^{(2)}$. Since

$$\Delta_z^{(1)} \subset \Delta_{z,p}^{(2)} \cap \Delta_{p,q}^{(2)} \cap \Delta_{q,z}^{(2)},$$

it follows that π_0 and π_k agree on $\Delta_z^{(1)}$. Since

$$x_0 \in R \subset \Delta_{x_{i-1},x_i}^{(2)}$$

for all $i \in [1, k]$, they also agree at x_0. By 10.5, therefore, π_0 and π_k agree on $\Delta_z^{(2)}$.   □

Lemma 10.14. *Let R and S be opposite residues of Δ of rank two and suppose that ω is a homomorphism from R to S such that u and $\omega(u)$ are opposite in Δ for every $u \in R$. Let $x, y \in R$, let γ be a gallery in R from x to y, let π be a full isometry from $\Delta_x^{(2)} \cup \Delta_{\omega(x)}^{(2)}$ to $\hat{\Delta}$. Then the full isometry from $\Delta_y^{(2)} \cup \Delta_{\omega(y)}^{(2)}$ to $\hat{\Delta}$ obtained from π by moving along γ according to 10.12 is independent of γ.*

Proof. Let ξ denote the full isometry from $\Delta_y^{(2)} \cup \Delta_{\omega(y)}^{(2)}$ to $\hat{\Delta}$ obtained by moving along γ according to 10.12. It suffices to show that if $x = y$, then $\xi = \pi$. Suppose, therefore, that $x = y$. Since $\omega(R) \subset S$, the isometries π and ξ and all the intermediate isometries agree on S. Hence, by 10.13 with $\omega(x)$ in place of z, the isometries π and ξ agree on $\Delta_{\omega(x)}^{(2)}$. Since π and ξ (and all the intermediate isometries) agree on R, they agree, in particular, on x. By 10.9, therefore, π and ξ agree also on $\Delta_x^{(2)}$.   □

Lemma 10.15. *Let $(x, z) \in \Delta \circ \Delta$, let π be a full isometry from $\Delta_x^{(2)} \cup \Delta_z^{(2)}$ to $\hat{\Delta}$, let Σ denote the unique apartment of Δ containing both x and z and let*

$$\omega = \mathrm{op}_\Sigma \cdot \mathrm{retr}_{\Sigma, x} .$$

(By 9.4, ω is a homomorphism from Δ to Σ such that u and $\omega(u)$ are opposite in Δ for all $u \in \Delta$; in particular, $\omega(x) = z$.) Then there exist full isometries π_u from $\Delta_u^{(2)} \cup \Delta_{\omega(u)}^{(2)}$ to $\hat{\Delta}$ for all $u \in \Delta$ such that $\pi_x = \pi$, $z^{\pi_z} = z^\pi$ and for every pair of adjacent chambers u, v of Δ, the isometries π_u and π_v agree on $\Delta_{u,v}^{(2)}$.

Proof. Let $u \in \Delta$, choose a minimal gallery γ from x to u and let π_u be the full isometry from $\Delta_{u,\omega(u)}^{(2)}$ to $\hat{\Delta}$ obtained from π by moving along γ according to 10.12. (Thus $\pi_u = \pi$ if $u = x$.) By 7.9, every minimal gallery from x to u can be obtained from γ by a sequence of elementary homotopies as defined in 7.6. By 9.4 and 9.10, the image under ω of a residue of Δ is contained in an opposite residue. By 10.14 (one application for each elementary homotopy), it follows that π_u is independent of the choice of γ.

Now suppose that u and v are adjacent chambers. If there is a minimal gallery from x to one of these two chambers which passes through the other, then by construction, π_u and π_v agree on $\Delta_{u,v}^{(2)}$. Suppose, instead, that there is no such gallery, i.e. that $\mathrm{dist}(x, u) = \mathrm{dist}(x, v)$. Let P denote the panel containing u and v, let $w = \mathrm{proj}_R x$, and let γ be a minimal gallery from x to w. By 8.22, (γ, u) and (γ, v) are both minimal galleries. Since π_u and π_v both agree with π_w on

$$\Delta_{u,v}^{(2)} = \Delta_{w,u}^{(2)} = \Delta_{w,v}^{(2)},$$

they agree with each other in this set. Thus π_u and π_v agree on $\Delta_{u,v}^{(2)}$ in every case.

By 9.1, x^π and z^π are opposite. Let

$$\gamma = (x_0, x_1, x_2, \ldots, x_d)$$

be a minimal gallery from x to z. By the conclusion of the previous paragraph,

$$(x_0^{\pi_{x_0}}, x_1^{\pi_{x_1}}, x_2^{\pi_{x_2}}, \ldots, x_d^{\pi_{x_d}})$$

is a gallery from x^π to z^{π_z} of the same type as γ. By 7.1 and 7.7 (ii), therefore, $\delta(x, z) = \hat{\delta}(x^\pi, z^{\pi_z})$. Hence x^π and z^{π_z} are opposite by 9.1. For all $i \in [0, d]$, $x_i^{\pi_{x_i}}$ and $\omega(x_i)^{\pi_{x_i}}$ are opposite chambers of $\hat{\Delta}$ (again by 9.1) and hence by 9.2, there is a unique apartment $\hat{\Sigma}_i$ containing $x_i^{\pi_{x_i}}$ and $\omega(x_i)^{\pi_{x_i}}$ (so $\hat{\Sigma}_0$ contains x^π and z^π and $\hat{\Sigma}_d$ contains z^{π_z}). By 8.9, $\gamma \subset \Sigma$. By 8.17, $\omega|_\Sigma = \mathrm{op}_\Sigma$. Thus, in particular, $\omega(\gamma) \subset \Sigma$. By repeated application of 10.8, therefore, $\hat{\Sigma}_i = \hat{\Sigma}_{i-1}$ for each $i \in [1, d]$. Thus, in particular, $z^{\pi_z} \in \hat{\Sigma}_0$. Hence z^π and z^{π_z} are both chambers of $\hat{\Sigma}_0$ which are opposite x^π. By 5.5, they are equal. $\square$

We can now complete the proof of 10.1. By 10.9, there is a unique extension of π (which we also denote by π) to a full isometry from $\Delta_x^{(2)} \cup \Delta_z^{(2)}$ to $\hat{\Delta}$. Let Σ denote the unique apartment of Δ containing x and z and let $\omega = \mathrm{op}_\Sigma \cdot \mathrm{retr}_{\Sigma, x}$. By 10.15, there exist full isometries π_u from $\Delta_u^{(2)} \cup \Delta_{\omega(u)}^{(2)}$ to $\hat{\Delta}$ for all $u \in \Delta$ such that $\pi_x = \pi$, $z^{\pi_z} = z^\pi$ and for every pair of adjacent chambers u, v of Δ, the isometries π_u and π_v agree on $\Delta_{u,v}^{(2)}$. Let ϕ be the map from Δ to itself given by $u^\phi = u^{\pi_u}$ for all $u \in \Delta$. Let R be a residue in $\mathrm{Res}_{\Delta,x}^{(2)}$ and let P be an arbitrary panel of Δ. Then π_u and π_v agree on R for all pairs u, v of adjacent chambers in R and π_u and π_v agree on P for all $u, v \in P$. Hence ϕ agrees with $\pi = \pi_x$ on R (since $\pi_x = \pi$ and R is connected) and ϕ agrees with π_u on P for each $u \in P$. Therefore ϕ is full and, since R is arbitrary, it agrees with π on $\Delta_x^{(2)}$. Hence ϕ agrees with π on $\Delta_x^{(2)} \cup \{z\}$ since $z^\phi = z^{\pi_z} = z^\pi$. Since the map ϕ is full, it is a special isomorphism from Δ to $\hat{\Delta}$ by 7.30. By 9.7, ϕ is uniquely determined. This completes the proof of 10.1.

As observed above, 10.2 follows from 10.1 and 10.6. The following small modification of 10.2 is also useful.

Theorem 10.16. *Let Δ and $\hat{\Delta}$ be thick irreducible spherical buildings of rank at least three having the same type and let $x \in \Delta$. Let Δ_x^{red} denote the set of all chambers of Δ contained in some irreducible residue in $\mathrm{Res}_{\Delta,x}^{(2)}$. Then every full map from Δ_x^{red} to $\hat{\Delta}$ has a unique extension to a full isometry from $\Delta_x^{(2)}$ to $\hat{\Delta}$. By 10.2, therefore, every full map from Δ_x^{red} to $\hat{\Delta}$ can be extended to a special isomorphism from Δ to $\hat{\Delta}$.*

Proof. Let π be a full isometry from Δ_x^{red} to $\hat{\Delta}$ and let $\hat{x} = x^\pi$. By 7.31, the restriction of π to each irreducible residue in $\text{Res}_{\Delta,x}^{(2)}$ is a special isomorphism to the residue in $\text{Res}_{\hat{\Delta},\hat{x}}^{(2)}$ of the same type. Choose $i, j \in \Pi$ such that $m_{ij} = 2$, i.e. such that the $\{i, j\}$-residue in $\text{Res}_{\Delta,x}^{(2)}$ is not irreducible. Let R denote this residue and let P_i and P_j denote the i- and j-panels of R containing x. By 7.15 and 7.17,

(i) every chamber of $R\backslash(P_i \cup P_j)$ is i-adjacent to a unique chamber in $P_j\backslash\{x\}$ and j-adjacent to a unique chamber of $P_i\backslash\{x\}$; and

(ii) for every pair $u \in P_i\backslash\{x\}$, $v \in P_j\backslash\{x\}$, there is a unique chamber of $R\backslash(P_i \cup P_j)$ which is i-adjacent to v and j-adjacent to u.

The analogous assertions hold for the $\{i, j\}$-residue $\hat{R}$ in $\text{Res}_{\hat{\Delta},\hat{x}}^{(2)}$, where $\hat{x} = x^\pi$. Since π maps P_i and P_j bijectively to the i- and j-panels of $\hat{\Delta}$ containing $\hat{x}$, it follows that the restriction of π to $P_i \cup P_j$ has a unique extension to a special isomorphism from R to $\hat{R}$. For each $u \in R\backslash(P_i \cup P_j)$, there is a minimal gallery of type ij from x to u, and thus by 7.21, R is the unique residue in $\text{Res}_{\Delta,x}^{(2)}$ containing u. Since the set $\{i, j\}$ is arbitrary, we conclude by 8.30 that π has a unique extension to a full isometry from $\Delta_x^{(2)}$ to $\hat{\Delta}$. $\qquad\square$

Chapter Eleven

The Moufang Property

Tits mentions the Moufang property for the first time in the addenda of [14], where he observes that it is a consequence of his Theorem 4.1.2 that this property holds for all thick irreducible spherical buildings of rank at least three. In 11.6 we give a proof of this fundamental result based on 6.13 and 10.1. In the rest of this chapter, we use the Moufang property to examine more deeply the structure of a spherical building and its automorphism group.

We begin with the principal definitions.

Definition 11.1. Let Δ be a spherical building of rank at least two, let α be a root of Δ (by which we mean a root of some apartment of Δ), and let U_α denote the subgroup of $\mathrm{Aut}^\circ(\Delta)$ consisting of all elements of $\mathrm{Aut}^\circ(\Delta)$ which act trivially on every panel of Δ which contains two chambers in α. The subgroup U_α is called the *root group* associated with the root α.

Let Δ, α and U_α be as in 11.1. By 3.14, a chamber of α lies on at most one panel which does *not* contain a second chamber in α. Since the rank of Δ (i.e. the number of panels containing a given chamber) is at least two, each chamber of α therefore lies on at least one panel which does contain a second chamber of α. It follows that the root group U_α acts trivially on α.

Definition 11.2. Let Δ be a spherical building of rank at least two. Then Δ has the *Moufang property* (equivalently, the building Δ satisfies the *Moufang condition*) if for each root α of Δ, the root group U_α acts transitively on the set of all apartments of Δ containing α. By 9.3, the following are equivalent.

(i) Δ has the Moufang property.

(ii) For each root α of Δ there is a panel P containing just one chamber of α such that U_α acts transitively on $P \backslash P \cap \alpha$ (i.e. on P with the one chamber in $P \cap \alpha$ removed).

(iii) For each root α of Δ and for each panel P containing just one chamber of α, U_α acts transitively on $P \backslash P \cap \alpha$.

Formally, these definitions apply also to non-spherical buildings. To be useful in the non-spherical case, however, they must be modified. See Chapter 6,

Section 4, of [7] as well as [17] and [18], where also a definition of a Moufang building of rank one (i.e. a 'Moufang set') is introduced.

11.3. Let Δ be a building of type $\bullet\!\!\xrightarrow{\ \ n\ \ }\!\!\bullet$ for some $n \geqslant 2$, let Γ be the corresponding generalized n-gon as defined in 7.15 and let $G = \mathrm{Aut}(\Gamma)$. By 7.16, we can also think of G as $\mathrm{Aut}(\Delta)$. For each vertex x of Γ (i.e. for each panel x of Δ), let Γ_x denote the set of vertices of Γ adjacent to x (i.e. the set of panels of Δ which contain a chamber in common with x), and let $G_x^{(1)}$ denote the pointwise stabilizer of $\{x\} \cup \Gamma_x$ in G (i.e. the pointwise stabilizer of the panel x, as a set of chambers, in G) as in 7.11. By 8.7, the set of edges on an apartment of Γ as defined in 7.12 is just the set of chambers of an apartment of Δ as defined in 8.3. A root of Δ is the collection of edges of Γ (i.e. chambers of Δ) contained in a path of Γ of length n. Let $(x_0, x_1, \ldots, x_{n-1}, x_n)$ be such a path, let α denote the root consisting of its edges, and let U_α denote the corresponding root group of Δ. Then U_α is just the subgroup

$$G_{x_1}^{(1)} \cap \cdots \cap G_{x_{n-1}}^{(1)}.$$

By 7.13 (i) (which is a special case of 9.3), Δ has the Moufang property if and only if for every path

$$(x_0, x_1, \ldots, x_{n-1}, x_n)$$

of length n in Γ, the subgroup

$$G_{x_1}^{(1)} \cap \cdots \cap G_{x_{n-1}}^{(1)}$$

acts transitively on $\Gamma_{x_n} \backslash \{x_{n-1}\}$.

The following consequence of 9.7 is essential.

Proposition 11.4. *Let Δ be an irreducible spherical building of rank at least two which has the Moufang property. Then for each root α of Δ and each panel P containing just one chamber of α, the root group U_α acts regularly[1] on $P \backslash P \cap \alpha$.*

Proof. Let α be a root of Δ and let P be a panel containing just one chamber of α. By 11.2, U_α acts transitively on $P \backslash P \cap \alpha$. Let v be an arbitrary chamber in $P \backslash P \cap \alpha$. By 4.12, $\alpha \neq \partial\alpha$. Let $u \in \alpha \backslash \partial\alpha$. By 11.1, $U_\alpha \subset G_u^{(1)}$, where $G = \mathrm{Aut}(\Delta)$ and $G_u^{(1)}$ is as defined in 9.6. By 9.3, there is a unique apartment Σ containing α and v. Thus $U_\alpha \cap G_v \subset G_u^{(1)} \cap G_\Sigma$ and hence $U_\alpha \cap G_v = 1$ by 9.7. $\qquad\square$

---

[1] A group acts *regularly* (or *simply transitively*) on a set X if it acts transitively on X and the stabilizer of each element of X is trivial.

11.5. Let Δ be a building of type $\bullet \quad \bullet$ and let Γ denote the corresponding generalized polygon. By 7.17, Γ is a complete bipartite graph. By 11.3, therefore, Δ has the Moufang property, but if some vertex of Γ has more than three neighbors, then it is not true that for each root α and each panel P containing just one chamber of α, the root group U_α acts regularly on $P \backslash P \cap \alpha$.

We come now to the main result of this chapter (Satz 1 in [15]). The proof we give is based on 6.13, 10.1 and 10.4.

Theorem 11.6. *Every thick irreducible spherical building of rank at least three has the Moufang property.*

Proof. Let Δ be a thick irreducible spherical building of rank at least three, let Σ be an apartment of Δ and let α be a root of Σ. By 6.13 (i), we can choose $x \in \alpha^{(2)}$, where $\alpha^{(2)}$ is as in 6.10. Let Σ' be an arbitrary apartment containing α, let $z = \mathrm{op}_\Sigma x$ and let $z' = \mathrm{op}_{\Sigma'} x$. By 9.3, there is a special isomorphism ξ from Σ to Σ' which is the identity map on α. By 5.5, $z^\xi = z'$. Choose $R \in \mathrm{Res}^{(2)}_{\Delta,x}$. By 6.10, $\Sigma \cap R \subset \alpha$. Thus ξ acts trivially on $\Sigma \cap R$. By 8.23, therefore,

$$\mathrm{proj}_R z = \mathrm{proj}_{\Sigma \cap R} z = \mathrm{proj}_{\Sigma \cap R} z' = \mathrm{proj}_R z'.$$

Hence, by 10.4, the map from $R \cup \{z\}$ to Δ which is the identity on R and sends z to z' is an isometry from $R \cup \{z\}$ to Δ. Since R is arbitrary, it follows that the map which acts as the identity map on $\Delta_x^{(2)}$ and sends z to z' is a full isometry from $\Delta_x^{(2)} \cup \{z\}$ to Δ. By 10.1, this map extends to a unique special automorphism of Δ which we denote by π. By 9.2, π sends Σ to Σ'. By 2.8, the restriction of π to Σ equals ξ and thus its restriction to α is the identity map. Hence π acts trivially on $\alpha \cup \Delta_x^{(2)}$. Since Σ' is arbitrary, it follows that the pointwise stabilizer of $\alpha \cup \Delta_x^{(2)}$ in $\mathrm{Aut}(\Delta)$ acts transitively on the set of apartments containing α. It will suffice, therefore, to show that this pointwise stabilizer lies in the root group U_α.

Let $G = \mathrm{Aut}(\Delta)$ and let $G_{\alpha,x}$ denote the pointwise stabilizer of $\alpha \cup \Delta_x^{(2)}$ in G for all $x \in \alpha^{(2)}$. Suppose that x and y are adjacent chambers in $\alpha^{(2)}$. Thus both $G_{\alpha,x}$ and $G_{\alpha,y}$ are contained in $G_x^{(1)}$, where $G_x^{(1)}$ is as in 9.6. Let $g \in G_{\alpha,x}$. By the conclusion of the previous paragraph, there exists $h \in G_{\alpha,y}$ such that $h^{-1}g$ maps Σ to itself. By 9.7, therefore, $g = h$. Hence $G_{\alpha,x} \subset G_{\alpha,y}$. By symmetry, it follows that $G_{\alpha,x} = G_{\alpha,y}$. By 6.13 (ii), therefore, the group $G_{\alpha,x}$ is independent of the choice of $x \in \alpha^{(2)}$.

Now let P be a panel of Δ which contains two chambers of α. By 6.13 (iii), there exists a residue S of rank two such that $P \subset S$, $S \cap \Sigma \subset \alpha$ (so $S \cap \Sigma =$

$S \cap \alpha)$ and $S \cap \Sigma$ contains a chamber w adjacent to a chamber $x \in \alpha^{(2)}$. Then

$$G_{\alpha,x} \subset G_w^{(1)} \cap G_{S \cap \alpha}.$$

By 8.13 (i), $S \cap \Sigma$ is an apartment of S. By 9.7 applied to S, therefore, $G_{\alpha,x}$ acts trivially on S and hence on P. Since P is arbitrary, it follows by the conclusion of the previous paragraph that $G_{\alpha,x}$ lies in U_α. $\square$

Definition 11.7. In light of 11.6, we will call a building *Moufang* in these notes[2] if it

  (i) is thick, irreducible and spherical;

 (ii) has rank at least two; and

(iii) satisfies the Moufang condition.

We observed in 11.5 that every building of type $\bullet \quad \bullet$ satisfies the Moufang condition. By 11.7, however, these buildings are not Moufang (since they are not irreducible).

By 11.6, every thick irreducible spherical building of rank at least three is Moufang. By 6.6.2 and 6.6.7 of [21], on the other hand, for every value of $n \geqslant 3$, there exist thick buildings of type $\bullet\!\!-\!\!\overset{n}{-}\!\!\bullet$ which are not Moufang. Nevertheless, we have the following important result.

Theorem 11.8. *Every irreducible residue of rank at least two of a Moufang building is a Moufang building.*

Proof. Let Δ be a Moufang building and let R be a residue of rank at least two. By 7.20, R is a subbuilding of Δ. Let Σ_0 be an apartment of R, let α_0 be a root of Σ_0 and let P be a panel of R containing just one chamber of α_0. By 8.13 (ii), $\Sigma_0 = \Sigma \cap R$ and $\alpha_0 = \alpha \cap R$ for some apartment Σ of Δ and some root α of Σ. Thus $\alpha_0 \cap P = \alpha \cap P$ (since $\alpha \cap P \subset \alpha \cap R \subset \alpha_0$). Since $U_\alpha \subset \text{Aut}^\circ(\Delta)$ acts trivially on α, it maps R to itself. The subgroup of $\text{Aut}^\circ(R)$ induced by the root group U_α acts trivially on every panel containing two chambers of α_0 and hence lies in the root group U_{α_0} (of R). By 11.2 and the hypothesis, U_α acts transitively on $P \backslash P \cap \alpha$. Therefore U_{α_0} acts transitively on $P \backslash P \cap \alpha_0$. Since α_0 is arbitrary, it follows that R is Moufang by a second application of 11.2. $\square$

Note that we have not used the irreducibility of R in the proof of 11.8. Thus we have really shown that every residue of rank at least two (irreducible or not)

---

[2] In [17], a more general class of Moufang buildings is introduced (see also § 4 in Chapter 6 of [7]).

of a Moufang building has the Moufang property (but we will not have any need of this more general result).

We now begin to show how the Moufang property can be used to examine the structure of a spherical building and its automorphism group.

11.9. For the rest of this book, we compose elements of a group G acting on a set X from left to right (the more usual convention in group theory) rather than from right to left and use x^g to denote the image of $x \in X$ by $g \in G$. Thus x^{gh} (for $x \in X$ and $g, h \in G$) is to be interpreted as $(x^g)^h$. The right-to-left convention seemed to be more natural in the context of Coxeter chamber systems, galleries and the types of galleries. Now, though, we will encounter calculations involving commutators, where it is better to conform to the convention used in [20]. In particular, we define the conjugates h^g and H^g to be $g^{-1}hg$ and $g^{-1}Hg$ and the commutator $[g, h]$ to be $g^{-1}h^{-1}gh$ for all elements g, h and all subgroups H of a group G.

The following result is an important inductive tool.

Proposition 11.10. *Let Δ be a Moufang building, let R be an irreducible residue of Δ of rank at least two and let Σ be an apartment of Δ such that $\Sigma \cap R \neq \emptyset$. (By 7.20 and 8.13 (i), R is a subbuilding of Δ and $\Sigma \cap R$ is an apartment of R.) Let α_0 be a root of $\Sigma \cap R$, let α be a root of Σ such that $\alpha_0 = \alpha \cap R$, and let P be a panel of R containing just one vertex x of α_0. Then the root groups U_α (of Δ) and U_{α_0} (of R) induce the same regular permutation group on $P \backslash \{x\}$ and are, therefore, canonically isomorphic.*

Proof. By 11.4 and 11.8, U_α and U_{α_0} both act regularly on $P \backslash \{x\}$. As we observed in the proof of 11.8, the group induced by U_α on $P \backslash \{x\}$ is contained in the group induced by U_{α_0}. It follows that these two groups are the same. $\quad\square$

Proposition 11.11. *Let Δ be a Moufang building, let $c \in \Delta$, let Σ be an apartment of Δ containing c, and let U_c^+ denote the subgroup generated by the root groups U_α for all roots α of Σ containing c. Then the following hold.*

(i) *If $(x_0, x_1, \ldots, x_d)$ is a minimal gallery in Σ from c to $\text{op}_\Sigma c$ (so $d = \text{diam } \Delta$) and α_i denotes the root $\Sigma_{(x_{i-1} \backslash x_i)}$ of Σ as defined in 3.15 for all $i \in [1, d]$,[3] then every element of U_c^+ has a unique representation as a product $g_1 \cdots g_d$, where $g_i \in U_{\alpha_i}$ for all $i \in [1, d]$.*

(ii) *The group U_c^+ acts regularly on the set of apartments containing the chamber c.*

---

[3] By 3.20 and 5.2, $\alpha_1, \ldots, \alpha_d$ are all the roots of Σ which contain c.

(iii) *The group U_c^+ contains U_α for all roots α of Δ containing c. Equivalently, U_c^+ is independent of the choice of the apartment Σ containing c.*

(iv) *The group U_c^+ acts transitively on the set of minimal galleries starting at c of a given type.*

Proof. Let P be a panel containing c. If α is a root of Σ containing c, then either P contains two chambers of α, in which case U_α acts trivially on P by 11.1, or $P \cap P \cap \alpha = \{c\}$, in which case α is uniquely determined by P by 3.15 and U_α acts regularly on $P \backslash \{c\}$ by 11.4. We conclude that any element of U_c^+ fixing a chamber in $P \backslash \{c\}$ acts trivially on P. Now let h be an element of U_c^+ fixing the apartment Σ. By 2.8, h acts trivially on Σ and hence fixes the two chambers in $\Sigma \cap P$. Thus h acts trivially on P. Since P is arbitrary, it follows that $h = 1$ by 9.7. Thus the stabilizer of Σ in U_c^+ is trivial.

Let $\gamma = (x_0, \ldots, x_d)$ be a minimal gallery in Σ from c to $\mathrm{op}_\Sigma c$ and let $\alpha_i = \Sigma_{(x_{i-1} \backslash x_i)}$ for all $i \in [1, d]$ as in (i). Let f denote the type of γ and, for all $i \in [1, d]$, let P_i denote the panel of Δ containing x_{i-1} and x_i. For each $i \in [1, d]$, the chambers x_j for all $j < i$ are nearer to x_{i-1} than to x_i (since γ is minimal), hence $(x_0, \ldots, x_{i-1})$ is contained in α_i and therefore $(x_0, \ldots, x_{i-1})$ is fixed by U_{α_i}. By 11.2, U_{α_i} acts transitively on $P_i \backslash \{x_{i-1}\}$ for all $i \in [1, d]$. It follows that if γ' is an arbitrary gallery of type f beginning at c (for instance, if $\gamma' = \gamma^{g^{-1}}$ for some $g \in U_c^+$), then there exist elements $g_i \in U_{\alpha_i}$ for $i \in [1, d]$ such that

$$(\gamma')^{g_1 g_2 \cdots g_d} = \gamma$$

(where the left-hand side of this equation is to be interpreted as in 11.9). Therefore U_c^+ acts transitively on the set of galleries of type f beginning at c, and for each $g \in U_c^+$, there exist $g_i \in U_{\alpha_i}$ for $i \in [1, d]$ such that the product $g^{-1} g_1 g_2 \cdots g_d$ maps γ to itself. By 2.5 and 9.2, every apartment containing c contains a unique gallery of type f starting at c and every gallery of type f starting at c is contained in a unique apartment. By the conclusion of the previous paragraph, therefore, (i) and (ii) hold. By (ii), (iii) also holds. By 8.6 and 8.9, every minimal gallery of Δ starting at c is contained in an apartment, and by 2.5 again, every gallery starting at c in a given apartment is the only gallery of its type starting at c in this apartment. Hence (ii) implies (iv). $\square$

Proposition 11.12. *Let Δ be a Moufang building and let $G^\dagger$ denote the subgroup of $\mathrm{Aut}^\circ(\Delta)$ generated by all the root groups of Δ. Then $G^\dagger$ acts transitively on the set of all pairs (Σ, c) such that Σ is an apartment of Δ and c a chamber of Σ.*

Proof. Let P be a panel and let x, y be two chambers of P. By 8.6, there exists an apartment Σ containing x and y. Let α denote the root $\Sigma_{(x \setminus y)}$ of Σ as defined in 3.15. By 11.2, the root group U_α acts transitively on $P \setminus \{x\}$. Since Δ is thick and $x \in P$ is arbitrary, it follows that the stabilizer of P in $G^\dagger$ acts transitively (in fact, 2-transitively, but this is not relevant here) on P. Since P is arbitrary, $G^\dagger$ contains elements which map each chamber of a gallery to its successor in the gallery. Since Δ is connected, it follows that $G^\dagger$ acts transitively on the set of chambers of Δ. The claim follows now by 11.11 (ii). $\square$

Proposition 11.13. *Let* (Δ, δ) *be a Moufang building and let G be a subgroup of* $\mathrm{Aut}^\circ(\Delta)$ *containing all the root groups of Δ. Then two ordered pairs* (x, y) *and* (u, v) *in* $\Delta \times \Delta$ *are in the same G-orbit if and only if* $\delta(x, y) = \delta(u, v)$.

Proof. Let (W, r) denote the Coxeter system corresponding to the type Π of Δ, let I denote the index set of Δ, and let (x, y) and (u, v) be two elements of $\Delta \times \Delta$. By 8.2, the group G consists of isometries from Δ to itself. This means that if (x, y) and (u, v) are in the same G-orbit, then $\delta(x, y) = \delta(u, v)$. Suppose, conversely, that $\delta(x, y) = \delta(u, v)$. Choose a reduced word $f \in M_I$ such that $\delta(x, y) = r_f$. By 7.1, there exist galleries γ and γ' of type f from x to y and from u to v. By 7.7 (ii), γ and γ' are both minimal. By 11.12, there exists an element of G mapping x to u. By 11.11 (iv), therefore, there exists an element of G which maps γ to γ' and therefore (x, y) to (u, v). $\square$

11.14. Let Δ be a Moufang building, let Σ be an apartment of Δ, let c be a chamber of Σ, let G be a subgroup of $\mathrm{Aut}^\circ(\Delta)$ containing all the root groups of Δ, let N denote the setwise stabilizer of Σ in G and let B denote the stabilizer of c in G (so the intersection $N \cap B$ is the pointwise stabilizer of Σ in N and the quotient group $N/N \cap B$ is isomorphic to the Weyl group of Δ). By (3.11) of [14] and 11.12, (B, N) is a Tits system (equivalently, BN-pair)[4] for the group G.

Definition 11.15. A *Tits system* (or BN-*pair*) for a group G is a pair of subgroups B and N such that for some set of generators $\{m_i \mid i \in I\}$ of N:

(i) $G = \langle B, N \rangle$;

(ii) H is normal in N and $m_i^2 \in H$ for all $i \in I$, where $H = N \cap B$;

(iii) $BwBm_i \subset Bwm_i B \cup BwB$ for all $w \in N$ and all $i \in I$;

(iv) $m_i B m_i \not\subset B$ for all $i \in I$.

---

[4] By 11.19 below, these BN-pairs are, in fact, *split*; that is to say, there exists a nilpotent normal subgroup U of B such that $B = U(N \cap B)$.

(As is shown in §2, Chapter 4, of [1], the subset $\{Hm_i \mid i \in I\}$ of N/H is uniquely determined by G, B and N, and the quotient group N/H is a Coxeter group with respect to this set of generators.[5])

Conversely, groups with a BN-pair give rise to buildings, and it is through this important connection that Tits showed how to associate a thick irreducible spherical building of rank ℓ to the group of k-rational points (k an arbitrary field) of a simple algebraic group of relative rank ℓ. Tits, in fact, discovered buildings through his investigations into this connection between geometry and algebraic groups (initially between geometry and Lie groups). The buildings of rank at least two which arise from algebraic groups in this way are Moufang. See Chapter 5 of [7], Chapters 3 and 5 of [14] and the Appendix of [20].

The following important result will be used in the proof of 11.20.

Proposition 11.16. *Let Δ be a Moufang building, let I denote the index set of Δ, let c be a chamber of Δ and let G be a subgroup of $\mathrm{Aut}°(\Delta)$ which contains all the root groups of Δ. Let B denote the stabilizer of c in G and for each subset $J \subset I$, let R_J denote the unique J-residue of Δ containing c and let B_J denote the setwise stabilizer of R_J in G (so $R_\emptyset = \{c\}$ and $B_\emptyset = B$). Then $R_J = c^{B_J}$ for all $J \subset I$ and the map $J \mapsto B_J$ is a bijection from the set of all subsets of I to the set of all subgroups of G containing B which preserves inclusions.*

Proof. Since $G \subset \mathrm{Aut}°(\Delta)$, each element of G maps each residue of Δ to a residue of the same type. It follows that $c^{B_J} = R_J$ for all $J \subset I$ (since G acts transitively on Δ by 11.12) and $B_J \subset B_K$ for all $J, K \subset I$ such that $J \subset K$. By 7.21, the set of chambers adjacent to c in R_J (for a given $J \subset I$) are precisely the chambers of Δ which are j-adjacent to c for some $j \in J$. It follows that the map $J \mapsto B_J$ is injective.

For each $i \in I$, let P_i denote the i-panel containing c. Let D be a subgroup of G containing B and let J denote the set of all $i \in I$ such that the setwise stabilizer of P_i in D acts transitively on P_i. We claim that $D = B_J$. Let $R = R_J$. The group D contains elements mapping c to every chamber which is i-adjacent to c for all $i \in J$. Since R is connected, this implies that $R \subset c^D$. Thus if $h \in B_J$, there exists $g \in D$ such that $g^{-1}h \in B$. Since $B \subset D$, it follows that $B_J \subset D$. From $R \subset c^D$ it follows that if $c^D \subset R$, then $c^D = R$ and hence $D \subset B_J$ (and thus $D = B_J$). We claim that, in fact, $c^D \subset R$.

---

[5] By [12] (p. 3 at the bottom), the condition '$m_i^2 \in H$ for all $i \in I$' in (ii) can be omitted if condition (iv) is replaced by '$m_i^{-1}Bm_i \not\subset B$'.

Let g be an element of D which does not fix c, let $x = c^g$, let

$$\gamma = (u_0, \ldots, u_{k-1}, u_k)$$

be a minimal gallery from c to x, let f denote the type of γ, and let $i \in I$ denote the last letter of f. We will prove by induction with respect to $|f|$ that $f \in M_J$ (and therefore $x \in R$). First note that by 11.2, B acts transitively on $P_i \backslash \{c\}$ (since $U_i \subset B$). It follows that $i \in J$ if and only if there is an element of D which fixes P_i but which does not fix c. If $|f| = 1$, then $x \in P_i$ and hence $P_i^g = P_i$ but $c^g = x \neq c$, so $i \in J$ and thus $f = i \in M_J$. Now suppose that $|f| > 1$. Let Q denote the i-panel containing x (so $Q = P_i^g$), let v denote an arbitrary element in $Q \backslash \{u_{k-1}, u_k\}$, and let $\gamma' = (u_0, \ldots, u_{k-1}, v)$. Then γ' is a gallery of type f from c to v. By 7.7 (ii) and 11.11 (iv), there is an element h of B mapping γ to γ'. Since h fixes u_{k-1}, it fixes Q. Since $B \subset D$, h lies in D. Thus the product ghg^{-1} (composed from left to right) is an element of D which fixes P_i (since $Q = P_i^g$) but which does not fix c (since $c^g = x$ is not fixed by h). Hence $i \in J$. By induction, we conclude that $f \in M_J$. Thus $x \in R$. Since g is arbitrary, it follows that $c^D \subset R$ and therefore $D = B_J$ as claimed. Since D is arbitrary, it follows that the map $J \mapsto B_J$ is surjective. $\qquad\square$

Proposition 11.17. *Let Δ be a Moufang building and let Σ be an apartment of Δ. Let $d = \operatorname{diam} \Delta$ and let*

$$(x_0, \ldots, x_d)$$

be a minimal gallery of length d in Σ. Let α_i denote the root $\Sigma_{(x_{i-1} \backslash x_i)}$ of Σ and let $U_i = U_{\alpha_i}$ for all $i \in [1, d]$. For all $i, j \in [1, d]$, let

$$U_{[i,j]} = \begin{cases} \langle U_i, U_{i+1}, \ldots, U_j \rangle & \text{if } i \leqslant j, \\ 1 & \text{otherwise.} \end{cases}$$

Then $U_{[i,j]} = U_i U_{i+1} \cdots U_j$ and

$$[U_i, U_j] \subset U_{[i+1, j-1]}$$

for all $i, j \in [1, d]$ such that $i < j$, where $[U_i, U_j]$ denotes the subgroup of $\operatorname{Aut}^\circ(\Delta)$ generated by all the commutators $[a, b] = a^{-1} b^{-1} ab$ such that $a \in U_i$ and $b \in U_j$.

Proof. We have $x_d = \operatorname{op}_\Sigma x_0$ and $x_0 = \operatorname{op}_\Sigma x_d$. Let $x_{d+i} = \operatorname{op}_\Sigma x_i$ for all $i \in [1, d-1]$ and let

$$\gamma = (x_0, x_1, \ldots, x_d, x_{d+1}, x_{d+2}, \ldots, x_{2d-1}, x_0).$$

By 5.11, γ is a gallery in Σ. For the rest of this proof, we will consider the subscripts of x as elements of $\mathbb{Z}_{2d}$. With this understanding, we observe that $(x_{i-d}, \ldots, x_i)$ is a minimal gallery and hence $(x_{i-d}, \ldots, x_{i-1})$ is contained in α_i and is thus fixed by U_i for all $i \in [1, d]$. Now choose $i, j \in [1, d]$ such that $i < j$. Then U_i and U_j both fix the gallery $(x_{j-d}, \ldots, x_{i-1})$. Let P denote the panel containing x_{i-1} and x_i. Since x_{i-1} and x_i are both in α_j, the root group U_j acts trivially on P. Since U_i maps P to itself, it follows that $[U_i, U_j]$ acts trivially on P. In particular, $[U_i, U_j]$ fixes x_i. By a similar argument, $[U_i, U_j]$ fixes x_{j-d-1}. Thus $[U_i, U_j]$ fixes

$$(x_{j-d-1}, \ldots, x_i).$$

Choose $g \in [U_i, U_j]$. By 11.2, for each $t \in [i + 1, j - 1]$, the group U_t, which fixes $(x_{j-d-1}, \ldots, x_{t-1})$, acts transitively on the set $P_t \backslash \{x_{t-1}\}$, where P_t denotes the panel containing x_{t-1} and x_t. It follows that there exist elements $g_t \in U_t$ for $t \in [i + 1, j - 1]$ such that the product

$$g^{-1} g_{i+1} \cdots g_{j-2} g_{j-1}$$

(composed from left to right) fixes the gallery $(x_{j-d-1}, \ldots, x_{j-1})$. Since x_{j-d-1} and x_{j-1} are opposite, the product $g^{-1} g_{i+1} \cdots g_{j-2} g_{j-1}$ therefore maps Σ to itself by 9.2 and hence

$$g = g_{i+1} \cdots g_{j-2} g_{j-1}$$

by 11.11 (ii) (since the roots $\alpha_i, \alpha_{i+1}, \ldots, \alpha_j$ all contain x_0). Thus $[U_i, U_j] \subset U_i U_{i+1} \cdots U_j$ for all $i, j \in [1, d]$ such that $i < j$. In particular, if $i, j \in [1, d]$ and $i < j$, then $ba \in a U_{[i+1,j]}$ for all $a \in U_i$ and all $b \in U_j$. Hence $U_{[i,j]} = U_i U_{[i+1,j]}$ and thus, by induction with respect to $j - i$,

$$U_{[i,j]} = U_i U_{i+1} \cdots U_j$$

for all $i, j \in [1, d]$ such that $i < j$. $\square$

Definition 11.18. Let G be a group. Let $G_0 = G$ and let $G_i = [G, G_{i-1}]$ for all $i \geqslant 1$. Then G is *nilpotent* if for some $k \geqslant 1$, the subgroup G_k is trivial. We will need three basic facts about nilpotent groups.

(i) If G is a non-trivial nilpotent group, then G is not perfect (i.e. $G \neq [G, G]$).

(ii) If G is nilpotent, then so is every quotient group of G.

(iii) A group generated by two nilpotent normal subgroups is itself nilpotent.

Fact (i) is an immediate consequence of the definition and fact (ii) is easy to check. Fact (iii) is well known in finite group theory, where it leads to the notion of the Frattini subgroup of a finite group. For a proof of (iii) which is valid for arbitrary groups, see (10.3.2) of [4].

The following result will be used in the proof of 11.20. The proof we give depends on our knowing (by the main results of [20]) that the root groups of a Moufang building of rank two are nilpotent.

Proposition 11.19. *Let Δ be a Moufang building, let Σ be an apartment of Δ, let c be a chamber of Σ and let U_c^+ be the subgroup defined in 11.11. Then U_c^+ is nilpotent.*

Proof. Let α be an arbitrary root of Σ. Choose a panel P containing just one chamber of α and an irreducible residue R of rank two containing P and let $\alpha_0 = \alpha \cap R$ (so α_0 is a root of the apartment $\Sigma \cap R$ of R). By (17.1) and (17.7) as well as (17.2), (17.4) and (17.5) (alternatively, (19.3), (21.3) and (29.8)) of [20], the root group U_{α_0} of R is nilpotent. By 11.10, therefore, U_α is nilpotent.

Let $d = \text{diam } \Delta$, choose a minimal gallery $(x_0, \ldots, x_d)$ in Σ from c to $\text{op}_\Sigma c$ and let $U_1, \ldots, U_d$ (and $U_{[i,j]}$) be as in 11.17 with respect to Σ and this gallery. By 11.11 (i), $U_c^+ = U_{[1,d]}$. We will show that $U_{[i,j]}$ is nilpotent for all $i, j \in [1, d]$ such that $i \leqslant j$ by induction with respect to $j - i$. By the conclusion of the previous paragraph, $U_{[i,j]}$ is nilpotent if $i = j$. Choose $i, j \in [1, d]$ such that $i < j$. Let $A = U_{[i,j-1]}$ and $B = U_{[i+1,j]}$. Then

$$U_{[i,j]} = \langle A, B \rangle = \langle A, U_j \rangle = \langle U_i, B \rangle.$$

By 11.17, $[U_t, U_j] \subset U_{[t+1,j-1]} \subset A$ for every $t \in [i, j-1]$ and $[U_i, U_s] \subset U_{[i+1,s-1]} \subset B$ for every $s \in [i+1, j]$. Thus U_j normalizes A and U_i normalizes B. Therefore both A and B are normal subgroups of $U_{[i,j]}$. By induction, A and B are nilpotent. By 11.18 (iii), therefore, $U_{[i,j]}$ is nilpotent. $\square$

The following result will be needed in the proof of 12.20 (see 11.21 as well as § 2 of Chapter 4 in [1]).

Lemma 11.20. *Let Δ be a Moufang building, let $G^\dagger$ denote the subgroup of $\text{Aut}^\circ(\Delta)$ generated by all the root groups of Δ as in 11.12 and suppose that $G^\dagger$ is perfect. Then $G^\dagger$ is a simple group.*

Proof. Let Π denote the type of Δ, let $[m_{ij}]$ denote the corresponding Coxeter matrix, and let I denote the vertex index set of Π. Let M be a normal subgroup of $G^\dagger$. Choose $c \in \Delta$ and let B denote the stabilizer of c in $G^\dagger$. Since M is normal in $G^\dagger$, the product BM is a subgroup of $G^\dagger$. By 11.16, there exists a subset J of I such that $c^{BM} = c^M$ is the unique J-residue of Δ containing c. We denote this residue by R. By 11.12, $G^\dagger$ acts transitively on Δ. Therefore $G^\dagger$ acts transitively on the set of all J-residues of Δ. Since M is normal in $G^\dagger$ and maps R to itself, it follows that M acts trivially on the set of all J-residues of Δ. If $J = \emptyset$, this means that M acts trivially on the set of chambers of Δ, i.e. $M = 1$. We can assume, therefore, that $J \neq \emptyset$.

Suppose that $J \neq I$. Since Π is irreducible, there exist $i, j \in I$ such that $i \notin J, j \in J$ and $m_{ij} > 2$. Since $c^M = R$, we can choose $g \in M$ mapping c to a chamber x which is j-adjacent to c. Choose a chamber u which is i-adjacent to c and let $v = u^g$. Then (u, c, x, v) is a gallery of type iji. Since $m_{ij} > 2$, the word iji is reduced and hence the gallery (u, c, x, v) is minimal by 7.7 (ii). Let S denote the unique J-residue of Δ which contains u. Since M acts trivially on the set of all J-galleries, not just $u \in S$ but also $v = u^g \in S^g = S$. By 7.21, every minimal gallery from u to v must be a J-gallery. Hence $iji \in M_J$. This contradicts the choice of i. With this contradiction, we conclude that $J = I$ and hence $R = \Delta$. Therefore M acts transitively on Δ.

For each $x \in \Delta$, let U_x^+ denote the subgroup of $G^\dagger$ generated by the root groups U_α for all roots α of Δ containing x as in 11.11 (see 11.11 (iii)). Since M is normal in $G^\dagger$, the product MU_c^+ is a subgroup of $G^\dagger$. Since M acts transitively on Δ, this subgroup contains U_x^+ for all $x \in \Delta$. Thus $MU_c^+ = G^\dagger$. Therefore

$$G^\dagger/M = MU_c^\dagger/M \cong U_c^+/U_c^+ \cap M.$$

By 11.18 (ii) and 11.19, $U_c^+/U_c^+ \cap M$ is nilpotent. Therefore $G^\dagger/M$ is nilpotent. Since $G^\dagger$ is perfect, also $G^\dagger/M$ is perfect. By 11.18 (i), therefore, $G^\dagger = M$. We conclude that $G^\dagger$ is simple. $\square$

11.21. It follows from the classification of Moufang buildings that the subgroup $G^\dagger$ is indeed perfect (and hence simple) except in three small cases. This is shown in (37.3) of [20] in the rank-two case (where the three exceptions occur) and in 12.20 for Moufang buildings of rank greater than two.

We now introduce the map μ_Σ. This map plays a central role in the study of Moufang buildings.

Proposition 11.22. *Let Δ be a Moufang building, let Σ be an apartment of Δ, let α be a root of Σ and let $-\alpha$ denote the root of Σ which is opposite α. Then for each $g \in U_\alpha^*$, there exists a unique element $\mu_\Sigma(g)$ in*

$$U_{-\alpha}^* g U_{-\alpha}^*$$

which maps Σ to itself and induces the reflection $\mathrm{refl}_\Sigma(\alpha)$ defined in 3.13 on Σ.

In particular,

(i) *the element $\mu_\Sigma(g)$ interchanges α and $-\alpha$;*

(ii) *for each panel P such that $|\alpha \cap P| = 1$, $\mu_\Sigma(g)$ is the unique element in $U^*_{-\alpha} g U^*_{-\alpha}$ which interchanges the two chambers in $P \cap \Sigma$.*

Proof. Let P be a panel of Δ such that $|\alpha \cap P| = 1$. Let x denote the unique chamber in $\alpha \cap P$, let y denote the unique chamber in $-\alpha \cap P$, let $x' = \mathrm{op}_\Sigma x$ and let $y' = \mathrm{op}_\Sigma y$. By 5.11, there is a panel Q containing x' and y'. By 5.2, $x' \in -\alpha$ and $y' \in \alpha$. Let $g \in U^*_\alpha$. By 11.4, U_α acts regularly on $P \backslash \{x\}$, so neither g nor g^{-1} fixes y, and $U_{-\alpha}$ acts regularly on $P \backslash \{y\}$, so there exist unique elements h_1 and h_2 in $U_{-\alpha}$ such that $x^{h_1} = y^{g^{-1}}$ and $y^{gh_2} = x$. Let $\mu_\Sigma(g) = h_1 g h_2$. Then $\mu_\Sigma(g)$ is the unique element in $U^*_{-\alpha} g U^*_{-\alpha}$ which interchanges x and y. Since $h_1, h_2 \in U_{-\alpha}$ fix $x' \in -\alpha$ and $g \in U_\alpha$ fixes $y' \in \alpha$, the element $\mu_\Sigma(g)$ maps Q to itself. Hence the apartment $\Sigma^{\mu_\Sigma(g)}$ contains x, y and $(x')^{\mu_\Sigma(g)} \in Q$. By 9.5, therefore, $\Sigma^{\mu_\Sigma(g)} = \Sigma$. By 3.13, $\mu_\Sigma(g)$ induces the reflection $\mathrm{refl}_\Sigma(\alpha)$ on Σ. If m is any element of $U^*_{-\alpha} g U^*_{-\alpha}$ which maps Σ to itself and induces the reflection $\mathrm{refl}_\Sigma(\alpha)$ on Σ, then m interchanges x and y and hence equals $\mu_\Sigma(g)$. By 3.11, (i) holds. Since P is arbitrary, (ii) holds. $\square$

The map μ_Σ in 11.22 depends on the root α as well as the apartment Σ and ought, properly, to have also α as a subscript. Omitting this subscript should not, however, cause any confusion.

Proposition 11.23. *Let Δ, Σ, α and μ_Σ be as in 11.22. Suppose that h is an automorphism of Δ mapping Σ to itself (setwise). Then $\mu_\Sigma(g^h) = \mu_\Sigma(g)^h$ for all $g \in U^*_\alpha$.*

Proof. Let $\beta = \alpha^h$ and $-\beta = (-\alpha)^h$. By 3.15, β is a root of Σ and $-\beta$ is its opposite. Thus, by 11.1, $U^h_\alpha = U_\beta$ and $U^h_{-\alpha} = U_{-\beta}$. Choose a panel P such that $|\alpha \cap P| = 1$, let x denote the unique chamber in $\alpha \cap P$, and let y denote the unique chamber in $-\alpha \cap P$. Let $g \in U^*_\alpha$. By 11.22 (ii), $\mu_\Sigma(g)$ is the unique element of $U^*_{-\alpha} g U^*_{-\alpha}$ which interchanges x and y. Hence $\mu_\Sigma(g)^h$ is the unique element of

$$U^*_{-\beta} g^h U^*_{-\beta}$$

which interchanges x^h and y^h. Since $g^h \in U^*_\beta$, $x^h \in \beta$, $y^h \in -\beta$ and x^h and y^h are contained in the panel P^h, it follows by 11.22 (ii) again (with β in place of α) that $\mu_\Sigma(g)^h = \mu_\Sigma(g^h)$. $\square$

Proposition 11.24. *Let Δ, Σ, α and μ_Σ be as in 11.22. Let κ_Σ and λ_Σ be the maps from U_α^* to $U_{-\alpha}^*$ such that $\mu_\Sigma(g) = \kappa_\Sigma(g) g \lambda_\Sigma(g)$ for all $g \in U_\alpha^*$. Then*

$$\mu_\Sigma(\kappa_\Sigma(g)) = \mu_\Sigma(\lambda_\Sigma(g)) = \mu_\Sigma(g)$$

for all $g \in U_\alpha^*$.

Proof. Let $g \in U_\alpha^*$ and let $\mu = \mu_\Sigma$, $\kappa = \kappa_\Sigma$ and $\lambda = \lambda_\Sigma$. By 11.22 (i), $\kappa(g)^{\mu(g)}$ and $\lambda(g)^{\mu(g)^{-1}}$ both lie in U_α^*, so

$$\mu(g) = \lambda(g)^{\mu(g)^{-1}} \kappa(g) g \in U_\alpha^* \kappa(g) U_\alpha^*$$

and

$$\mu(g) = g \lambda(g) \kappa(g)^{\mu(g)} \in U_\alpha^* \lambda(g) U_\alpha^*.$$

By 11.22, $\mu(\kappa(g))$ is the unique element of $U_\alpha^* \kappa(g) U_\alpha^*$ which maps Σ to itself and acts like $\mathrm{refl}_\Sigma(\alpha) = \mathrm{refl}_\Sigma(-\alpha)$ on Σ. Hence $\mu(\kappa(g)) = \mu(g)$. Similarly, $\mu(\lambda(g)) = \mu(g)$. $\qquad\square$

For the rest of this chapter, we will examine the following set-up.

Notation 11.25. Let Δ be a Moufang building, let Π denote the type of Δ, let $[m_{ij}]$ denote the corresponding Coxeter matrix, and let I denote the index set of Δ (which is also the vertex set of Π). Let Σ be an apartment of Δ and let c be a chamber of Σ. For each $i \in I$, let c_i denote the unique chamber of Σ which is i-adjacent to c, let α_i denote the root $\Sigma_{(c \backslash c_i)}$ of Σ as defined in 3.15 and let U_i denote the root group U_{α_i}.

Notation 11.26. Let Δ, Σ, c, c_i, α_i, m_{ij}, etc., be as in 11.25. Let $\{i, j\}$ be a two-element subset of I, let $n = m_{ij}$ and let R be the unique residue of Δ of type $\{i, j\}$ containing c. Let $t \mapsto x_t$ be the unique map from the integers $\mathbb{Z}$ to $\Sigma \cap R$ such that $x_n = c$, $x_{n+1} = c_i$, and for all $t \in \mathbb{Z}$, x_t is adjacent to x_{t-1} and distinct from x_{t-2}. (Thus $x_{n-1} = c_j$, $x_0 = \mathrm{op}_{\Sigma \cap R} c$ and $x_s = x_t$ whenever $s \equiv t \pmod{2n}$.) By 8.13 (ii), there is a unique root ω_t of Σ such that

$$\omega_t \cap R = \{x_t, x_{t+1}, \ldots, x_{t+n-1}\}$$

for each $t \in \mathbb{Z}$. Then $\omega_1 \cap R = \alpha_i \cap R$ and $\omega_n \cap R = \alpha_j \cap R$, so $\omega_1 = \alpha_i$ and $\omega_n = \alpha_j$, and

$$\omega_1 \cap R, \ldots, \omega_n \cap R$$

are all the roots of $\Sigma \cap R$ containing c. By 8.13 (i), therefore, $\omega_1, \ldots, \omega_n$ are all the roots of Σ which contain c but not all of $\Sigma \cap R$. We will call $\omega_1, \ldots, \omega_n$ the *canonical ordering of these roots from α_i to α_j*.

Proposition 11.27. *Let* Δ, Σ, c, c_i, α_i, m_{ij}, *etc., be as in 11.25, let* $\{i, j\}$ *be a two-element subset of* I, *let* $n = m_{ij}$, R, $t \mapsto x_t$ *and* $t \mapsto \omega_t$ *be as in 11.26 and let* $U_t = U_{\omega_t}$ *for all* $t \in \mathbb{Z}$. *Then the following hold.*

(i) $\langle U_t, U_{t+1}, \ldots, U_{t+n-1} \rangle$ *acts faithfully on* R *for all* t.

(ii) *Suppose that* $n \geqslant 3$ *and that*

$$[e_t, e_{t+n-1}^{-1}] = e_{t+1} \cdots e_{t+n-2}$$

for some t, *where* $e_s \in U_s$ *for all* $s \in [t, t + n - 1]$ *and both* e_t *and* e_{t+n-1} *are non-trivial. Then* $e_{t+1} = e_{t+n-1}^{\mu_\Sigma(e_t)}$ *(so* e_{t+1} *is also non-trivial),* $\lambda_\Sigma(e_t) \in U_{t+n}^*$ *and*

$$[e_{t+1}, \lambda_\Sigma(e_t)^{-1}] = e_{t+2} \cdots e_{t+n-1},$$

where μ_Σ *and* λ_Σ *are as in 11.22 and 11.24.*

Proof. Choose t, let $X = \{\omega_t, \ldots, \omega_{t+n-1}\}$ and let $z = x_{t+n-1}$. Thus X is the set of all roots of Σ which contain z but not all of $\Sigma \cap R$. Let

$$M = \langle U_t, U_{t+1}, \ldots, U_{t+n-1} \rangle$$

and let g be an element of M which acts trivially on R. Choose $s \in [t, t+n-1]$, let $\omega = \omega_s$, let $u = x_s$ and let $v = x_{s-1}$. By 3.15 and 8.9,

$$\omega = \{y \in \Sigma \mid \mathrm{dist}(y, u) < \mathrm{dist}(y, v)\}.$$

Since $z \in \omega$, we can thus choose a minimal gallery γ from v to z which passes through u. Choose $k \in I \backslash \{i, j\}$, let w be the unique chamber of Σ which is k-adjacent to z, and let P denote the panel of Δ containing z and w. By 7.26, $P \cap R = \{z\}$. By 8.25, $\mathrm{proj}_P v = z$. By 8.22, therefore, (γ, w) is a minimal gallery. Thus $\mathrm{dist}(w, u) < \mathrm{dist}(w, v)$ and hence $w \in \omega$, so $|P \cap \omega| = 2$. By 11.1, therefore, U_ω acts trivially on P. Since $k \in I \backslash \{i, j\}$ and $s \in [t, t + n - 1]$ are arbitrary, we conclude that M acts trivially on the set of chambers adjacent to z and not in R. Since $g \in M$ acts trivially on R, it therefore acts trivially on the set of all chambers adjacent to z. No root in X contains x_{t-1} $(= \mathrm{op}_{\Sigma \cap R} z)$. Thus, by 5.2, every root in X contains $\mathrm{op}_\Sigma x_{t-1}$. Hence M fixes $\mathrm{op}_\Sigma x_{t-1}$. Since g acts trivially on R, it fixes x_{t-1}. By 9.2, it follows that g fixes Σ. By 9.7, we conclude that $g = 1$. Thus (i) holds.

By 11.10, we can apply the maps $\mu_{\Sigma \cap R}$ and $\lambda_{\Sigma \cap R}$ to elements of U_t^*. By 4.10 and 11.22, $\mu_{\Sigma \cap R}(g)$ restricted to R equals $\mu_\Sigma(g)$ and thus $\lambda_{\Sigma \cap R}(g) = \lambda_\Sigma(g)$

for all $g \in U_t^*$. By (6.4) of [20], therefore, the elements e_{t+1} and $e_{t+n-1}^{\mu_\Sigma(e_t)}$ agree on the residue R as do the elements $[e_{t+1}, \lambda_\Sigma(e_t)^{-1}]$ and $e_{t+2} \cdots e_{t+n-1}$. Since

$$e_{t+n-1}^{\mu_\Sigma(e_t)} \in U_{t+1}^* \quad \text{and} \quad \lambda_\Sigma(e_t) \in U_{t+n}^*,$$

we conclude that $e_{t+1} = e_{t+n-1}^{\mu_\Sigma(e_t)}$ and

$$[e_{t+1}, \lambda_\Sigma(e_t)^{-1}] = e_{t+2} \cdots e_{t+n-1}$$

by (i) with $t + 1$ in place of t. $\qquad\qquad\qquad\qquad\qquad\qquad\qquad\qquad\qquad\qquad\square$

Proposition 11.28. *Let Δ, Σ, c, etc., be as in 11.25, let $\{i, j\}$ be a two-element subset of I, let $n = m_{ij}$, R, $t \mapsto x_t$ and $t \mapsto \omega_t$ be as in 11.26 (so $\omega_1 = \alpha_i$ and $\omega_n = \alpha_j$), and let $U_{\Sigma,c}^{i,j}$ denote the subgroup*

$$\langle U_{\omega_1}, \ldots, U_{\omega_n} \rangle.$$

Let $m_k \in \mu_\Sigma(U_{\alpha_k}^*)$ for $k = i$ and j, where μ_Σ is as in 11.22, and for each $p \geqslant 1$, let $m_i^{(p)}$ denote the product $m_i m_j m_i \cdots$ in $\mathrm{Aut}^\circ(\Delta)$ having p factors, and let $m_j^{(p)}$ denote the product $m_j m_i m_j \cdots$ having p factors. Then the following hold.

(i) *Every element of $U_{\Sigma,c}^{i,j}$ has a unique representation as a product $g_1 \cdots g_n$, where $g_t \in U_{\omega_t}$ for all $t \in [1, n]$.*

(ii) $m_i^{(n)} = m_j^{(n)}$.

(iii) $[U_i, U_j] = [m_i, U_j] = [U_i, m_j] = 1$ *if $n = 2$.*

Proof. Suppose first that $n = 2$, so

$$U_{\Sigma,c}^{i,j} = \langle U_{\alpha_i}, U_{\alpha_j} \rangle.$$

Let P_k denote the panel containing c and c_k for $k = i$ and j. Since c and c_j both lie in α_i, the root group U_{α_i} acts trivially on P_j. Similarly, the root group U_{α_j} acts trivially on P_i. Since U_{α_k} maps P_k to itself for $k = i$ and j, it follows that the commutator subgroup $[U_{\alpha_i}, U_{\alpha_j}]$ acts trivially on $P_i \cup P_j$. Let $x \in R$. By 7.15 and 7.17, $x \in P_i \cup P_j$ or x is adjacent to a unique chamber u in P_i and a unique chamber v in P_j and c and x are the only two chambers of R adjacent to both u and v. Hence $[U_{\alpha_i}, U_{\alpha_j}]$ fixes x. Since x is arbitrary, $[U_{\alpha_i}, U_{\alpha_j}]$ acts trivially on R. Therefore $[U_{\alpha_i}, U_{\alpha_j}] = 1$ by 11.27 (i). In particular, (i) holds. In fact, our argument shows that $[U_{\beta_1}, U_{\beta_2}] = 1$ whenever $\beta_1 \cap R$ and $\beta_2 \cap R$ are any two distinct but not opposite roots of $\Sigma \cap R$. Thus $[U_{\epsilon_i \alpha_i}, U_{\epsilon_j \alpha_j}] = 1$ for all choices of $\epsilon_i = \pm$ and $\epsilon_j = \pm$. By 11.22, $m_k \in \langle U_{\alpha_k}, U_{-\alpha_k} \rangle$ for $k = i$ and j. Therefore (ii) (i.e. $m_i m_j = m_j m_i$) and (iii) hold.

Now suppose that $n \geqslant 3$. By 11.11 (i) and 11.27 (i), (i) holds. Let $U_t = U_{\omega_t}$ for all $t \in \mathbb{Z}$ as in 11.27. Since $m_k \in \mu_\Sigma(U_{\alpha_k}^*)$ for $k = i$ and j, there exist

$$e_1 \in U_1^* = U_{\alpha_i}^* \quad \text{and} \quad e_n \in U_n^* = U_{\alpha_j}^*$$

such that

$$m_i = \mu_\Sigma(e_1) \quad \text{and} \quad m_j = \mu_\Sigma(e_n).$$

We have $\omega_t = \Sigma_{(x_{t+n-1} \setminus x_{t+n})}$ for all t. By 11.17 and 11.27 (i), therefore, there exist $e_s \in U_s$ for all $s \in [2, n-1]$ such that

$$[e_1, e_n^{-1}] = e_2 \cdots e_{n-1}.$$

By repeated application of 11.27 (ii), $e_s \neq 1$ for all $s \in [2, n-1]$ and there exist $e_t \in U_t^*$ for all $t > n$ such that $e_{t+n} = \lambda_\Sigma(e_t)$,

$$[e_t, e_{t+n-1}^{-1}] = e_{t+1} \cdots e_{t+n-2}$$

and $e_{t+1} = e_{t+n-1}^{\mu_\Sigma(e_t)}$ for all $t \geqslant 1$. Let $g_t = \mu_\Sigma(e_t)$ for all $t \geqslant 1$. Then $g_1 = m_i$ and $g_n = m_j$. By 11.24, $g_t = g_{t+kn}$ for all $t, k \geqslant 1$. By 11.23, therefore,

$$\begin{aligned}
g_{t+1} &= \mu_\Sigma(e_{t+1}) \\
&= \mu_\Sigma(e_{t+n-1}^{\mu_\Sigma(e_t)}) \\
&= g_{t+n-1}^{g_t} = g_{t-1}^{g_t}
\end{aligned}$$

for all $t \geqslant 2$ and hence

$$g_1 g_2 = g_2 g_3 = g_3 g_4 = \cdots.$$

Therefore

$$\begin{aligned}
m_i^{(n)} &= g_1 g_n g_1 \cdots g_1 g_n \\
&= g_1 \cdot g_n g_{n+1} \cdot g_n g_{n+1} \cdots g_n g_{n+1} \cdot g_n \\
&= g_1 \cdot g_2 g_3 \cdot g_4 g_5 \cdots g_{n-2} g_{n-1} \cdot g_n \\
&= g_1 g_2 \cdot g_3 g_4 \cdots g_{n-1} g_n \\
&= g_n g_{n+1} \cdot g_n g_{n+1} \cdots g_n g_{n+1} \\
&= g_n g_1 \cdot g_n g_1 \cdots g_n g_1 \\
&= m_j^{(n)}
\end{aligned}$$

if n is even, and

$$
\begin{aligned}
m_i^{(n)} &= g_1 g_n g_1 \cdots g_n g_1 \\
&= g_1 \cdot g_n g_{n+1} \cdot g_n g_{n+1} \cdots g_n g_{n+1} \\
&= g_1 \cdot g_2 g_3 \cdot g_4 g_5 \cdots g_{n-1} g_n \\
&= g_1 g_2 \cdot g_3 g_4 \cdots g_{n-2} g_{n-1} \cdot g_n \\
&= g_n g_{n+1} \cdot g_n g_{n+1} \cdots g_n g_{n+1} \cdot g_n \\
&= g_n g_1 \cdot g_n g_1 \cdots g_n g_1 \cdot g_n \\
&= m_j^{(n)}
\end{aligned}
$$

if n is odd. Thus (ii) holds. $\square$

In the next sequence of results 11.30–11.36, we work with the following subgroups.

Notation 11.29. Let Δ, Σ, I, c, etc., be as in 11.25. Let H denote the pointwise stabilizer of Σ in $\mathrm{Aut}^\circ(\Delta)$. For each $i \in I$, let $-\alpha_i$ denote the root of Σ opposite α_i, let U_{-i} denote the root group $U_{-\alpha_i}$, let U_c^+ be as in 11.11 and let $U_c^{(i)}$ denote the subgroup of U_c^+ generated by the root groups U_α for all roots α of Σ containing c except α_i. Let

$$
H_i = \langle \mu_\Sigma(a)\mu_\Sigma(b) \mid a, b \in U_i^* \rangle
$$

for all $i \in I$, where μ_Σ is as in 11.22. Let $G^\dagger$ be as in 11.12, let

$$
H^\dagger = \langle H_i \mid i \in I \rangle
$$

(so $H^\dagger \subset H \cap G^\dagger$), and let $B^\dagger = \langle H^\dagger, U_c^+ \rangle$. Choose $m_i \in \mu_\Sigma(U_i^*)$ for all $i \in I$ and let

$$
M = \langle m_i \mid i \in I \rangle.
$$

Proposition 11.30. *Let Δ, Σ, c, M, $H^\dagger$, etc., be as in 11.29. Then M normalizes $H^\dagger$ and acts transitively on Σ and $H^\dagger$ is the stabilizer of c in $MH^\dagger$.*

Proof. Let $i, j \in I$ and let $h \in H_j$. Then h^{-1} normalizes U_i and hence by 11.23, $m_i^{h^{-1}} \in \mu_\Sigma(U_i^*)$. Thus $m_i^{-1} \cdot m_i^{h^{-1}} = m_i^{-2} \cdot m_i m_i^{h^{-1}} \in H_i$, so

$$
h^{m_i} = m_i^{-1} \cdot m_i^{h^{-1}} \cdot h \in H_i H_j.
$$

Since i, j and h are arbitrary, it follows that $H^\dagger$ is normalized by M. Therefore $MH^\dagger$ is a subgroup.

Let X denote the stabilizer of c in $MH^\dagger$. By 11.22 (i), $c^{m_i} = c_i$ for all $i \in I$. Since Σ is connected, it follows that M acts transitively on Σ. Therefore

$$|MH^\dagger/X| = |\Sigma|.$$

The image of m_i^2 in $MH^\dagger/H^\dagger$ is trivial for each $i \in I$. Hence, by 11.28 (ii), the elements of the generating set $\{m_i H^\dagger \mid i \in I\}$ of $MH^\dagger/H^\dagger$ satisfy all the relations defining the Weyl group of Δ. Therefore

$$|MH^\dagger/H^\dagger| \leqslant |\Sigma|.$$

Since $H^\dagger \subset X$, we conclude that $H^\dagger = X$. $\qquad\square$

Proposition 11.31. *Let Δ, Σ, m_i, $H^\dagger$, etc., be as in 11.29. Then*

$$H^\dagger \langle U_{-i}, U_i \rangle = H^\dagger U_{-i} m_i \cup H^\dagger U_{-i} U_i$$

for all $i \in I$.

Proof. Choose $i \in I$, let $K = H^\dagger U_{-i}$, let $L = H^\dagger \langle U_{-i}, U_i \rangle$, and let $Q = Km_i \cup KU_i$. The subgroup $H^\dagger$ normalizes U_{-i} and U_i. Thus K and L are subgroups and Q is a union of right cosets of K in L. To show $Q = L$, it will suffice to show that $QL \subset Q$. By 11.22 (i), $U_{-i} = U_i^{m_i}$ and hence $L = H^\dagger \langle m_i, U_i \rangle$. Also, $m_i^{-1} \in m_i H_i \subset m_i H^\dagger$. It will thus suffice, in fact, to show that $QX \subset Q$ for $X = H^\dagger$, U_i and m_i.

By 11.30, m_i normalizes $H^\dagger$, so $Km_i \cdot H^\dagger \subset Km_i$. Since $H^\dagger$ normalizes U_i, we have $KU_i \cdot H^\dagger \subset KU_i$. Thus $QH^\dagger \subset Q$. If $g \in U_i$, then

$$m_i g = g^{m_i^{-1}} m_i \in U_{-i} m_i,$$

so $Km_i g \subset KU_{-i} m_i = Km_i$. It follows that $Km_i \cdot U_i \subset Km_i$ and hence $QU_i \subset Q$.

Again let $g \in U_i^*$. By 11.22, $\mu_\Sigma(g) = a^{-1} g b^{-1}$ for some $a, b \in U_{-i}^*$ and $b^{m_i} \in U_i^*$. Moreover, $\mu_\Sigma(g) m_i \in H_i \subset K$. Thus $a\mu_\Sigma(g) m_i \in K$ and hence

$$Kgm_i = Ka\mu_\Sigma(g) bm_i = Ka\mu_\Sigma(g) m_i \cdot b^{m_i} = Kb^{m_i} \subset KU_i^*.$$

Therefore $KU_i^* \cdot m_i \subset KU_i^*$. Since $m_i^2 \in H_i \subset K$, we have $Km_i \cdot m_i = K$. Thus $Qm_i \subset Q$. $\qquad\square$

Lemma 11.32. *Let Δ, Σ, c, $U_c^{(i)}$, U_{-i}, etc., be as in 11.29. Then $U_c^{(i)}$ is normalized by $\langle U_i, U_{-i} \rangle$ for each $i \in I$.*

Proof. Let $d = \text{diam } \Delta$ and choose $i \in I$. By 3.6 and 8.9, we can choose a minimal gallery

$$\gamma = (x_0, x_1, \ldots, x_d)$$

in Σ from c to $\text{op}_\Sigma c$ such that $x_1 = c_i$. Let $x_{d+1} = \text{op}_\Sigma c_i$. Thus x_{d+1} is adjacent to x_d by 5.11, $x_{d+1} \in \alpha_i$ by 5.2 since $c_i \notin \alpha_i$ (by 11.25), and $x_d \in -\alpha_i$ by 5.2 since $x_0 \in \alpha_i$. Let β_i denote the root $\Sigma_{(x_{i-1} \backslash x_i)}$ of Σ for all $i \in [1, d+1]$. By 3.20 and 5.2, $\beta_1, \ldots, \beta_d$ are all the roots of Σ containing c. By 3.15, $\alpha_i = \beta_1$ and $-\alpha_i = \beta_{d+1}$. Therefore

$$U_c^{(i)} = \langle U_{\beta_2}, U_{\beta_3}, \ldots, U_{\beta_d} \rangle$$

and, by 11.17,

$$[U_i, U_{\beta_t}] = [U_{\beta_1}, U_{\beta_t}] \subset \langle U_{\beta_2}, \cdots, U_{\beta_{t-1}} \rangle \subset U_c^{(i)}$$

and

$$[U_{\beta_t}, U_{-i}] = [U_{\beta_t}, U_{\beta_{d+1}}] \subset \langle U_{\beta_{t+1}}, \cdots, U_{\beta_d} \rangle \subset U_c^{(i)}$$

for all $t \in [2, d]$. Hence both U_i and U_{-i} normalize $U_c^{(i)}$.   □

Proposition 11.33. *Let $\Delta, \Sigma, c, M, B^\dagger$, etc., be as in 11.29. Then*

$$B^\dagger w B^\dagger m_i \subset B^\dagger w m_i B^\dagger \cup B^\dagger w B^\dagger$$

for each $w \in M$ and each $i \in I$.

Proof. Let $w \in M$ and $i \in I$. The chamber c^w lies either in α_i or in $-\alpha_i$. Thus either $\alpha_i^{w^{-1}}$ or $-\alpha_i^{w^{-1}}$ contains the chamber c. We have

$$U_i^{w^{-1}} \subset U_c^+ \text{ in the first case } \quad \text{and} \quad U_{-i}^{w^{-1}} \subset U_c^+ \text{ in the second.}$$

Since $U_{-i}^{m_i^{-1}} = U_i$, we can thus choose $z \in \{w, wm_i\}$ such that $U_{-i}^{z^{-1}} \subset U_c^+$. With this choice of z, we have

$$z U_{-i} \subset U_c^+ z \subset B^\dagger z.$$

By 11.31, we have

$$H^\dagger \langle U_{-i}, U_i \rangle = H^\dagger U_{-i} m_i \cup H^\dagger U_{-i} U_i,$$

and by 11.30, z normalizes $H^\dagger$. Therefore

$$z H^\dagger \langle U_{-i}, U_i \rangle = z(H^\dagger U_{-i} m_i \cup H^\dagger U_{-i} U_i)$$
$$\subset B^\dagger z m_i \cup B^\dagger z U_i$$

by the choice of z. By 11.32, we have

$$\langle U_{-i}, B^{\dagger}\rangle = H^{\dagger}\langle U_{-i}, U_i\rangle U_c^{(i)}$$

since $H^{\dagger}$ normalizes U_{-i} and U_c^+. Thus

$$\begin{aligned}
B^{\dagger}z \cdot \langle m_i\rangle B^{\dagger}m_i &\subset B^{\dagger}z \cdot \langle U_{-i}, B^{\dagger}\rangle \\
&= B^{\dagger}z \cdot H^{\dagger}\langle U_{-i}, U_i\rangle U_c^{(i)} \\
&\subset (B^{\dagger}zm_i \cup B^{\dagger}zU_i)U_c^{(i)} \\
&\subset B^{\dagger}zm_i B^{\dagger} \cup B^{\dagger}zB^{\dagger}.
\end{aligned}$$

Since $m_i^2 \in H_i \subset B^{\dagger}$, we have $B^{\dagger}wm_i^2 B^{\dagger} = B^{\dagger}wB^{\dagger}$. Therefore

$$\begin{aligned}
B^{\dagger}wB^{\dagger}m_i &\subset B^{\dagger}z \cdot \langle m_i\rangle B^{\dagger}m_i \\
&\subset B^{\dagger}zm_i B^{\dagger} \cup B^{\dagger}zB^{\dagger} \\
&= B^{\dagger}wm_i B^{\dagger} \cup B^{\dagger}wB^{\dagger}
\end{aligned}$$

since $w \in z\langle m_i\rangle$ and $z = w$ or wm_i.   □

Proposition 11.34. *Let Δ, Σ, M, $G^{\dagger}$, $B^{\dagger}$, etc., be as in 11.29. Then $G^{\dagger} = B^{\dagger}MB^{\dagger}$.*

Proof. Let $D = B^{\dagger}MB^{\dagger}$ and let $E = \langle M, B^{\dagger}\rangle$. Then

$$DB^{\dagger} \subset D \subset E$$

and, by 11.33, $Dm_i \subset D$ for all $i \in I$. Since $m_i^2 \in B^{\dagger}$ for all $i \in I$, it follows that $DE \subset D$ and hence $D = E$. In particular, D is a subgroup of $G^{\dagger}$. By 11.30, M acts transitively on Σ. By 8.6 and 11.11 (ii), every chamber of Δ is mapped to a chamber of Σ by some element of U_c^+. Therefore D acts transitively on Δ. Since $U_c^{\dagger} \subset B^{\dagger}$, it follows that $U_x^+ \subset D$ for all $x \in \Delta$. Thus D contains all the roots groups of Δ.   □

Theorem 11.35. *Let Δ, Σ, c, M, $G^{\dagger}$, $B^{\dagger}$, $H^{\dagger}$, etc., be as in 11.29. Then $B^{\dagger}$ is the stabilizer of the chamber c in $G^{\dagger}$, $H^{\dagger}$ is the pointwise stabilizer of Σ in $G^{\dagger}$, and $MH^{\dagger}$ is the setwise stabilizer of Σ in $G^{\dagger}$.*

Proof. By 11.34, $G^{\dagger} = B^{\dagger}MB^{\dagger}$. Let $a, b \in B^{\dagger}$ and $w \in M$ and suppose that awb fixes c. Then w fixes c. By 11.30, therefore, $w \in H^{\dagger} \subset B^{\dagger}$. Therefore $B^{\dagger}$ is the stabilizer of c in $G^{\dagger}$. By 11.11 (ii), $H^{\dagger}$ is the stabilizer of Σ in $B^{\dagger} = H^{\dagger}U_c^+$. Thus $H^{\dagger}$ is the pointwise stabilizer of Σ in $G^{\dagger}$. By 11.30, M acts transitively on Σ and normalizes $H^{\dagger}$. It follows that the product $MH^{\dagger}$ is the setwise stabilizer of Σ in $G^{\dagger}$.   □

If Δ, $B^\dagger$, M and $H^\dagger$ are as in 11.29, then by 11.14 and 11.35, $(B^\dagger, MH^\dagger)$ is a Tits system for $G^\dagger$ as defined in 11.15. Note that this observation also follows directly from 11.33, 11.34 and 11.35.

Theorem 11.36. *Let Δ, Σ, c, $G^\dagger$, H, $H^\dagger$, etc., be as in 11.29. Then $G^\dagger$ is a normal subgroup of $\mathrm{Aut}(\Delta)$, $H^\dagger$ is a normal subgroup of H and*

$$\mathrm{Aut}^\circ(\Delta)/G^\dagger \cong H/H^\dagger.$$

(See also 7.23.)

Proof. By 8.10, each element of $\mathrm{Aut}(\Delta)$ maps apartments to apartments. Hence, by 3.15, each element of $\mathrm{Aut}(\Delta)$ maps roots to roots. It follows that $G^\dagger$ is normal in $\mathrm{Aut}(\Delta)$. By 11.12, $\mathrm{Aut}^\circ(\Delta) = HG^\dagger$. Therefore

$$\mathrm{Aut}^\circ(\Delta)/G^\dagger = HG^\dagger/G^\dagger \cong H/H \cap G^\dagger.$$

By 11.35, $H \cap G^\dagger = H^\dagger$. $\square$

We now introduce a set which plays a central role in the construction of Moufang buildings given in [9] and in Chapter 40 of [20]. Our goal is to prove 11.43.

Definition 11.37. Let Δ, Σ, Π, U_i, etc., be as in 11.25 and let M_I^{red} denote the set of words in M_I which are reduced (with respect to Π) including the empty word. For each non-empty word $f = i_1 \cdots i_k$ in M_I^{red}, let S_f denote the set of sequences $(a_1, \ldots, a_k)$, where $a_j \in U_{i_j}$ for all $j \in [1, k]$. Let $S_\emptyset$ consist of just the empty sequence and let S_Δ denote the disjoint union of the sets S_f for all $f \in M_I^{\mathrm{red}}$. The elements of S_f will be called the elements of S_Δ *of type* f. Let 1_f denote the unique element of S_f all of whose entries are the identity for each $f \in M_I^{\mathrm{red}}$ (so $1_\emptyset$ is the empty sequence) and let

$$S_\Delta^\# = \{1_f \mid f \in M_I^{\mathrm{red}}\}.$$

Proposition 11.38. *Let Δ, Σ, c, S_Δ, $S_\Delta^\#$, etc., be as in 11.37 and let $m_i \in \mu_\Sigma(U_i^*)$ for each $i \in I$, where μ_Σ is as in 11.22. For each non-empty $f = i_1 \cdots i_k \in M_I^{\mathrm{red}}$, each $a = (a_1, \ldots, a_k) \in S_f$ and each $t \in [1, k]$, let*

$$a^{(t)} = (a_1, \ldots, a_t)$$

(an element in $S_{i_1 \cdots i_t}$), let

$$\phi(a^{(t)}) = m_{i_t} a_t m_{i_{t-1}} a_{t-1} \cdots m_{i_2} a_2 m_{i_1} a_1$$

(an element of $\mathrm{Aut}^\circ(\Delta)$*), let* $x_t = c^{\phi(a^{(t)})}$*, and let*

$$\psi(a) = (x_0, x_1, \ldots, x_k),$$

where $x_0 = c$*. Let* $\psi(\emptyset) = (c)$*. Then we have the following.*

(i) ψ *is a bijection from* S_Δ *to the set of minimal galleries of* Δ *starting at* c *and* ψ *maps elements of* S_Δ *of any given type to galleries of the same type.*

(ii) $\psi(a) \subset \Sigma$ *if and only if* $a \in S_\Delta^\#$.

Proof. Let f be a word in M_I^{red} and let $k = |f|$. By 11.22 (i), $c^{m_i} = c_i$ and hence $c^{m_i u g} \sim_i c^{u g} = c^g$ for all $u \in U_i$, for all $i \in I$ and for all $g \in \mathrm{Aut}^\circ(\Delta)$ (see 11.9). It follows that if $a \in S_f$, then $\psi(a)$ is a gallery of type f beginning at c. To prove that ψ is a bijection from S_f to the set of galleries of type f beginning at c, we proceed by induction with respect to the length k of f. Since $\psi(\emptyset) = (c)$, the claim holds for $k = 0$, i.e. for $f = \emptyset$. Suppose that $k > 0$ and let $f = i_1 \cdots i_{k-1} i_k$. Let $(x_0, \ldots, x_k)$ be a gallery of type f such that $x_0 = c$. By induction, there is a unique element $b \in S_g$ such that $\psi(b) = (x_0, \ldots, x_{k-1})$, where $g = i_1 \cdots i_{k-1}$. Thus

$$x_{k-1} = c^{\phi(b^{(k-1)})}.$$

Since x_k is i_k-adjacent to x_{k-1}, the chamber $x_k^{\phi(b^{(k-1)})^{-1}}$ is i_k-adjacent to c and hence equals $c_k^{a_k} = c^{m_k a_k}$ for a unique element $a_k \in U_k$ by 11.4. Let $a = (b, a_k)$. Then a is the unique element of S_f which ψ maps to $(x_0, \ldots, x_k)$. Thus (i) holds.

Since the element m_i maps Σ to itself for all $i \in I$, $\psi(a) \subset \Sigma$ for all $a \in S_\Delta^\#$. By 2.5, Σ contains a unique gallery starting at c of any given type. Hence (i) implies (ii). $\qquad\qquad\square$

Proposition 11.39. *Let* Δ*,* Σ*,* c*,* S_f*,* 1_f*, etc., be as in 11.37 and let* $m_i \in \mu_\Sigma(U_i^*)$*, where* μ_Σ *is as in 11.22, and let* ψ *and* ϕ *be as in 11.38. Let* (i, j) *be an ordered pair of distinct elements of* I*. Then there is a unique bijection* ρ_{ij} *from* $S_{p(i,j)}$ *to* $S_{p(j,i)}$ *such that for every* $a \in S_{p(i,j)}$*, the elements* a *and* $\rho_{ij}(a)$ *have the same image under* ϕ*. The map* ρ_{ij} *sends* $1_{p(i,j)}$ *to* $1_{p(j,i)}$ *and for every* $a \in S_{p(i,j)}$*,* $\rho_{ij}(a)$ *is the unique element of* $S_{p(j,i)}$ *whose image under* ψ *is a gallery having the same last chamber as the gallery* $\psi(a)$*. If* $m_{ij} = 2$*, then* $\rho_{ij}(a_1, a_2) = (a_2, a_1)$ *for all* $(a_1, a_2) \in S_{p(i,j)} = S_{ij}$*.*

Proof. Let $n = m_{ij}$ and $\omega_1, \ldots, \omega_n$ be as in 11.26 and let $m_i^{(p)}$ and $m_j^{(p)}$ for $p \geqslant 1$ and $U_{\Sigma,c}^{i,j}$ be as defined in 11.28. Then

$$\phi(a) = m_j a_n m_i a_{n-1} m_j a_{n-2} \cdots$$
$$= m_j^{(n)} a_n^{m_i^{(n-1)}} a_{n-1}^{m_j^{(n-2)}} a_{n-2}^{m_i^{(n-3)}} \cdots$$

for all $a = (a_1, \ldots, a_n) \in S_{p(i,j)}$, and

$$\phi(b) = m_i b_n m_j b_{n-1} m_i b_{n-2} \cdots$$
$$= m_i^{(n)} b_n^{m_j^{(n-1)}} b_{n-1}^{m_i^{(n-2)}} b_{n-2}^{m_j^{(n-3)}} \cdots$$

for all $b = (b_1, \ldots, b_n) \in S_{p(j,i)}$. By 11.28 (ii), $m_i^{(n)} = m_j^{(n)}$. By 11.22 (i), the ordered n-tuple of roots

$$\left(\alpha_j^{m_i^{(n-1)}}, \alpha_i^{m_j^{(n-2)}}, \alpha_j^{m_i^{(n-3)}}, \ldots \right)$$

equals either $(\omega_1, \ldots, \omega_n)$ or $(\omega_n, \ldots, \omega_1)$ (depending on the parity of n) as does the ordered n-tuple

$$\left(\alpha_i^{m_j^{(n-1)}}, \alpha_j^{m_i^{(n-2)}}, \alpha_i^{m_j^{(n-3)}}, \ldots \right).$$

Thus, by 11.28 (i), as stated or with i and j interchanged, the maps

$$(a_1, \ldots, a_n) \mapsto a_n^{m_i^{(n-1)}} a_{n-1}^{m_j^{(n-2)}} a_{n-2}^{m_i^{(n-3)}} \cdots$$

and

$$(b_1, \ldots, b_n) \mapsto b_n^{m_j^{(n-1)}} b_{n-1}^{m_i^{(n-2)}} b_{n-2}^{m_j^{(n-3)}} \cdots$$

are bijections from $S_{p(i,j)}$ to $U_{\Sigma,c}^{i,j}$ and from $S_{p(j,i)}$ to $U_{\Sigma,c}^{i,j}$ mapping $1_{p(i,j)}$ and $1_{p(j,i)}$ to 1 and, if $m_{ij} = 2$, mapping (a_1, a_2) to $a_2 a_1 = a_1 a_2$ and (b_1, b_2) to $b_2 b_1 = b_1 b_2$ by 11.28 (iii). Let ρ_{ij} denote the first of these bijections followed by the inverse of the second. Then ρ_{ij} is a bijection from $S_{p(i,j)}$ to $S_{p(j,i)}$ mapping $1_{p(i,j)}$ to $1_{p(j,i)}$ such that for each $a \in S_{p(i,j)}$, the elements a and $\rho_{ij}(a)$ have the same image under ϕ and, if $m_{ij} = 2$, $\rho_{ij}(a_1, a_2) = (a_2, a_1)$ for all $(a_1, a_2) \in S_{p(i,j)}$. By 7.7 (iii) and 11.38 (i), for every element $a \in S_{p(i,j)}$, $\rho_{ij}(a)$ is the unique element of $S_{p(j,i)}$ whose image under ψ is a gallery having the same last chamber as the gallery $\psi(a)$. $\qquad\square$

Definition 11.40. Let Δ, Σ, c, S_Δ, etc., be as in 11.37. An *elementary homotopy* in the set S_Δ is a transformation of an element

$$(a_1, b, a_2) \in S_f$$

for some $f \in M_I^{\text{red}}$ of the form $f_1 p(i, j) f_2$ (for some distinct $i, j \in I$), where $a_k \in S_{f_k}$ for $k = 1$ and 2 and $b \in S_{p(i,j)}$, into the element

$$(a_1, \rho_{ij}(b), a_2)$$

in $S_{f_1 p(j,i) f_2}$, where ρ_{ij} is the map from $S_{p(i,j)}$ to $S_{p(j,i)}$ defined in 11.39. We say that two elements of S_Δ are *homotopic* if one can be transformed into the other by a finite sequence of elementary homotopies.

Proposition 11.41. *Let Δ, Σ, c, S_Δ, etc., be as in 11.37, let ψ be as in 11.38 and let a and a' be two elements of S_Δ. Then a' can be obtained from a by an elementary homotopy as defined in 11.40 if and only if $\psi(a')$ can be obtained from $\psi(a)$ by an elementary homotopy as defined in 7.6. In particular, a and a' are homotopic elements of S_Δ if and only if $\psi(a)$ and $\psi(a')$ are homotopic galleries.*

Proof. This holds by 11.38–11.40. $\square$

Definition 11.42. Let Δ, Σ, c, S_Δ, 1_f, etc., be as in 11.37 and let ψ be as in 11.39. Let Ω denote the set of homotopy classes in S_Δ. We make Ω into a chamber system with index set I by declaring that $x \sim_i y$ for $x, y \in \Omega$ whenever x contains an element $a = (a_1, \ldots, a_s)$ whose type we denote by f and y contains an element $b = (b_1, \ldots, b_t)$ whose type we denote by g such that either

(i) $s = t - 1$, $a = (b_1, \ldots, b_s)$ and g ends in i or

(ii) $s = t$, $(a_1, \ldots, a_{s-1}) = (b_1, \ldots, b_{t-1})$ but $a_s \neq b_t$ and both f and g end in i or

(iii) $t = s - 1$, $(a_1, \ldots, a_t) = b$ and f ends in i.

(In all three cases, $\psi(a)$ and $\psi(b)$ do not have the same last chamber, hence a and b are not homotopic by 11.41 and thus $x \neq y$.) Let $S_\Delta^\# = \{1_f \mid f \in M_I^{\text{red}}\}$ and let $\Omega^\#$ denote the set of elements of Ω containing some element of $S_\Delta^\#$ (and hence, by 11.39, containing only elements of $S_\Delta^\#$).

Theorem 11.43. *Let Δ, c, S_Δ, ψ, etc., be as in 11.38 and let Ω and $\Omega^\#$ be as in 11.42. Then the following hold.*

   (i) *There is a unique special isomorphism Φ from Ω to Δ such that for each $\boldsymbol{a} \in S$, Φ maps the homotopy class of $\boldsymbol{a}$ to the last chamber of the gallery $\psi(\boldsymbol{a})$.*

   (ii) *$\Phi(x) \in \Sigma$ if and only if $x \in \Omega^\#$, where Φ is as in (i).*

Proof. By 11.41, two elements of S_Δ are in the same homotopy class if and only if their images under ψ are homotopic galleries. By 7.7 (ii) and 7.9, there is a bijection Φ from Ω to Δ such that the images under ψ of all the elements of S_Δ contained in a given $x \in \Omega$ are precisely the minimal galleries from c to $\Phi(x)$. By 8.32 and 11.42, two chambers of Ω are i-adjacent in Ω if and only if their images under Φ are i-adjacent in Δ. Thus (i) holds. By 8.9 and 11.38 (ii), (ii) holds. $\qquad\square$

Chapter Twelve

Root Group Labelings

In this last chapter, we give an overview of the classification of thick irreducible spherical buildings of rank at least three and sketch the way this classification is carried out in Chapter 40 of [20]. By 10.16, the structure of a thick irreducible building Δ of rank at least three is uniquely determined by the set of its irreducible residues of rank two containing a fixed chamber c (each of which, by 11.6 and 11.8, is Moufang) together with the way the panels of a given type containing c in pairs of these residues are identified to form a single panel in Δ. We will describe these identifications through the notion of a root group labeling (defined in 12.9).

We begin by recalling some results from Parts I–III of [20], in which Moufang polygons are classified. A *Moufang polygon* Γ is a generalized polygon such that the corresponding building of rank two is

(i) thick and

(ii) irreducible and

(iii) has the Moufang property.

The first of these conditions means that $|\Gamma_x| \geqslant 3$ for every vertex x of Γ, where Γ_x is as in 7.11, the second means that diam $\Gamma \geqslant 3$ (i.e. that Γ is a generalized n-gon for some $n \geqslant 3$) and the third means, by 11.3, that for every path $(x_0, x_1, \ldots, x_{n-1}, x_n)$ of length n in Γ, the group

$$G_{x_1}^{(1)} \cap \cdots \cap G_{x_{n-1}}^{(1)}$$

(where $G = \mathrm{Aut}(\Gamma)$) acts transitively on $\Gamma_{x_n} \backslash \{x_{n-1}\}$.

Root group sequences, which we define in 12.1, were introduced in Chapter 8 of [20]. There is a natural correspondence (up to isomorphism) between root group sequences and Moufang polygons (equivalently, Moufang buildings of rank two) which we summarize in 12.2 and 12.3.

Definition 12.1. Let U_+ be a group and let $U_1, \ldots, U_n$ be non-trivial subgroups of U_+ for some $n \geqslant 3$. For all $i, j \in [1, n]$, let

$$U_{[i,j]} = \begin{cases} \langle U_i, U_{i+1}, \ldots, U_j \rangle & \text{if } i \leqslant j, \\ 1 & \text{otherwise.} \end{cases}$$

The $(n + 1)$-tuple $(U_+, U_1, \ldots, U_n)$ is called a *root group sequence* if the following four conditions hold.

(i) $[U_i, U_j] \subset U_{[i+1,j-1]}$ for all $i, j \in [1, n]$ such that $i < j$,

where $[U_i, U_j]$ denotes the subgroup generated by the commutators $[a, b] = a^{-1}b^{-1}ab$ for all $a \in U_i$ and $b \in U_j$.

(ii) The product map $(g_1, \ldots, g_n) \mapsto g_1 \cdots g_n$ is a bijection from the direct product $U_1 \times \cdots \times U_n$ to U_+ (so, in particular, $U_+ = U_{[1,n]}$).

By (i), U_1 normalizes $U_{[2,n]}$ and U_n normalizes $U_{[1,n-1]}$. For each $g \in U_n$ and each $h \in U_1$, let $\tilde{g}$ denote the element $x \mapsto g^{-1}xg$ of $\text{Aut}(U_{[1,n-1]})$ and let $\tilde{h}$ denote the element $x \mapsto h^{-1}xh$ of $\text{Aut}(U_{[2,n]})$. Let $\tilde{U}_n$ denote the image of the map $g \mapsto \tilde{g}$ in $\text{Aut}(U_{[1,n-1]})$ and let $\tilde{U}_1$ denote the image of the map $h \mapsto \tilde{h}$ in $\text{Aut}(U_{[2,n]})$.

(iii) For some subgroup $\tilde{U}_0$ of $\text{Aut}(U_{[1,n-1]})$, there exists for each $g \in U_n^*$ an element $\mu(g)$ in $\tilde{U}_0^* \tilde{g} \tilde{U}_0^*$ such that $U_i^{\mu(g)} = U_{n-i}$ for all $i \in [1, n-1]$ and all $g \in U_n^*$, and for some $g \in U_n^*$, $\tilde{U}_i^{\mu(g)} = \tilde{U}_{n-i}$ for $i = 0$ and n.

(iv) For some subgroup $\tilde{U}_{n+1}$ of $\text{Aut}(U_{[2,n]})$, there exists for each $h \in U_1^*$ an element $\mu(h)$ in $\tilde{U}_{n+1}^* \tilde{h} \tilde{U}_{n+1}^*$ such that $U_i^{\mu(h)} = U_{n+2-i}$ for all $i \in [2, n]$ and all $h \in U_1^*$, and for some $h \in U_1^*$, $\tilde{U}_i^{\mu(h)} = \tilde{U}_{n+2-i}$ for $i = 1$ and $n + 1$.

Let $\Theta = (U_+, U_1, \ldots, U_n)$ be a root group sequence. The number n is called the *index* of Θ and the subgroups $U_1, \ldots, U_n$ are called the *terms* of Θ. Let $\Theta^{\text{op}} = (U_+, U_n, \ldots, U_1)$; Θ^{op} is also a root group sequence. We say that Θ and Θ^{op} are *opposites*. An *isomorphism* from Θ to another root group sequence $(U'_+, U'_1, \ldots, U'_n)$ is an isomorphism from U_+ to U'_+ which maps U_i to U'_i for all $i \in [1, n]$. An *automorphism* of Θ is an isomorphism from Θ to itself.

Note that in 12.1 (ii) we are not asserting that the product map is an isomorphism (equivalently, that $[U_i, U_j] = 1$ for $i \neq j$); by 12.3 below and (5.7) of [20], this is, in fact, never the case.

Proposition 12.2. *Let Δ a Moufang building of type* $\bullet\!\!-\!\!^{n}\!\!-\!\!\bullet$ *for some $n \geqslant 3$, let Σ be an apartment of Δ and let c be a chamber in Σ. Let the index set I of Δ be labeled by the numbers 1 and 2 (i.e. let the elements of I be assigned the names 1 and 2) and let c_i, α_i and U_i for $i = 1$ and 2 be as in 11.25. Let $\omega_1, \cdots, \omega_n$ be the set of roots of Σ containing c in the canonical ordering from α_1 to α_2 as defined in 11.26 and let U_c^+ be the subgroup of $\mathrm{Aut}(\Delta)$ generated by the root groups $U_{\omega_1}, \cdots, U_{\omega_n}$ as in 11.11. Let Θ denote the $(n+1)$-tuple of subgroups*

$$(U_c^+, U_{\omega_1}, \cdots, U_{\omega_n}).$$

Then Θ is a root group sequence as defined in 12.1; it is called the root group sequence of Δ associated with the pair (Σ, c) and the labeling of I. The root group sequence associated with the same pair (Σ, c) but the other labeling of I by the numbers 1 and 2 is Θ^{op}, the opposite root group sequence as defined in 12.1. By 11.12, the root group sequence associated with another pair (Σ', c') but the same labeling of I is isomorphic to Θ via conjugation by a special automorphism of Δ.

Proof. Since Δ is thick and has the Moufang property, the groups $U_{\omega_1}, \ldots, U_{\omega_n}$ are non-trivial by 11.2. Condition (i) of 12.1 holds by 11.17, condition (ii) by 11.11 (i) and conditions (iii) and (iv) by 11.22. $\square$

Proposition 12.3. *For each root group sequence Θ of index $n \geqslant 3$ as defined in 12.1, there exists a Moufang building Δ of type* $\bullet\!\!-\!\!^{n}\!\!-\!\!\bullet$ *and a labeling of its index set I by the numbers 1 and 2 such that for every apartment Σ of Δ and every chamber c of Σ, Θ is isomorphic to the root group sequence of Δ associated with the pair (Σ, c) and the labeling of I as in 12.2. The building Δ is unique up to a special isomorphism (i.e. an isomorphism which preserves the labeling of I).*

Proof. This holds by (7.5) and (8.11) of [20]. $\square$

Now let

$$\Theta = (U_+, U_1, \ldots, U_n)$$

be a root group sequence. By conditions (i) and (ii) of 12.1, the group U_+ is uniquely determined by the subgroups $U_1, \ldots, U_n$ (i.e. the terms of Θ) and commutator relations expressing $[a_i, a_j] = a_i^{-1} a_j^{-1} a_i a_j$ as an element of $U_{[i+1, j-1]}$ for all $i, j \in [1, n]$ such that $i < j$, all $a_i \in U_i$ and all $a_j \in U_j$. Note that if $i \in [1, n-1]$ and $j = i + 1$, then by 12.1 (i), $[U_i, U_j] = 1$.

Our next goal is to describe in 12.4–12.7 four families of root group sequences and thus four families of the Moufang polygons (equivalently, four families of

Moufang buildings of rank two). These are precisely the Moufang polygons which appear, it turns out, as residues of rank two of a thick irreducible spherical building of rank greater than two.

We describe these root group sequences in 12.4–12.7 by giving $U_1, \ldots, U_n$ and commutator relations defining U_+. We use the convention that $[U_i, U_j] = 1$ for all pairs $i, j \in [1, n]$ such that $i < j$ for which we do not give explicit formulas. For the proofs that the given commutator relations really define root group sequences, we refer the reader to Chapter 32 of [20].

12.4. The Moufang triangles $A_2(K)$

Let K be an alternative division ring (so by the theorem of Bruck–Kleinfeld, K is a field or a skew-field or an octonion division algebra, or equivalently, a Cayley–Dickson division algebra; see, for example, Chapter 9 of [20] for the definitions of these terms). Let U_1, U_2, U_3 be three groups isomorphic to the additive group of K and choose isomorphisms $t \mapsto x_i(t)$ from the additive group of K to U_i for all $i \in [1, 3]$ (so $x_i(s)x_i(t) = x_i(s + t)$ for all $s, t \in K$ and all $i \in [1, 3]$). There is a unique root group sequence $\Theta_{A_2(K)}$ of index three having U_1, U_2, U_3 as its terms such that

$$[x_1(s), x_3(t)] = x_2(st)$$

for all $s, t \in K$. We denote the corresponding Moufang triangle by $\mathcal{T}(K)$ or $A_2(K)$. Here and in 12.5–12.7, we give two names to the same Moufang polygon. The first is meant to suggest the Moufang polygon itself and the second is meant to suggest the corresponding building together with the labeling of its index set by the numbers 1 and 2 given by 12.3, i.e. with the two elements of I distinguished.

12.5. The Moufang quadrangles $B_2(K, L_0, q)$

Let (K, L_0, q) be an anisotropic quadratic space. Thus K is a field, L_0 is a non-trivial vector space over K, and q is an anisotropic quadratic form on L_0, i.e. q is a map from L_0 to K such that, for some bilinear form f on L_0 (which is uniquely determined by q),

   (i) $q(u + v) = q(u) + q(v) + f(u, v)$,

   (ii) $q(tu) = t^2 q(u)$, and

   (iii) $q(u) = 0$ only if $u = 0$

for all $u, v \in L_0$ and all $t \in K$. Let U_1, U_2, U_3, U_4 be four groups such that U_1 and U_3 are isomorphic to the additive group of K and U_2 and U_4 are isomorphic to L_0 (as an additive group). Choose isomorphisms $t \mapsto x_i(t)$ from the additive group of K to U_i for $i = 1$ and 3 and isomorphisms $u \mapsto x_i(u)$ from L_0 to U_i for $i = 2$ and 4. There is a unique root group sequence $\Theta_{B_2(K,L_0,q)}$ of index four having U_1, U_2, U_3, U_4 as its terms such that

$$[x_2(u), x_4(v)^{-1}] = x_3(f(u, v)),$$
$$[x_1(t), x_4(v)^{-1}] = x_2(tv)x_3(tq(v))$$

for all $t \in K$ and all $u, v \in L_0$. We denote the corresponding Moufang quadrangle by $\mathcal{Q}_{\mathcal{Q}}(K, L_0, q)$ or $B_2(K, L_0, q)$.

12.6. The Moufang quadrangles $C_2(K, K_0, \sigma)$

Let $\Xi = (K, K_0, \sigma)$ be an involutory set as defined in (11.1) of [20]. Thus K is a field or a skew-field, σ is an involution of K (i.e. σ is an anti-automorphism of K such that $\sigma^2 = 1$), and K_0 is an additive subgroup of K containing 1 such that

$$K_\sigma \subset K_0 \subset \mathrm{Fix}_K(\sigma),$$

where $K_\sigma = \{a + a^\sigma \mid a \in K\}$, and

$$a^\sigma K_0 a \subset K_0$$

for all $a \in K$. Let U_1, U_2, U_3, U_4 be four groups such that U_1 and U_3 are isomorphic to K_0 and U_2 and U_4 are isomorphic to the additive group of K. Choose isomorphisms $t \mapsto x_i(t)$ from K_0 to U_i for $i = 1$ and 3 and isomorphisms $u \mapsto x_i(u)$ from the additive group of K to U_i for $i = 2$ and 4. There is a unique root group sequence $\Theta_{C_2(K,K_0,\sigma)}$ of index four having U_1, U_2, U_3, U_4 as its terms such that

$$[x_2(u), x_4(v)^{-1}] = x_3(u^\sigma v + v^\sigma u)),$$
$$[x_1(t), x_4(v)^{-1}] = x_2(tv)x_3(v^\sigma tv)$$

for all $t \in K_0$ and all $u, v \in K$. We denote the corresponding Moufang quadrangle by $\mathcal{Q}_{\mathcal{I}}(K, K_0, \sigma)$ or $C_2(K, K_0, \sigma)$.

12.7. The Moufang quadrangles $BC_2(K, K_0, \sigma, L_0, q)$

Let (K, K_0, σ, L_0, q) be an anisotropic skew-hermitian pseudo-quadratic space as defined in (11.17) of [20]. Thus (K, K_0, σ) is an involutory set as defined in 12.6, L_0 is a right vector space over K, and q is a map from L_0 to K such that for some skew-hermitian form f on L_0 (by which we mean that f

is a bi-additive map from $L_0 \times L_0$ to K such that $f(u, vt) = f(u, v)t$ and $f(u, v)^\sigma = -f(v, u)$ for all $u, v \in L_0$ and all $t \in K$),

(i) $q(u + v) \equiv q(u) + q(v) + f(u, v) \pmod{K_0}$,

(ii) $q(ut) \equiv t^\sigma q(u)t \pmod{K_0}$, and

(iii) $q(u) \equiv 0 \pmod{K_0}$ only if $u = 0$,

for all $u, v \in L_0$ and all $t \in K$. (By (11.19) of [20], the skew-hermitian form f is uniquely determined by q.) Let

$$T = \{(u, t) \in L_0 \times K \mid q(a) - t \in K_0\}$$

and

$$(u, s) \cdot (v, t) = (u + v, s + t + f(v, u))$$

for all $(u, s), (v, t) \in T$. By (11.24) of [20], T endowed with the multiplication $\cdot$ is a group. Let U_1, U_2, U_3, U_4 be four groups such that U_1 and U_3 are isomorphic to T and U_2 and U_4 are isomorphic to the additive group of K. Choose isomorphisms $(v, t) \mapsto x_i(v, t)$ from T to U_i for $i = 1$ and 3 and isomorphisms $u \mapsto x_i(u)$ from the additive group of K to U_i for $i = 2$ and 4. There is a unique root group sequence $\Theta_{BC_2(K, K_0, \sigma, L_0, q)}$ of index four having U_1, U_2, U_3, U_4 as its terms such that

$$[x_1(u, s), x_3(v, t)^{-1}] = x_2(f(u, v)),$$
$$[x_2(a), x_4(b)^{-1}] = x_3(0, a^\sigma b + a^\sigma b),$$
$$[x_1(v, t), x_4(a)^{-1}] = x_2(ta)x_3(va, a^\sigma ta)$$

for all $(u, s), (v, t) \in T$ and all $a, b \in K$. We denote the corresponding Moufang quadrangle by $\mathcal{Q}_{\mathscr{P}}(K, K_0, \sigma, L_0, q)$ or $BC_2(K, K_0, \sigma, L_0, q)$.

This completes our description of the four families of Moufang polygons which appear as rank-two residues of a thick irreducible spherical building of rank at least three. The families described in 12.5–12.7 are not completely disjoint; this matter is discussed in Chapter 38 of [20]. There are three further families of Moufang quadrangles: the indifferent quadrangles, the quadrangles of type E_6, E_7 and E_8, and the quadrangles of type F_4, as well as Moufang hexagons and Moufang octagons (see Chapter 16 of [20]). (That hexagons and octagons do not arise as residues of thick irreducible spherical buildings of higher rank is an immediate consequence of 5.18.)

It will be useful, before we go on, to extend the definition of the operator C_2 given in 12.6 as follows.

12.8. The Moufang quadrangles $C_2(K, F, \sigma)$

Let (K, F, σ) be an honorary involutory set and let N denote its norm as defined in (38.11) and (38.12) of [20]. Thus K is an octonion division algebra with center F and standard involution σ, and the triple (F, K, N) is an anisotropic quadratic space. We set $\Theta_{C_2(K,F,\sigma)} = \Theta_{B_2(F,K,N)}$ and $C_2(K, F, \sigma) = B_2(F, K, N)$ and observe that the commutator relations given in 12.5 with respect to (F, K, N) are the same as the commutator relations given in 12.6 with respect to (K, F, σ) if we were to treat (K, F, σ) as an involutory set, which it is not, however, since K is not associative (hence 'honorary').

Our next goal is to describe how the Moufang polygons in 12.4–12.8 can be glued together to make up the sub-chamber system Δ_x^{red} of a thick irreducible spherical building Δ (which, by 10.16, determines Δ uniquely). We do this through the notion of a root group labeling.

Definition 12.9. Let Π be a Coxeter diagram with vertex set I such that all the entries of the corresponding Coxeter matrix $[m_{ij}]$ are finite, let $E(\Pi)$ denote the set of edges of Π, and let $DE(\Pi)$ denote the set of ordered pairs (i, j) such that $\{x, y\} \in E(\Pi)$, i.e. the set of 'directed edges' of Π. Let ν be a labeling of I and let Θ and θ be two labelings of the set $DE(\Pi)$ such that

(i) $\nu(i)$ is a group for each $i \in I$,

(ii) Θ_{ij} is a root group sequence of index m_{ij} for each $(i, j) \in DE(\Pi)$, and

(iii) θ_{ij} is an isomorphism from $\nu(i)$ to the first term of Θ_{ij} for each $(i, j) \in DE(\Pi)$.

A *root group labeling* of Π is a triple (ν, Θ, θ) of such labelings such that $\Theta_{ji} = \Theta_{ij}^{\text{op}}$ for all $(i, j) \in DE(\Pi)$. Let (ν, Θ, θ) and (ν', Θ', θ') be two root group labelings of Π. An *isomorphism* from the first to the second is a collection of isomorphisms ψ_i from $\nu(i)$ to $\nu'(i)$ for each $i \in I$ and ψ_{ij} from Θ_{ij} to Θ'_{ij} for each $(i, j) \in DE(\Pi)$ such that

$$\theta'_{ij} \cdot \psi_i = \psi_{ij} \cdot \theta_{ij}$$

(composition from right to left) for all $(i, j) \in DE(\Pi)$.

In the next two paragraphs, we describe the connection between root group labelings and spherical buildings.

12.10. Let Π be an irreducible spherical Coxeter diagram of rank at least two with vertex set I and let (ν, Θ, θ) be a root group labeling of Π as defined in 12.9. Choose $\{i, j\}$ in $E(\Pi)$ and let $n = m_{ij}$. By 12.3, there is a building

R_{ij} of type $\bullet\!\!\xrightarrow{\;\;n\;\;}\!\!\bullet$ with index set $\{i, j\}$ such that for each apartment Σ_{ij} of R_{ij} and each chamber x_{ij} of Σ_{ij}, the root group sequence associated with the pair (Σ_{ij}, x_{ij}) and the labeling of the index set $\{i, j\}$ of R_{ij} which assigns to i the name 1 and to j the name 2 (as described in 12.2) is isomorphic to Θ_{ij} (and thus the root group sequence associated with the same pair (Σ_{ij}, x_{ij}) but the other labeling of the index set $\{i, j\}$ by 1 and 2 is isomorphic to $\Theta_{ij}^{\mathrm{op}} = \Theta_{ij}$). Choose an apartment Σ_{ij} of R_{ij} and a chamber x_{ij} of Σ_{ij}. For both $k = i$ and $k = j$, let x_{ij}^k denote the unique chamber of Σ_{ij} which is k-adjacent to x_{ij} and let P_{ij}^k denote the panel of R_{ij} containing x_{ij} and x_{ij}^k. By 11.4 and 12.2, the map $g \mapsto (x_{ij}^i)^g$ is a bijection from the first term of Θ_{ij} to $P_{ij}^i \backslash \{x_{ij}\}$. Let $\pi_{ij}(a) = (x_{ij}^i)^{\theta_{ij}(a)}$ for all $a \in \nu(i)$. Thus π_{ij} is a bijection from $\nu(i)$ to $P_{ij}^i \backslash \{x_{ij}\}$. (Similarly, the map π_{ji} given by $\pi_{ji}(a) = (x_{ij}^j)^{\theta_{ji}(a)}$ for all $a \in \nu(j)$ is a bijection from $\nu(j)$ to $P_{ij}^j \backslash \{x_{ij}\}$.) Now let X be the chamber system obtained from the union

$$\bigcup_{\{i,j\} \in E(\Pi)} R_{ij}$$

of all the R_{ij} in two steps: first we identify all the x_{ij} with a single chamber we call x and then, for all $i, j, k \in I$ such that (i, j) and (i, k) are in $DE(\Pi)$, we identify the i-panel $P_{ij}^i \backslash \{x\}$ with the i-panel $P_{ik}^i \backslash \{x\}$ via $\pi_{ik} \cdot \pi_{ij}^{-1}$. (Equivalently, for each $i \in I$, we identify $P_{ij}^i \backslash \{x\}$ with $\nu(i)$ via π_{ij}^{-1} and, in particular, x_{ij}^i with the identity element of $\nu(i)$ for each $j \in I$ adjacent to i in Π, so that $\nu(i) \cup \{x\}$ becomes the i-panel of X containing x.) By 11.12, the pair (X, x) is (up to a special isomorphism) independent of the choice of the R_{ij}, Σ_{ij} and x_{ij} and, in fact, depends only on the isomorphism class of (ν, Θ, θ). We will say that the root group labeling (ν, Θ, θ) of Π is *realizable* (or *realized by* Δ) if there exists a building Δ of type Π such that there is a full map from X to Δ whose image is Δ_c^{red} for some $c \in \Delta$. By 10.16, such a building, if it exists, is unique (up to a special isomorphism).

In 12.11, we observe that for each Moufang building Δ of type Π, there exists a root group labeling of Π which is realized by Δ.

12.11. Suppose that Δ is a Moufang building of type Π and let I denote the index set of Δ. Choose an apartment Σ of Δ and a chamber c of Σ and let c_i, α_i and U_i for $i \in I$ be as in 11.25. Let $\nu(i) = U_i$ for all $i \in I$. For each $\{i, j\} \in E(\Pi)$, let R_{ij} denote the unique $\{i, j\}$-residue in $\mathrm{Res}_{\Delta, c}^{(2)}$ and let $\Sigma_{ij} = \Sigma \cap R_{ij}$, an apartment of R_{ij} by 8.13 (i). By 11.8, the residues R_{ij} all have the Moufang property. For each $(i, j) \in DE(\Pi)$, let Θ_{ij} denote the root group sequence of R_{ij} associated with (Σ_{ij}, c) and the labeling $i \mapsto 1$ and $j \mapsto 2$ of the index set $\{i, j\}$ of R_{ij} as defined in 12.2. By 11.10, for each

$(i, j) \in DE(\Pi)$, the map from U_i to the first term of Θ_{ij} which sends each element of U_i to its restriction to R_{ij} is an isomorphism which we denote by θ_{ij}. Then (v, Θ, θ) is a root group labeling of Π which is realized by Δ in the sense defined in 12.10.

From 12.10 and 12.11 we deduce that to classify thick irreducible spherical buildings of rank $\ell \geqslant 3$ (i.e. to prove the main results of [14]), it suffices to classify realizable root group labelings for all the irreducible spherical Coxeter diagrams of rank ℓ given in 5.17. This classification is carried out as an application of the classification of Moufang polygons in Chapter 40 of [20].

In 12.13–12.19 we describe all the realizable root group labelings of spherical Coxeter diagrams of rank at least three which come out of the classification using the following conventions.

12.12 (The root group labeling Λ). In 12.13–12.19, we give a parameter system (a field, an involutory set, etc.) and a Coxeter diagram Π (and thus, implicitly, also a Coxeter matrix $[m_{ij}]$) by means of a picture together with a labeling of the vertices of Π by the integers $1, 2, \ldots, \ell$. For certain ordered pairs $(i, j) \in DE(\Pi)$, we then set Θ_{ij} equal to one of the root group sequences given in 12.4–12.7. Let X denote the set of ordered pairs (i, j) for which we define Θ_{ij}. Then $(j, i) \in X$ for all $(i, j) \in DE(\Pi)$ which are not in X and no two ordered pairs X have the same first coordinate. We can thus extend Θ to a root group labeling of Π as follows. First let $\Theta_{ij} = \Theta_{ji}^{op}$ for all $(i, j) \in DE(\Pi)$ not in X. Then for each $(i, j) \in X$, we set $v(i)$ equal to the parameter group which is the domain of the map $t \mapsto x_1(t)$ given in the description of Θ_{ij} in 12.4–12.7 and we set θ_{ij} equal to this map. Finally, for each $(i, j) \in X$, we observe that $v(j)$ is precisely the parameter group which is the domain of the map $t \mapsto x_n(t)$, where $n = m_{ij}$, given in the definition of Θ_{ij} in 12.4–12.7, and we set θ_{ji} equal to this map. Thus θ_{ji} maps the parameter group $v(j)$ to the last term of Θ_{ij}, which is also the first term of Θ_{ji}. Let Λ denote the root group labeling (v, Θ, θ) of the Coxeter diagram Π.

12.13. The buildings $A_\ell(K)$

Let Π be the Coxeter diagram A_ℓ for some $\ell \geqslant 3$ with its vertices numbered as follows:

$$\underset{1}{\bullet} \!-\!\!-\! \underset{2}{\bullet} \!-\!\!-\! \underset{3}{\bullet} \; \cdots \; \underset{\ell-2}{\bullet} \!-\!\!-\! \underset{\ell-1}{\bullet} \!-\!\!-\! \underset{\ell}{\bullet}$$

Let K be a field or a skew-field, let $\Theta_{i,i+1} = \Theta_{A_2(K)}$ for all $i \in [1, \ell - 1]$ and then let Λ be the root group labeling of Π described in 12.12 based on these choices. The root group labeling Λ is realized by a building we denote by $A_\ell(K)$.

12.14. The buildings $B_\ell(K, L_0, q)$

Let Π be the Coxeter diagram C_ℓ for some $\ell \geqslant 3$ with its vertices numbered as follows:

$$\underset{1}{\bullet} \quad \underset{2}{\bullet} \quad \underset{3}{\bullet} \quad \cdots \quad \underset{\ell-2}{\bullet} \quad \underset{\ell-1}{\bullet} = \underset{\ell}{\bullet}$$

Let (K, L_0, q) be an anisotropic quadratic space, i.e. a triple as in 12.5, let $\Theta_{i,i+1} = \Theta_{A_2(K)}$ for all $i \in [1, \ell - 2]$, let $\Theta_{\ell-1,\ell} = \Theta_{B_2(K,L_0,q)}$, and then let Λ be the root group labeling of Π described in 12.12 based on these choices. The root group labeling Λ is realized by a building we denote by $B_\ell(K, L_0, q)$.

12.15. The buildings $C_\ell(K, K_0, \sigma)$

Let $\Pi = C_\ell$ for some $\ell \geqslant 3$ again (with the same numbering of the vertices as above), let (K, K_0, σ) be a proper, quadratic or honorary involutory set as defined in (35.3) and (38.11) of [20] and let K^{op} denote the opposite ring of K (as defined, for example, in (2.11) of [20]). Suppose, too, that $\ell = 3$ if (K, K_0, σ) is honorary. Let $\Theta_{i,i+1} = \Theta_{A_2(K^{op})}$ for all $i \in [1, \ell-2]$ if (K, K_0, σ) is proper, let $\Theta_{i,i+1} = \Theta_{A_2(K)}$ for all $i \in [1, \ell-2]$ if (K, K_0, σ) is quadratic or honorary, let $\Theta_{\ell,\ell-1} = \Theta_{C_2(K,K_0,\sigma)}$ as defined in 12.6 or 12.8 in all three cases and let Λ be the root group labeling of Π described in 12.12 based on these choices. The root group labeling Λ is realized by a building we denote by $C_\ell(K, K_0, \sigma)$.

12.16. The buildings $BC_\ell(K, K_0, \sigma, L_0, q)$

Let $\Pi = C_\ell$ for some $\ell \geqslant 3$ again (with the same numbering of the vertices as above) and let (K, K_0, σ, L_0, q) be a proper anisotropic skew-hermitian pseudo-quadratic space as defined in (35.5) of [20]. Let $\Theta_{i,i+1} = \Theta_{A_2(K^{op})}$ for all $i \in [1, \ell - 2]$, let

$$\Theta_{\ell,\ell-1} = \Theta_{BC_2(K,K_0,\sigma,L_0,q)},$$

and let Λ be the root group labeling of Π described in 12.12 based on these choices. The root group labeling Λ is realized by a building we denote by $BC_\ell(K, K_0, \sigma, L_0, q)$.

12.17. The buildings $D_\ell(K)$

Let Π be the Coxeter diagram D_ℓ for some $\ell \geqslant 4$ with its vertices numbered as follows:

Let K be a (commutative) field, let $\Theta_{i,i+1} = \Theta_{A_2(K)}$ for all $i \in [1, \ell - 2]$, let $\Theta_{\ell,\ell-2} = \Theta_{A_2(K)}$ and let Λ be the root group labeling of Π described in 12.12

based on these choices. The root group labeling Λ is realized by a building we denote by $\mathsf{D}_\ell(K)$.

12.18. The buildings $\mathsf{E}_\ell(K)$ for $\ell = 6, 7$ and 8

Let Π be the Coxeter diagram E_ℓ for $\ell = 6$, 7 or 8 with its vertices numbered as follows:

Let K be a (commutative) field, let $\Theta_{i,i+1} = \Theta_{\mathsf{A}_2(K)}$ for all $i \in [1, 2]$ and all $i \in [5, \ell - 1]$, let $\Theta_{4,3} = \Theta_{\mathsf{A}_2(K)}$, let $\Theta_{3,5} = \Theta_{\mathsf{A}_2(K)}$, and let Λ be the root group labeling of Π described in 12.12 based on these choices. The root group labeling Λ is realized by a building we denote by $\mathsf{E}_\ell(K)$.

12.19. The buildings $\mathsf{F}_4(K, F, \sigma)$

Let Π be the Coxeter diagram F_4 with its vertices numbered as follows:

Let (K, F, σ) be a quadratic or honorary involutory set as defined in (38.11) of [20]. Let $\Theta_{1,2} = \Theta_{\mathsf{A}_2(F)}$, let $\Theta_{2,3} = \Theta_{\mathsf{C}_2(K,F,\sigma)}$, let $\Theta_{3,4} = \Theta_{\mathsf{A}_2(K)}$, and let Λ be the root group labeling of Π described in 12.12 based on these choices. The root group labeling Λ is realized by a building we denote by $\mathsf{F}_4(K, F, \sigma)$. The $\{1, 2, 3\}$-residues of this building are isomorphic to $\mathsf{B}_3(K, F, N)$, where N is the norm of (K, F, σ), and the $\{2, 3, 4\}$-residues are isomorphic to $\mathsf{C}_3(K, F, \sigma)$.

These are all the thick irreducible spherical buildings of rank at least three. Notice that there are none of type

$$\mathsf{H}_3 = \bullet \!\!\!\!\!-\!\!\!\!\!- \bullet \overset{5}{-\!\!\!\!\!-} \bullet$$

or

$$\mathsf{H}_4 = \bullet \!\!\!\!\!-\!\!\!\!\!- \bullet \!\!\!\!\!-\!\!\!\!\!- \bullet \overset{5}{-\!\!\!\!\!-} \bullet \;.$$

An immediate consequence of the classification is the following.

Theorem 12.20. *Let Δ be a Moufang building of rank at least three and let $G^\dagger$ denote the subgroup of $\mathrm{Aut}^\circ(\Delta)$ generated by all the root groups of Δ as in 11.12 and 11.20. Then $G^\dagger$ is a simple group.*

Proof. By 11.20, it suffices to show that $G^\dagger$ is perfect. Let $[m_{ij}]$ denote the Coxeter matrix associated with Δ and choose an apartment Σ containing c.

Let (v, Θ, θ) denote the root group labeling of Π associated with Σ and c as described in 12.11. By the classification, (v, Θ, θ) is isomorphic to one of the root group labelings given in 12.13–12.19. For all $i \in I$, let c_i denote the chamber of Σ which is i-adjacent to c, let α_i denote the root $\Sigma_{(c \backslash c_i)}$ of Σ and let $U_i = U_{\alpha_i}$ as in 11.25. By 11.12, every root of Δ can be mapped by an element of $G^\dagger$ to α_i for some $i \in I$ and hence every root group of Δ is conjugate in $G^\dagger$ to U_i for some $i \in I$. It thus suffices to show that $U_i \subset [G^\dagger, G^\dagger]$ for all $i \in I$. Choose $i \in I$. Suppose first that $m_{ij} = 3$ for some $j \in I$. This means that the $\{i, j\}$-residue containing c is isomorphic to $\mathsf{A}_2(K)$ for some alternative division ring K. Choose $m \in \mu_\Sigma(U_j^*)$, where μ_Σ is as in 11.22. Then m acts on the $\{i, j\}$-residue of Σ containing c like the reflection interchanging c and c_j, from which it follows that U_i^m is the middle term of Θ_{ij}. By 12.4, this group equals $[U_i, U_j]$. Hence $U_i \subset [G^\dagger, G^\dagger]$. Now suppose that $m_{ij} \neq 3$ for all $j \in I$. Then $\Pi = \mathsf{C}_\ell$ for some $\ell \geqslant 3$, $m_{ij} = 4$ for some $j \in I$, and (since $m_{jk} = 3$ for some $k \in I$) $U_j \subset [G^\dagger, G^\dagger]$. This time, we choose $m_k \in \mu_\Sigma(U_k^*)$ for both $k = i$ and $k = j$. Then $U_i^{m_j}$ is the third term of Θ_{ij} and $U_j^{m_i}$ is the second term of Θ_{ij}. Thus the second term of Θ_{ij} is contained in $[G^\dagger, G^\dagger]$. The commutator relations involving $[U_i, U_j]$ (or those involving $[U_j, U_i]$) are as in 12.4, 12.6 or 12.7. Since the second term of Θ_{ij} is contained in $[G^\dagger, G^\dagger]$, it follows from these relations that also the third term of Θ_{ij} lies in $[G^\dagger, G^\dagger]$. Hence $U_i \subset [G^\dagger, G^\dagger]$. $\square$

We close this chapter by sketching how the classification of realizable root group labelings of irreducible spherical Coxeter diagrams of rank at least three is deduced from the classification of Moufang polygons in Chapter 40 of [20]. Let $\Delta, \Pi, I, \Sigma, c$ and (v, Θ, θ) be as in 12.11. We want to show that (v, Θ, θ) must be isomorphic to one of the root group labelings given in 12.13–12.19. Let H_i for $i \in I$ and $H^\dagger$ be the subgroups of $\mathrm{Aut}^\circ(\Delta)$ defined in 11.29 with respect to Σ.

Proposition 12.21. $[H_i, H_j] = 1$ for all $i, j \in I$ such that $m_{ij} = 2$, i.e. for all non-adjacent pairs of vertices i, j of Π.

Proof. This holds by 11.28 (ii). $\square$

Now choose $(i, j) \in \mathrm{DE}(\Pi)$. By 11.10 and 11.22, the action of H_i on U_k for $k = i$ and j is determined by Θ_{ij} alone and is therefore as in (33.10)–(33.15) of [20]. Suppose, for example, that $\Theta_{ij} = \Theta_{\mathsf{A}_2(K)}$, as defined in 12.4, for some alternative division ring K. Then by (33.10) of [20], we have the following result.

Lemma 12.22. *With respect to the parametrizations of the first term U_i and the last term U_j of Θ_{ij} by the additive group of K given in 12.4, the action of H_i on U_j is generated by the maps $a \mapsto ta$ (from K to itself) for all $t \in K^*$ and the action of H_j on U_i is generated by the maps $a \mapsto at$ for all $t \in K^*$.*

Corollary 12.23. *The group $H^\dagger$ acts transitively on both U_i^* and U_j^*.*

Proof. This holds by 12.22. □

These facts are enough to handle the case $\Pi = A_\ell$.

Proposition 12.24. *If $\Pi = A_\ell$ for some $\ell \geqslant 3$, then (v, Θ, θ) is isomorphic to the root group labeling of Π described in 12.13 for some field or skew-field K.*

Proof. Let the vertices of Π be numbered as in 12.13. Suppose first that $\ell = 3$. By the classification of Moufang polygons, we can assume that $\Theta_{1,2} = \Theta_{A_2(K)}$ and $\Theta_{2,3} = \Theta_{A_2(K')}$ for alternative division rings K and K'. The group U_2 is both the last term of $\Theta_{1,2}$ and the first term of $\Theta_{2,3}$. This allows us to identify the additive group of K with the additive group of K'. By 12.23, we can assume, in fact, that the multiplicative identities of K and K' are the same. Let $\cdot$ denote the multiplication of K and let $*$ denote the multiplication of K'. Now let $t, u \in K^*$. By 12.22, there is an element $h_1 \in H_1$ which acts on U_2 via the map $a \mapsto t * a$ and an element $h_3 \in H_3$ which acts on U_2 via the map $a \mapsto a \cdot u$. By 12.21, therefore,

$$(t * a) \cdot u = t * (a \cdot u)$$

for all $a \in K$. Setting $a = 1$, we have $t \cdot u = t * u$. Since t and u are arbitrary, it follows that $* = \cdot$ (i.e. that $K' = K$). Therefore $(t \cdot a) \cdot u = t \cdot (a \cdot u)$ for all $a, t, u \in K$, so K is associative. An alternative division ring which is associative is automatically a field or a skew-field. We conclude that (v, Θ, θ) is isomorphic to the root group labeling described in 12.13. The claim holds for arbitrary ℓ by induction. □

This is, of course, only the first case. All the remaining irreducible spherical diagrams and all possible Moufang polygons for all the Θ_{ij} remain to be considered. Surprisingly, however, the only tools needed to produce the list 12.13–12.19 are 12.21, the action of H_i and H_j on U_i and U_j, and a few other facts about the $\mathrm{Aut}(\Theta_{ij})$ for all the Θ_{ij} under consideration.

This leaves the question of the realizability of the root group labelings described in 12.13–12.19. Suppose that (v, Θ, θ) is one of them. Let S_Δ denote the set defined in 11.37, let ψ be as in 11.38, let ρ_{ij} be as in 11.39 for each $(i, j) \in \mathrm{DE}(\Pi)$, and let Ω be as in 11.42. In Chapter 11, all of these things are described in terms of a building Δ, but, in fact, they are completely determined by the root group labeling (ν, Θ, θ) alone. (In (32.15) of [20], explicit formulas for the maps ρ_{ij} corresponding to each irreducible residue of rank two of each of the root group sequences under consideration can be found. If $m_{ij} = 2$, then ρ_{ij} is given explicitly in 11.39.) If (ν, Θ, θ) is realized by a building Δ, then by 11.43, there is a special isomorphism from Ω to Δ and, in particular, Ω is a building. By (40.19) of [20], the converse holds: if Ω is a building, then (ν, Θ, θ) is realizable (and, in fact, it is realized by Ω). By (39.48), (40.19) and (40.55) of [20] (see [9] and [16] for the original versions of these results), Ω is a building if for each $a \in S$, a itself is the only element of S_Δ which is homotopic to a and of the same type as a, and, remarkably, it suffices to check this condition only for all the root group labelings obtained by restricting to irreducible subdiagrams of Π of rank three; even more, for each root group labeling of an irreducible Coxeter diagram of rank three, it suffices to check the condition only for elements of S_Δ of one fixed type with respect to one fixed sequence of elementary homotopies (which depends only on the Coxeter diagram). Note that in 12.13–12.19, there are not so many different restrictions to irreducible subdiagrams of rank three, and with the explicit formulas for the different maps ρ_{ij}, the required calculations are easily carried out (see (40.54) of [20]).

All the buildings described in 12.13–12.19 arise from algebraic or classical groups.[1] These connections are described in [16] and in Chapters 41 and 42 of [20].

---

[1] Just one family—the buildings $F_4(K, F, \sigma)$ for K/F a field extension in characteristic two such that $F \neq K$ and $\sigma(K) \subset F$, where $\sigma(x) = x^2$ for all $x \in K$—represents a small exception to the general pattern (see 10.3 of [16]).

References

[1] Bourbaki, N. 1981 *Groupes et algèbres de Lie*, chapters 4, 5 and 6. Masson, Paris.

[2] Brown, K. 1989 *Buildings*. Springer.

[3] Coxeter, H. S. M. 1935 The complete enumeration of finite groups of the form $R_i^2 = (R_i R_j)^{k_{ij}} = 1$. *J. Lond. Math. Soc.* **10**, 21–25.

[4] Hall Jr, M. 1959 *The theory of groups*. Macmillan, New York.

[5] Humphreys, J. E. 1990 *Reflection groups and Coxeter groups*. Cambridge University Press.

[6] Mühlherr, B. and Ronan, M. 1995 Local to global structure in twin buildings. *Invent. Math.* **122**, 71–81.

[7] Ronan, M. 1989 *Lectures on buildings*. Academic Press, New York.

[8] Ronan, M. 2000 Local isometries of twin buildings, *Math. Z.* **234**, 435–455.

[9] Ronan, M. and Tits, J. 1987 Building buildings. *Math. Annalen* **278**, 291–306.

[10] Scharlau, R. 1995 Buildings. In *Handbook of incidence geometry* (ed. F. Buekenhout). Elsevier, Amsterdam.

[11] Tits, J. 1964 Algebraic and abstract simple groups. *Ann. Math.* **80**, 313–329.

[12] Tits, J. 1965 *Structures et groupes de Weyl*, Séminaire Bourbaki, exp. no. 288.

[13] Tits, J. 1969 Le problème des mots dans les groupes de Coxeter. In *Symposia Mathematica (INDAM, Rome, 1967/1968)*, vol. 1, pp. 175–185. Academic Press, London.

[14] Tits, J. 1974 *Buildings of spherical type and finite BN-pairs*. Lecture Notes in Mathematics, vol. 386. Springer.

[15] Tits, J. 1977 Endliche Spiegelungsgruppen, die als Weylgruppen auftreten. *Inventiones Math.* **43**, 283–295.

[16] Tits, J. 1981 A local approach to buildings. In *The geometric vein (Coxeter Festschrift)* (ed. C. Davis, B. Grünbaum and F. A. Sherk), pp. 519–547. Springer.

[17] Tits, J. 1987 Uniqueness and presentation of Kac–Moody groups over fields. *J. Algebra* **105**, 542–573.

[18] Tits, J. 1990 Twin buildings and groups of Kac–Moody type. In *Groups, combinatorics and geometry (Durham, 1990)* (ed. M. Liebeck and J. Saxl). London Mathematical Society Lecture Note Series, vol. 165, pp. 249–286. Cambridge University Press.

[19] Tits, J. 2001 Note concerning Jacques Tits. In *Wolf prize in mathematics* (ed. S. S. Chern and F. Hirzebruch), vol. 2, pp. 703–754. World Scientific, Singapore.

[20] Tits J. and Weiss, R. M. 2002 *Moufang polygons*. Springer.

[21] Van Maldeghem, H. 1998 *Generalized polygons*. Birkhäuser.

Index

adjacent, 1
alternative division ring, 120
anisotropic
    pseudo-quadratic space, 121
    quadratic space, 120
apartment
    of a building, 62
    of a generalized polygon, 52
automorphism
    of a chamber system, 6
    of a Coxeter diagram, 56
    of a graph, 51
    of a root group sequence, 118
    σ-automorphism, 6
    special, 6

bipartite, 51
BN-pair, 97, 98
    split, 97
building, 47
    irreducible, 51
    spherical, 51
    Weyl group of, 47
    Weyl-distance, 47

Cayley–Dickson division algebra, 120
center
    of a retraction, 67
chamber, 2
chamber system, 3
    connected, 2
    rank of, 2
    sub-chamber system, 3
complete
    bipartite graph, 51
    graph, 1
complex, 48
concatenation, 5
connected, 2
contractible, 27
contraction, 17
convex, 5, 25, 54, 65

Coxeter
    chamber system, 12
    diagram, 9
        of a building, 47
        spherical, 14
    group, 9
    matrix, 9
    system, 9

deletion, 18
diameter
    of an edge-colored graph, 2
direct product
    of buildings, 58
    of chamber systems, 4
distance, 2
    Weyl-distance, 47

edge coloring, 1
edge-colored graph, 1
elementary homotopy
    in S_Δ, 114
    of galleries, 49
    of words, 17
endomorphism, 6
    σ-endomorphism, 6
    special, 6
equivalent words, 17
exchange condition, 25
expansion, 17

folding, 23
free group, 18
free monoid, 2
free-equivalent, 18
full map, 57

gallery, 2
    length of, 2
    minimal, 2
    type of, 2
generalized
    n-gon, 52
    polygon, 52